THE EMERGING SOUTH

The Emerging South

SECOND EDITION

THOMAS D. CLARK

OXFORD UNIVERSITY PRESS
London   Oxford   New York
1968

OXFORD UNIVERSITY PRESS
Oxford   London   New York
Glasgow   Toronto   Melbourne   Wellington
Cape Town   Salisbury   Ibadan   Nairobi   Lusaka   Addis Ababa
Bombay   Calcutta   Madras   Karachi   Lahore   Dacca
Kuala Lumpur   Hong Kong   Tokyo

To the Memory of

WILLIAM KENNETH BOYD
and
CHARLES SACKETT SYDNOR

Preface to the Second Edition

In 1961 when I entitled this book *The Emerging South* I realized, of course, that it could not be said positively that the South had emerged to the extent that its efforts in most categories equaled the national achievement. I meant nevertheless to express the belief that the region was undergoing enormous change, and that much of the change promised to be for the better. With the passage of three quarters of a decade several aspects of modern southern development have come more fully into focus. For better or worse, the South in the years since 1945 has lost many of its traditional regional characteristics.

In the field of economic change there has been marked advancement. More and more the regional thrust has become that of industrial and commercial America in general. The South has been engaged in a relentless crusade to claim a greater share of the national industry, and to raise the level of personal incomes. This it is gradually accomplishing.

By 1961 it was self-evident that the old southern agricultural system of the yeoman farmer had all but vanished. There remained islands where men still struggled in their clumsy and inefficient way to survive socially and economically. They, however, carried on a losing battle. Toward the close of the decade it was clear that much southern farming had become a capital business. Farms continued to grow in size, and to become more highly mechanized. Never in the history of the region was so little human energy engaged in crop production. By the same token there was never so much human displacement in the South from the old areas of employment. Census statistics for 1960 revealed this fact, but the latter part of this decade has witnessed the great social impact of this condition. Conversely the potential of total agricultural production has risen steadily. Advertisements and special articles in southern agricultural journals all promise a much higher degree of mechanization, wider uses of chemicals, and a vastly increased profit from the harvest. Implement manufacturers and dealers, as well as agricultural scientists, are determined to see that this comes about. They have synchronized their financing program with the changing approaches of the farmers themselves. They show only slight interest in the little farmer.

The South may have failed in the past two decades to equal national expansion in the industrial field, but this is not an overweening fact. Phenomenal industrial progress has come about. Hundreds of plants producing a wide variety of goods have been located in the South. Towns and villages have become industrial sites. The more meaningful sociological fact really lies in the remaining wide margins of improperly exploited human energy and natural resources. The greater emphases placed upon education promises to make the human resource far more productive. Only now can southerners gain a meaningful perspective of what conserving and replenishing some resources since 1930 has really accomplished. Land which in 1933 was well-nigh worthless has advanced in value a hundred fold in many areas. Young trees are now growing in forests which by the latter decades of this century will supply the fourfold increased demand for cellulose products.

These are the material things. What of advances made in education, political needs, revision of religious attitudes, and race relations? Education is, as it has been since 1865, the most demanding need of the South. There is not a single southern state in which the rising costs of education are not about to wreck the present outmoded fiscal structures. This is the bear which the modern South has by the tail. At the same time social advances made in other areas over the past two decades have added strong pressures to improve public services. Educational progress has been greatly hindered by the emotional furore over desegregation of schools and public facilities. No one can possibly know at present how costly in terms of educational achievement this resistance has been. There is not at present any appreciable number of perceptive southerners who believe this battle has not finally been lost both in Congress and the courts.

Aside from their fiscal and educational challenges the southern states face the enormous task of bringing about the revision of their outmoded constitutions. In this area they are caught on dead center between two political and economic ages. The rise of urban centers and of a new industrial society has magnified constitutional weaknesses. At the same time a fear prevails that old centers of political control will be destroyed.

Much southern church leadership has demonstrated precious little understanding of the basic nature of this age. For southerners who resent the court decisions, and civil rights legislation, and changes wrought by the economic revolution, there is only one haven to which they can retreat and that is the church. Most of the organized church bodies had made pronouncements which recognize the demands of the times, but aggressive leadership has been too rarely exerted in social and moral areas which should be a primary concern of the religious man. It may not be too extreme to say that many southern congregations harbor some of the bitterest prejudices and hatred. Ku Klux Klansmen, for instance, make strong professions of religious faith while they prepare to destroy the very foundations of freedom of worship. As yet the church in the South has failed to meet the challenge of the age.

Taking a dim view of southern accomplishments in the field of race relations since 1954, one could itemize a considerable list of failures. Again, political and social leadership has had a great opportunity to improve race relations, and it has failed in large part to do so. It has not failed completely of course. Southerners no doubt have made more progress in this area than other Americans. No matter how far the Negro still has to go to consolidate his gains, he too has come further in less time than even the most charitable observer could have believed possible in 1950. The significance of this lies not so much in precise gains as in the fact that southerners have come to view their racial attitudes in a new context. Indicative of this was the attitude endorsed by all but two governors in the Southern Governors' Conference in 1967 that the time had come to give serious support to Negro higher education.

Preface to the Second Edition

There are reasons to share the views of the 1967 study of the Twentieth Century Fund that the South has gained much momentum. The region has emerged from many of the dark recesses of its past, and it promises to revise its history further in the immediate future.

Lexington, Kentucky   T.D.C.
April 1968

Acknowledgments

In the preparation of the manuscript for a book of this sort scores of people are of genuine service to an author. I could not begin here to list the names of people who in some way have helped me. I traveled over the South several times and found that people were always generous with their time in discussing various phases of the changing South and in giving frank and objective answers to my questions. By examination of the bibliography, which is far from being an orthodox one, the reader can readily see how varied were my sources of information.

I would like to acknowledge the assistance of Dr. MacDonald Horne of the National Cotton Council who supplied me with considerable materials on the present cotton situation. Mr. Paul Flowers of the Memphis *Commercial Appeal* supplied me with the published sources describing his paper's Plant-to-Prosper program. Mr. William New and Mr. Paul Evans of the Tennessee Valley Authority made available to me a storehouse of information on the Authority's activities. The late Mr. William Poe of the *Progressive Farmer* gave me very genuine assistance in reading the agricultural chapters. Mr. Robert Coker and Mr. James Neely of Hartsville, South Carolina, were most helpful in commenting on the same chapters.

Dr. J. R. Meyers of the Stoneville, Mississippi, Cotton Experiment Station was patient in explaining the work of the cotton geneticists. Officers of the various state health departments in the South were obliging in supplying materials relating to public health. So were the personnel managers of at least a dozen corporations which have moved into the South in the past two decades. I am grateful to the superintendents of public instruction in the southern states for their co-operation.

ACKNOWLEDGMENTS

Mr. James Dahir read my chapter on communities and gave me constructive advice. I am indeed grateful to the late Pat Kerr of the East Tennessee Exposition and Fair for helping me with the early history of the community improvement projects in East Tennessee. Mr. Charles Robinson of Gallatin, Tennessee, was able to show me some of the community projects in the process of development. One of the most useful sources of information was the staff members of the Tennessee Extension Service. Mr. Crosby Murray read my chapter on communities. Mr. Barrett Shelton of Decatur, Alabama, was a highly informed source on the kind of changes that have occurred in a progressive community once industrialization began.

Judge Tom P. Brady of Brookhaven, Mississippi, graciously permitted me to quote from his book *Bloody Monday*. Mr. Lambert Davis, Director of the University of North Carolina Press, gave me permission to use material from that press's publications.

I am deeply indebted to Dr. H. C. Nixon of Vanderbilt University for reading my manuscript and making highly constructive suggestions. Dr. Rembert Patrick of the University of Florida performed an expert reading chore for me that saved me from several pitfalls. I found ready co-operation from Dr. Ernest Trice Thompson of the Union Theological Seminary in Richmond, Virginia. Dr. James Angell and Dr. William Garner of Lexington, Kentucky, likewise gave me useful assistance on the chapter on the churches. Messrs. Herbert Finch, Thomas Ramage, Thomas Nelson, and Fred Moffett read the same chapter.

My colleagues J. Merton England, Holman Hamilton, James F. Hopkins, W. Clement Eaton, A. D. Albright, Lee Coleman, and A. D. Kirwan hold me deeply in their debt for their most patient assistance. No author can ever really acknowledge the services of those who work with a manuscript as typist, as did Mrs. Neva Armstrong, Miss Judy Withers, and Mrs. Genevieve Carroll.

No one mentioned in these acknowledgments is responsible for the points of view, the nature of organization, or the conception of this book. I alone bear the responsibility for the text.

T.D.C.

Lexington, Kentucky
February 1961

Introduction

Slightly more than a century ago Frederick Law Olmsted, a New Yorker, visited the South on three different occasions. In three extensive volumes he described life in the older coastal area, in the back country, and in Texas. Olmsted viewed the South through eyes which could see no good in slavery, and he failed to perceive much that could be labeled progress.

Though the great bulk of his comment was negative in nature, Olmsted tried to identify and describe a southern culture. Many other books written specifically about the South have attempted the same complex task. But clearly there is no single pattern of southern culture, and no single set of facts will describe the region. By its very historical nature the South is a land of complexities which does not reveal itself fully to any single observer. If one were to select a single condition which has struck most viewers of the South it would be that of crisis. A region which has experienced civil war, reconstruction, and a long, unresolved agricultural depression could hardly fail to produce a crisis picture. In addition, there are the many complex facts which have made up the region's racial, political, and social history. In particular, there has been the problem of the Negro. Olmsted viewed the South in crisis over slavery; subsequent observers have seen it in crisis over the race problem.

Sentimentalists have viewed the South from another perspective. They have seen it suffering from the well-nigh irreparable damage of fratricidal war followed by a senseless period of reconstruction. To them the thread of cultural continuity was broken in this horrible period. This segment of the New South has struggled constantly to recapture a moment of former glory. For nostalgic southerners the advances the region has made have only accentuated the loss of its distinct regional character. The whole modern period has seemed to them to represent the destruction of the "southern way of life." These southerners have never denied that there was something fundamentally lacking in the South's culture pattern, but they have always hoped that in some way time would solve the region's deep-seated problems.

Opposed to this point of view are those realists who have understood that the South's problems could not be solved either by the passage of time or by its people looking the other way. Harsher critics have seen the region as one bound and gagged by a slavocracy and by a conscienceless political-industrial-capitalistic oligarchy. So long as the South remained the victim of an economic and political colonialism, there was no hope that it could ever attain the degree of independence of free development necessary for its advancement, so their argument ran. Wilbur J. Cash in his *Mind of the South,* Howard W. Odum in his monumental *Southern Regions* (which was in fact Hinton Rowan Helper's *Impending Crisis* brought up to date), Marvin Skaggs in the *Southern Oligarchy,* and Stetson Kennedy in *Southern Exposure,* and scores of southern novelists, political scientists, historians, sociologists, journalists, and economists have raised doubts whether the southern way of life was stable and mature enough to maintain itself.

Social analysts like Rupert B. Vance, Charles Johnson, Guy B. Johnson, Ben U. Ratchford, John Dollard, and others have approached interpretations of the South with mountains of statistical and social data. They have succeeded in establishing a solid foundation of fact which is difficult, if not impossible, for critics to undermine. Each year the Bureau of the Census releases new statistical evidence of how the South lags behind other regions of the nation, and state government agencies supply their own data which buttress these arguments.

Maybe the South has been, and still is, all of the things which observers, scholars, and sentimentalists have said it is. Maybe its story is basically one of recurring crisis. But since 1920 there have come deep changes. A modern observer could hardly view the race problem today as containing anything resembling the serious implications of slavery in 1856. To Olmsted, over a century ago, the crisis both in the South and in the nation as a whole was impending sectional war. The modern observer sees in the frequent resort to the courts for settlement of social issues an almost certain indication that in time the South's most serious social problem will be resolved within the framework of law.

On every hand it seems clear that many of the traditional southern powers, labeled "slavocracy" or "readjustor oligarchy," are now fighting a rearguard action. They are beset on one side by the shrinking importance of the old agrarian system, and on the other by a rising industrialism and unrelenting federal court system. No one can possibly know how far the forces of change will ultimately push the South, but already many of the old institutions have been by-passed. A rising industry brings with it a new way of life which often refuses to accept many old social and political customs.

Frederick Law Olmsted scarcely mentioned the attitude of the world toward the South, but today the region is subjected to enormous pressure from world opinion. World social and political opinion confronts the South with challenges which both anger and stagger it. For the first time in history southerners seek a world market for manufactured goods, and so feel the competition of foreign manufacturers with their own economic system. They also seek international good will.

However, it is within the southern system itself that the impact of change has had its most noticeable effects. Rural electrification has brought virtually a great spiritual rebirth to the region. Availability of cheap electrical power has touched every phase of southern human existence, from methods of farming to standards of health, from the quality of local communities to public education. Regional life has acquired new stamina and texture. In the same manner, a revolution in agriculture has closed the ledger on the Old South. The facts of change lie not alone in agrarian revolution but in keen anticipation of an immediate industrial future.

The whole fabric of southern life is caught in the great web of revolt against the past. Whatever may be the professed fears of those who resist the details of the revolution which has occurred, their deeper fears are that the regional structure will become hopelessly involved in the inevitable changes of the future. A great, sprawling geographic region of deeply sentimental people faces revolution with little or no basic preparation for a new way of life. White and black alike find themselves torn away from the past; both are startled at what has happened.

This may be the wrong time to attempt to assess the present state of the South. It may be that the region is in such great labor of change that neither the forms of the past nor the promises of the future can be brought into focus. There are, however, certain landmarks already clear. Agriculture has experienced a revolution. Industry has planted itself where once it was unknown; courts and legislators have spoken frequently and forcibly on race questions; towns and cities have felt the impact of an enormous shifting of population; regional public health has been improved; the old plantation system has been dealt a death blow in having its base rudely shifted; the southern political oligarchy is being challenged within the South itself and is under fire both in Washington and in foreign capitals; and the educational system has set for its ideal the national rather than regional standards of achievement.

For the South, the great revolution started with the end of the crop year 1920. Forty years later, southerners can look back, as would a mountain climber, and determine the shape of the terrain up which they have climbed. The South may not yet have lifted itself far above the foot of the numerous census tables that reflect the state of national welfare and growth, but it has made phenomenal progress when compared with its position in 1920. The South's accomplishments at this point in the twentieth century are not to be evaluated in terms of actual achievements so much as in the certain belief that it may well claim the remainder of the twentieth century as an era of regional advancement. The South's future course will depend largely on the nature of its basic decisions within this present decade.

I want to say emphatically that this is not a history of the modern South in the orthodox sense. It is in no sense definitive; it makes no attempt to recount the political events of these forty important years. However, I have attempted to investigate the sources about the region's growth which were available. And I believe I have seen more of the South than Olmsted or any other traveler since his time has seen. I know personally what it meant to face heartbreak and frustration at the end of the cotton-picking season of 1920. I have sat for long hours interviewing people about the

New South. I have gone through the new factories. I have seen the lights come on in humble homes where previously nothing stronger than a smoky kerosene lamp had burned. I have seen towns and country villages change their personalities within a decade. I have seen people who now enjoy good health where their parents were parasite- and malaria-ridden. And I have seen people red in the face with anger at both the changing times and the Supreme Court.

So far as has been possible I have let the people themselves present the different points of views on individual issues. I have tried to write objectively, but at times I have felt completely inadequate to the task of fathoming the meaningful impulses running through the modern South. I do believe that the South will claim its share of the rest of this century. For the region to fail to do so would be ignominious self-defeat.

Contents

CONTENTS

THE EMERGING SOUTH

I

A South in Transition

*The difficulty of giving anything like an intelligent and exact estimate
of the breeding of any people or of any class of people is almost insurmountable, owing to the vagueness of the terms which must be
used, or rather to the quite different ideas which different readers will
attach to these terms. The very word which I have employed to desig-
nate my present subject has itself such a varied signification that it
needs to be defined at the outset. I mean to employ it in that sense
wherein, according to Webster, it covers the ground of "nurture, instruction, and the formation of manners." It is something more than
"manners and customs" then, and includes, or may include, qualities
which, if not congenital, are equally an essential part of character with
those qualities which are literally in-bred of a man, or a child growing
to be a man, is usually unconscious, and of which he cannot be independent if he would.*

OLMSTED, A JOURNEY IN THE BACK COUNTRY, p. 411

Only yesterday I drove down the main street of a Mississippi
county seat town, going westward into country which I once
knew intimately, as a boy gets to know country that he traversed
countless times. I had hauled thousands of feet of pine lumber
and crossties over the muddy roads which in fact extended main
street into the backcountry. Every mudhole, rutted hillside, and
rickety bridge had to be negotiated according to its own peculiar
bit of treachery. I hauled cotton to the gin and market on this
road. Atop a swaying cotton wagon I guided a team of panting
mules between the mud and the dust pockets, always hoping I
would meet no one and be spared the ordeal of passing. This five-

3

or six-mile haul consumed a day, and sometimes involved part of the evening too.

In the old days the roadside was dotted with cabins and cotton fields. Everywhere wasteful methods of cultivation had gutted the hills. The fingers of hill cotton poverty were embedded in the economic throats of the people. On the land there were more Negroes than whites, and new cabins appeared with the regularity of common law marriages. Occasionally a shabby frame Negro church teetered on tall blocks. Grounds about these fragile structures were pounded bare by trampling feet and gashed by pounding Gulf country rainstorms. Churches of the whites were only slightly more attractive and sat on but little firmer foundations.

In almost every bend of the road I could recall traveling with my father and meeting neighboring farmers who stopped to complain of the bad conditions they faced. Up and down that mudbound road the causes of unhappiness were common to all — cheap cotton, boll-weevil damage, and costly meat and mule feed. Many times had I ridden this way on sacks of "sweet feed" of indifferent quality bought at unreasonably dear prices. This was feed for cotton mules.

Halfway between my home and town lived an aged white-haired man whose corrugated neck was deeply burned by three-score years of cotton planting. Persistent frustration had made him a confirmed pessimist. Sitting in a splint bottom chair by the road he awaited his victims. Too old and worn to work in sun-scorched fields, and too stubborn to die, he delighted in making gloomy predictions. He was ready at the creak of a cotton wagon to discuss the ills of the times, not only those in the county but in the world at large, but the world he talked most about ended at his entry in a fat account book in a farm furnishing store in town. He did know, however, about a narrow strip of creation which ran from his rickety mail box to the order desks of Sears, Roebuck and Company in Chicago. The disillusioned old man, who interspersed farmers' visits with vicarious shopping excursions through a dog-eared catalog that displayed a bewildering assortment of cash-priced merchandise, had made an effective comparative study of prices charged by local furnishing merchants and those asked by Richard Sears. His solution for the South's ills was

4

childishly simple — dam up Main Street and fill it with Sears, Roebuck catalogs so the people could learn the economic facts of life. There was a catch to Uncle Neely's solution; for hauling the Sears' orders the railroads took a hefty bite out of the farmers' savings. Too, the Chicago house did not sell meat, meal, and molasses, and it was obstinate about granting twelve months' credit secured by well-nigh worthless cotton lien notes.

I drove past the place where the old man used to sit breathing in the dust of the road. He and his house were both gone now, and so were the mud and dust. Instead there was a surfaced road with a dividing white stripe almost like a string laid down to guide frustrated cotton farmers to a better world. I am sure that if the old Sears disciple were sitting beside the road today he would be grieving over the fact that Main Street was never flooded with mail order catalogs, but he could take comfort in the piles of C.O.D. packages which accumulate weekly in the local post-office awaiting return when the customers fail to bring cash in hand to claim them.

Gone on with Uncle Neely are the occupants of other old houses along the road. Clusters of crumpled oaks and cedars and of insect-damaged fruit trees droop over the crumbling mounds that were once homeplaces. Negro cabins long ago melted into the ground, but more important the ebony faces which once crowded doors and windows to stare at passers-by have moved "up North some place" or now live in town. Fields which they deprived of soil and substance no longer bear cotton. Stands of pines or pastures obliterate cotton rows. Hereford and Angus cattle roam over the land in about the same proportion as white and Negro once populated it. Mule barns have either rotted down or been converted to tractor sheds, and cotton houses have been replaced by feed bins for cattle.

One part of the old scene remains. Bottom-land cornfields still flourish. Like a furrowed sea, slender cornstalks crowd rows, casting up oily black fronds in ranks unknown to the pioneers who cleared those fields. Hybrid seed stocks adapted to conditions of soil and climate have within two decades more than doubled the yields.

The master of an old cotton farm of other years now rests on his front porch. Once his fields were scenes of intense activity.

His Negro houses were occupied by large families, and every one of his stables sheltered a mule. Now the cabins have vanished, together with the voices that once turned that place into a bedlam of sound. Much of the land is registered in the Soil Bank, and the farmer today is assured more profit without working than he realized in past seasons from exhausting labor. Because of improved seed stocks and the availability of higher grade fertilizers, the old place can yield four or five times as much cotton per acre as it did in 1920.

We sat on the farmer's front porch and looked into the fields both of us had known all our lives, I as a child growing up, and he as a young farmer struggling with the land. There arose before us the conical dome of a field we had seen cleared from the virgin woods. Once its cotton rows, starting at the base, wound in a spiral up to the top. We could reconstruct in our minds the scene of cotton choppers assaulting grass on that hill with the same vigor a son from that farm helped subdue the Moros in the Philippines. In the fall, platoons of cotton pickers dragged fattening sacks around that dome as though they were climbing the golden stairs to glory. Now white-faced cattle picked their way gingerly through the matting kudzu. This ravenous vine had obliterated cotton rows, blocked gullies, and now stretched tendrils out to ensnare the R.E.A. pole at the apex of the hill.

Some of the old fields were growing pines. Loblollies shot up in an apparent attempt to outgrow the destruction that had laid waste their parental stock. This land, said the old farmer, had advanced enormously in price. Good roads had made it more accessible, and wood-using corporations were buying every acre available. In the bitter years of depression good lands could be bought for less than ten dollars an acre, and vast submarginal and cut-over tracts could be had for fifty cents an acre, but now they were almost unobtainable.

The land has changed physically. More important, however, the human structure of the community has undergone greater changes. Brothers and sisters of my old neighbor have wandered away to other places in the state, and even away from the South. The old homeplace has fallen into other hands. Younger members of this numerous family have sought better opportunities away from the land.

Negroes went to only God knows where. The retreat of cotton during the bitter years of the depression sent them flocking to southern towns, to eastern and midwestern cities, and even to California. Old Columbus's sons went North. Harmon's boys went to work in the planing mill, and the last anyone knew of Simon's brood they were in Detroit. Every year fewer Negroes remained on the land, and almost none lived on places where they were born.

Once southerners had a fierce attachment for the soil. To them it was a source of livelihood. It was, in fact, in affection only a step removed from motherhood itself. With pride they went from one patch to another watching crops grow. They knew where every fertile spot of loam lay blanketed in mulch in the woods. Homey landmarks were monuments to nostalgia, and sometimes to frustration and heartache. For young southerners, patches and fields were open chapters in their lives. There they had labored and dreamed. Today mechanization has destroyed the laborious pace by which men moved about the land; tractors have leveled the ancient boundaries of fields. Pasture sod has glazed over the old gullies where once boys wore the seats of their breeches slick and thin sliding down their muddy sides. Now a great mass of southerners no longer knows deep love for the soil and, in this respect, stands in a new relationship to the South itself.

Industry, on the other hand, has helped many families keep their land. Farmers work for wages and till their farms on the side. Surface roads permit farmer-laborers to go farther to work daily than their fathers traveled in a lifetime. For the present generation the struggle is to balance the old way of life with the insistent demands of the new. Machines — tractors, electric motors, automatic cultivators and harvesters, water pumps, electric washers and refrigerators — have brought a revolution to farm life.

Back in town equally phenomenal changes have occurred. Weeds have overgrown much of the railroad yards; the old lumber yard is covered with small houses; and the crosstie lanes are stacked with pulpwood. The roundhouse is abandoned; the passenger station is closed to public use; and the community of railroad workers has shrunk to a fraction of its former population. Two or three diesel-drawn trains a day haul more freight than four times that number of noisy steam-driven freights did three decades ago. Trucks haul most of the local goods and much of the lumber and heavy goods.

Rings of new streets are inhabited by people who once grew cotton but are now dependent upon service and industrial employment for survival. The population of the town has not grown in proportion to the rate of its physical changes. Old-timers along main street have taken a close look and they say, "A new class of people has moved into town." Original families have either died or moved on, and their children have gone away to school never to return.

This is the story everywhere in the South. Talented young men and women with education and training have gone away to greener fields. Sociologists at Mississippi State University say that "since the turn of the century, Mississippi has lost over two million people. This loss is about the size of the state's population at the present time. During the first half of this century, the yearly losses have averaged about 40,000 people. Since the South as a whole has lost many people through migration, Mississippi is not alone. The long duration of this trend, its magnitude and implications, however, make it a matter of concern."

The more education young southerners obtain, the greater is the temptation to leave the South to find better jobs. On every hand sons and daughters have moved away. Once they populated sprawling cotton farms, but now families have become scattered. Corporations, devoid of human sentiments, are buying the lands, and homesteads are left to weeds and bushes, and grandpa's grave is often as badly lost as the addresses of his descendants.

What of the people who lived in the sharecropper cabins? Where did the fecund, red-necked, white farmers and their colored neighbors go? Some went to Memphis, Birmingham, Atlanta, Chattanooga, and Norfolk, but possibly as many went to Detroit, Akron, St. Louis, Baltimore, and Chicago. Occasionally one returns in a high-priced automobile, bought on credit, bearing an impressive alien license tag. Sometimes social columns in local papers announce the marriages of sons and daughters who have formed alliances with families far-removed from the scenes of their origins.

My native Mississippi community is a microcosm in the South.

In its long tradition of agricultural and lumbering economy it failed to feel the full impact of change which came over the nation. In mid-twentieth century it suddenly found itself deeply involved in the social and economic revolution of the nation and the world. People in this community, like southerners generally, hoped sentimentally to cling to the ways of the past. Nevertheless they were forced to accept the realities of the moment with full knowledge that they could neither recall the past nor shape the future.

The meanings of change in conditions of southern life go deep. Regional economy has become co-ordinated with that of the industrial world. Tremors which disturb American and world market places now rattle windows along southern main streets. The states' rights arguments are no less realistic now than a century ago, but the questions are different. How far this argument can be carried without injuring the new southern way of life is an open question. How much, for instance, would the chambers of commerce, the Jaycees, and the service clubs really want to argue the issue? The stakes are higher now, and political issues become economically more important. Red-necks no longer run the southern farms, and, even if they did, they are already a political minority. Farming has become a capital operation requiring business acumen if farmers are to succeed. It is important that farmers know about government, with its multiplicity of regulations and sources of aid. Demagogues like James K. Vardaman and Theodore G. Bilbo would be befuddled by the thinking of modern Mississippi audiences. Their listeners may still have limited knowledge of political theories, but they are informed about applied government.

In this age of transition the South is forced to reconsider the past in light of the immediate future. There are deep subleties in this moment in the fields of education, public health, economics, and social relationships. Southern society has suddenly found itself in a situation where it can ignore neither the exigencies nor promises of this age. The place and rights of the individual in this new South have assumed greater importance than ever before.

II

Like a Shadow on the Heart

If these slopes were thrown into permanent terraces, with turfed or stone-faced escarpments, the fertility of the soil might be preserved, even with constant tillage. In this way the hills would continue for ages to produce annual crops of greater value than those which are at present obtained from them at such destructive expense — from ten to twenty crops of cotton rendering them absolute deserts. But with negroes at $1000 a head and fresh land in Texas at $1 an acre, nothing of this sort can be thought of. The time will probably come when the soil now washing into the adjoining swamps will be brought back by our descendants, perhaps on their heads, in pots and baskets, in the manner Huc describes in China, which may be seen also in the Rhenish vineyards, to be relaid on the sunny slopes, to grow the luxurious cotton in.

OLMSTED, A JOURNEY IN THE BACK COUNTRY, p. 20

Forces of change, like the ravages of malignant disease, have long been at work in the South, even though they appear to have developed overnight. In the fall of 1919, southern cotton whitened with the richest harvest in almost a decade. Farmers had stayed the ravages of the boll weevil to produce more than a half crop. Prices were high and, so far as anyone between plow handles knew, prosperity would endure. The spirit of the moment was gauged by the optimism which prevailed in cotton buyers' offices and in the stores of farm furnishing merchants.

At the shoe counters and shelves of fancy dress goods, farmers' wives and daughters claimed rewards for their help in producing the new crop. Farther north, tobacco farmers threw reason to the wind. Leaf prices soared upward to unprecedented levels, and the next year's crop was projected on a bigger scale. New automobiles, bought with cotton and tobacco money, threshed mud and dust in country roads that never before knew greater agitation than that caused by a trotting buggy team.

The first decade of the twentieth century was an unhappy one for southern cotton and tobacco farmers. They faced disaster from declining prices, foreign competition, and, for cotton farmers, the boll-weevil plague. Had it not been for the occurrence of World War I a reckoning might have come early. Clearly the old economic way of the South lived on borrowed time. Despite the breathing spell of war prosperity, cotton farming was in for a revolution. Briefly during the war it seemed that cotton was an important southern mainstay. Southern fields yielded an indispensable raw material. In the minds of farmers the success of the American war effort could be traced in part to the end of a hoe handle and the mouth of a cotton sack, or to stripping rooms in tobacco barns.

In these four flush years of war prosperity the most evil word that could have been uttered where cotton and tobacco farmers came to receive fat wartime checks was "depression." But the germ of change only lay dormant. Signs of disaster which appeared before 1912 became ominous in 1921.

Travelers coming south in the 1920s saw a region that was outwardly prosperous as compared with its immediate past. These visitors, however, detected that the old social evils described by other visitors remained. Natural resources were improperly utilized, and the South as a whole seemed to be a stupefied giant that some day might be awakened to its possibilities. Farming was still the way of life for most people. Land bore deep gall marks of successively poor farming seasons and faltering cotton and tobacco prices. Forests were slashed to pieces, roads were miserable, and homes were tumbled down and shabby.

The depth of agricultural despair could be seen in the anxiety for the location of industries in the South. There was hope that in peace temporary war industries would flourish. High farm prices in 1919 did not obscure the fact that much of the southern wartime income had not come from industrial employment. Industry not agriculture held promise for the future.

If in 1921 an introspective southerner had sat on his front porch and examined thoughtfully the tables of the *Statistical Abstract* of the Census Bureau or, better still, read the fuller census reports, he would have at least detected the shape of the South's struggle. A few comparisons of conditions in the South with those in other areas of the United States would have encouraged him. He could not have known that 1919 and 1920 were as sharply transitional as single years can be in history. These things happened: the farm furnishing merchant and his usurious credit system were dying; cotton culture had reached an apex of influence on human lives; virgin timber was almost exhausted; and the old rough-and-ready lumbering days were numbered. Already the automobile was giving greater mobility to southerners, and migrant workers wandered away in sufficient numbers to affect population statistics. One might even have defined the economic colonial status of the South, and discovered that it, too, was changing. Cash wages for day labor had sharply delineated the differences between the haphazard economics of the old system of sharecropping and industrial employment.

Since 1914 both prices and levels of agricultural production had soared. Armies of women and children able and old enough to drag hoes and shoulder cotton sacks helped to produce bumper crops. Worn-out lands were snatched from pine and persimmon to be returned to cultivation. Cotton acreage again equaled the big years before 1910. So joyful was the revival of cotton farming during these years that farmers almost forgot the bloody costs of war. Again the South was in the ancient whirl of "growing more cotton to buy more mules, to hire more Negroes . . ."

Red-necked farmers were so certain that prosperity would prevail that many of them either hoarded their cotton or bought heavily of cotton futures. Within a year their farms were for sale to bail themselves out of a declining cotton market.

Since the southern economic focus was overwhelmingly agricultural, the plight of the region was largely that of the farmer. Physical travail of the South was eloquently portrayed in the troubled, sun-grooved faces of its cotton farmers who realized in 1920 once again they were caught in the ancient bind. Whereas the preceding year general economic prospects were cheerful, settling time in 1920 was calamitous. Few wives and daughters fussed over new shoes and dresses, or pawed over the fancy-goods counters. Cotton wagons rattled home with ominous sounds of emptiness. Everywhere in the South in that year crop yields were high; in fact acreage planted and the yield were greater than in 1914, but prices dropped disastrously.

Southern farmers had never come to understand the meaning of statistics as applied to their future. Cold facts recorded in both merchants' ledgers and official statistical sources revealed that the number of farm owners was shrinking at an alarming rate. Mortgages had increased significantly, and the ancient regional blight of sharecropping had spread like wildfire. None of that mattered in 1919 under the stimulus of war prosperity. To simple men glorying in good crops, the old way of life was restored. Their most immediate worries were getting their ex-soldier sons to settle down on the farm and to forget the unsettling diversions of battlefields and Paris streets, and of persuading local road officials to improve enough highway on which to drive their Model Ts. Few of them indeed had notions of the dynamics of economic and social change, and none foresaw the bump over which they would tumble disastrously in December 1920.

Alabama farmers in that year harvested 662,669 bales of cotton from 2,858,000 acres. At the "settling up" counters the cold facts of disaster were revealed in sharply reduced cash returns of $60,590,000, or $70,850,000 less than was paid over the same counters the preceding year. These farmers had picked an average of four acres to gather a bale. Everywhere that cotton was grown in the South the story was the same. War prosperity had ended, and the farmers found they had overplanted their land and overextended their credit.

Farmers in this important year did not understand, of course, that it was not so much a decline of cotton culture as it was the decline of marginal farming. At last the incurable economic disease, cost of production, was taking its toll. The human factors in cotton culture were headed for revolution. Plant breeding and sufficient application of chemical fertilizers and insecticides, coupled with increasing mechanization, placed cotton growing largely in the field of capital farming.

Change in economic conditions of little cotton and tobacco farmers was one of the decisive moments in southern history. Never again was King Cotton to rule the lives of so many people.

Tobacco prices in 1919 had brought unbelievably high prices. Across the landscape new curing barns reared expensive roofs to shelter the new crop of 1920. Banks extended generous credit, and the future looked bright from the perspective of spring plant beds. In Kentucky, where burley farmers had battened on a $195,584,000 crop in 1919, they were in deep misery because a slightly smaller crop brought only $71,400,400 in 1920.

Rugged individualism, if it ever prevailed in southern staple agriculture, all but vanished with the descent of farm prices in 1920–21. Southerners had experienced threescore years of lean prices and economic uncertainty, but none was so fundamental as the postwar years of the 1920s. In this period, Thomas Stribling's trilogy was a remarkably precise social document. He revealed the South in a highly troubled pose and, distorted though much of his material was, prefaced a revolution. *The Unfinished Cathedral* was as prophetic as the *Statistical Abstracts*, and Colonel Milatides Vaiden symbolized a vanishing regional way of life as much as did the vanishing furnishing system. Where Stribling painted a fictional profile of human life in the frustrated southern cotton belt in the 1920s, Rupert Vance portrayed it in concrete terms in his *Human Factors in Cotton Culture.*

Each year farm tenantry ensnared a greater number of human beings. A close look at the statistical picture revealed a social system which was out of hand. Tenantry was living on borrowed time, awaiting only a severe depression, the sociologists, and the New Deal analysts to expose it. The severity of economic failure of staple agriculture in the South translated into effects on human beings became one of the frightening experiences of the region. Farmers without land were not only a threat to regional economy, they involved the whole southern agrarian tradition in social tragedy and disillusionment.

A positive manifestation was the appearance of stores in the region selling merchandise at clearly marked prices. They offered deadly competition to the furnishing merchants, though the new stores did not grant credit. As more southerners earned cash wages during boom sawmill years they were weaned away from the abusive credit system and its arbitrary scale of prices. Merchants in the new stores no longer sold goods at prices that took into consideration the customer's ability to pay. Clarence Saunders of Memphis helped to change the old system of merchandising with his self-service, cash-priced chain stores.

Sharecropping was not new to the South. There were tenants among the pioneers who penetrated the great free-land frontier. The disastrous increase in tenants in the 1920s, however, threatened the entire southern agricultural system with bankruptcy. Never before were there so many landless farmers, or so great a mire of rural poverty. The stability of the southern home was seriously threatened. In Alabama in 1920 only 124,000 homes were free of mortgage, and 379,756 out of 508,769 families lived in rented houses. In every southern state approximately three out of five families lived either in mortgaged homes or were at the mercy of landlords. Farming as a way of life had failed these people, and for many in this decade it threatened social and economic calamity.

In the decade of the 1920s southerners still lived in the country in overwhelming numbers. Of 145 cities in the United States with more than 50,000 population only 21 were south of the Potomac, and 5 of these had moved into the larger category during boom war years. Only five states — Virginia, Tennessee, the Carolinas, and Kentucky — had population densities of more than 50 persons per square mile, and Arkansas and Florida had only 33.4 and 17.7 respectively. Massachusetts had 479.4, New Jersey 420, Pennsylvania, 278.4, and Illinois 115.7. Approximately six out of seven Mississippians lived in the country, and, for the South as a whole, the figure was about two out of three. In population density, the South seemed to be just breaking the frontier barrier. In the Lower South less than 50 per cent of the land could be classified as improved, and for older parts of the region the percentage was not much higher. This was in sharp contrast to 85.4 per cent in Illinois, 79.8 in Ohio, and 56.4 in Wisconsin, all agricultural states of approximately the same age as the younger southern states.

A closer scrutiny of farm statistics in 1920 would reveal that the South was well below its fellow agrarian states in the value of its farm lands and property. Real property in the South Atlantic states was valued at $2,916,141,222 as compared with $12,346,-673,000 in the East-North Central area. Most of the southern states in the first decades of the century had seen a relatively small increase in number and size of farms. Sizes of farms declined from 120.5 acres in 1900 in the East-South Central states to 75 acres in 1920, and from 125.6 to 84.4 in the South Atlantic area. These figures indicated a trend toward smaller farms and more intensive practices of cultivation. An observer in 1920 could hardly have discovered these facts from land statistics. However, the day of the large plantation was definitely ended, land in vast acreage would go back to the forest, and the traditional term "improved lands" would have little meaning.

World War I had its most marked effect upon the South in the uprooting of a provincial folk culture. Local interests and attitudes were now being shaped by enormous national and international influences. Many old prejudices which had kept southerners from identifying themselves emotionally with complete nationalism were destroyed. Experiences of southern boys in military service abroad changed the region's peculiar isolationism, and added a new dimension to the southern perspective.

If old folk patterns were disrupted by the war, the whole relationship of people to nature was also changed. It mattered little that a maze of streams pitched down from mountain to sea, or that great rivers plowed wide courses southward carrying incalculable volumes of water on their nearly profitless courses, or that southern lands were adaptable to other uses, and that the soil with reasonable care and management would grow almost any crop. Nature was prodigal in her gifts to the South, but southerners learned the hard lesson that nature's bounties are measured by the efficiency of their use. If land that would produce year-round pastures or grain and vegetables in unlimited quantities was not put to raising those things, it was no better than sterile soil. If monotonous production of staple crops meant that top soil was swept away to choke magnificent streams and rivers, if once clear streams became stagnant and mud-choked wallows, abundance of fresh water had little meaning. A quiet stream chuckling away in a mountain fastness or in willow-bound isolation had little meaning to lands that needed moisture and humus, or industries that needed water and power. If a million people in Alabama struggled in 1920 to gather a meager bale of cotton from every four acres of land, instead of more than a bale an acre as they did in 1955, offended nature had the upper hand and saddled its human tormentors with poverty and heartbreak. The secret of man's happier relationship with nature in the South after 1920 lay not in his slow folksy responses to its pressures, but in the profitable and non-exhaustive utilization of land and resources. This was the hard lesson the South eventually learned. The forces of nature in the region governed its future, and man in a remarkably short time was brought to account for his sinful waste of both human and natural resources. In breaching these southern folkways the South made a significant departure from the past.

Both casual visitor and social analyst failed to see in the South of the 1920s the approaching revolution in utilization of regional resources. Lumbering seemed to be reaping diminishing returns. The end was revealed in woods that were stripped of their virgin stands. Dirt roads were gashed and scarred with the constant knifings given them by overloaded log and lumber wagons. From Richmond to Shreveport both big and little mills butchered their stands, and by 1925 many of them were idle. The so-called great pine barrens of Georgia, Alabama, Mississippi, and Louisiana now deserved the name. Little landholders had laid their lean hillside woods bare by selling timber on the flourishing war market. The recession of 1920 and 1921, however, had a chastening influence. If southern timber lands were again to be profitable, new methods of conservation had to be practiced, and a more diversified market created for timber products. Statistics on southern pulpwood for paper stock were missing from the census of 1920. So far as anyone knew it would not be a factor in southern economy for a long time to come, if ever.

At the war's end lumbering no longer promised the necessary economic returns to balance a sagging agricultural income with industrial wages in the cotton South. No longer did mill whistles, like rural calliopes, arouse people long before daybreak, or whistle down the sun in the evening. Gone, or subdued, were rowdy sawmill workers who had hustled southern lumber onto a world market. Gone too were strings of suffering mules and swearing skinners who had hauled millions of feet of heart lumber over impossibly muddy roads to finishing mills and rail sidings. Even the big mills, like those at Bogalusa, Louisiana, Laurel,

Mississippi, Sumter, Alabama, and Georgetown, South Carolina, had either reduced their activities or ceased operation. No longer did as many trains roar away to distant markets burdened with lumber. By 1926 the slackening of lumbering was as injurious to southern economy as the lagging of cotton production.

Sawmill man and cotton farmer alike had wasted their resources. Lumbermen operated on the philosophy that virgin timber stands had matured for exploitation by a single generation. Few southerners stopped to think how long it took to produce the giant trees that they were so ruthlessly destroying. Southerners produced the staggering cut of 18,450,000,000 board feet of lumber in 1915, and 14,437,500,000 in 1920. There is missing from the earlier statistics, however, the fact that much of this lumber was of extraordinary quality.

There was a close correlation between stripping timber from the land and disastrous loss of top soil. Cotton lands in large areas were exhausted, and abused wooded areas were gullied by storms. Historians have often overlooked the fact that there was almost as close a relationship between lumbering and the conditions of southern society in the first quarter of this century as between cotton and society. In a more limited way the lumber industry created a new southern aristocracy. These millmen, some of whom became prominent in state politics, were almost to a man arch-conservatives. Many of them had come from outside the South. Northwesterners and easterners from the older lumbering belts of the nation found their way southward to the great virgin pine stands. Native sons entered the lumbering business and quickly gained wealth and the social status once monopolized by cotton barons. This industry depended upon bountiful supplies of cheap and willing labor. The cheaper the timber could be processed the larger the profits from the business. Lumbermen have tended to resist importation of competitive manufacturing industries, and they have abhorred organized labor.

For common laborers, white and black, sawmilling was the first major industry to break the cotton monopoly. It brought weekly pay days to the rural South without disrupting the established social pattern. Farmers turned wage hands still lived on the farm, or they moved away to flimsy shacks in temporary sawmill camps. Lumbering also contributed heavily to the breaking of the old credit system. The company store with its special system of credit granting replaced the country furnishing store. Once southern labor had received cash wages, paid steadily through most of the year, it was never satisfied to return to the back-breaking labor of the cotton fields and the frustrating uncertainties of the farm. When southern laborers migrated northward, sawmill workers were among the first to leave.

It was from this era of frustration and change, 1920 to 1940, that the South launched itself into the turbulent mid-twentieth century. Since 1880 southerners have nurtured the idea that they possess a distinctive and superior culture. For those who neither knew nor cared about statistical discrepancies between the South and the rest of the country, the old way of life seemed secure and satisfying. Some placed their faith in the Jeffersonian philosophy of agrarianism, which meant that the way of life was farm-based and farm-conditioned. For those who read the lessons of the tables a little more thoughtfully, the South's future hinged on reforms in the use of its vast human and natural resources. The necessity of reform for a sagging agrarian system had long been overlooked.

There were southerners in the 1920s who were less touched by sentimental nostalgia and philosophy than by poverty. Their fate was centered in the vicious system of credit furnishing and its constant threat of peonage. Since 1866 this had been a central theme of their economic lives. This fact was clearly brought home in 1920. The peak of wartime inflation was a perspective from which failures of the old system could be viewed; it was also a perspective from which to see that the impending doom of 1912 once again gripped the southern economy.

Industrial development in much of the South was hardly advanced enough in the immediate postwar years to permit an appraisal of the meaning of industry to the region. Textile manufacturing was expanding, but it was still secondary to that in the East. Nearly every textile manufacturing plant had increased the number of spindles in operation. Out of 36,617,584 spindles in the United States in 1920, southerners operated 15,719,712 of them. But this industry, despite expansion, showed a decline in the number of bales of cotton consumed because of a sagging consumer market. The southern textile industry was beset in the first postwar decade by both labor troubles and the ravages of outside competition. In other areas the southern industrial picture was equally as obscure. Out of a total of 9,006,372 individuals employed in the South, only 1,146,438 were engaged in industry.

Before the end of the 1920–30 decade, southerners were to search national statistics for answers to their plight. These findings revealed not only economic weaknesses but likewise the end of an era. Social displacement created by widespread tenant farming was the most startling fact in early twentieth-century southern history.

In time this wasteful system of farming was to bring crashing down a significant portion of the old southern economic and social system. The so-called poor white element dramatized the South's economic weaknesses. Evidence of the costliness of this social lag was to be found in low industrial employment, a minimum cash income, loss of population by migration, a shrinking farm and lumbering economy, and limited bank deposits.

Only an imaginative program of general industrialization promised the South economic betterment, and this change could come only by redirecting the course of southern life. Natural resources awaited proper utilization. Large quantities of raw materials were hauled away to be processed elsewhere and to enrich people in other regions. The South depended on outside capital and management to develop its resources and to provide employment for its people. Failure to produce adequate native capital and native management was a major sin of the southern system in the first half of the twentieth century.

The South waited out a troubled period between 1920 and 1939. Economic changes, if not failures, had all but made it economically weak. Its people wandered away to seek employment beyond the South. Many migrants were illiterate and created enormous social problems in their new homes; they provoked ill-will, if not ridicule, for the South itself. At the opposite extreme, intelligent young southerners who were trained in the region went elsewhere to spend productive lives. Some of them became key individuals in major industrial and capital enterprises, thus refuting the folk belief that southerners were incapable of business management.

At home, some religious fundamentalists raised wails of protest that made sensational press headlines. Their antics, brought on in part by economic failures of the old southern system, gave the impression that the South was populated largely by illiterates who adhered to a social primitivism which was little short of tribal worship. At the same time noisy extremists of rising religious sects made professions of faith in "unknown tongues," and confirmed their fidelity by handling poisonous snakes. It was in this period that Erskine Caldwell wrote *Tobacco Road*, the Dayton trial occurred, and the crime of lynching was being severely arraigned before the nation.

In a broader field, ethnic rivalries in the South have been between white and Negro instead of among groups of foreign origin. Politicians have developed organizations within the framework of a white native-born society. Unlike their eastern and midwestern colleagues, they have made no special appeals to various national groups, but rather to racial elements. An office-seeker makes his strongest appeal while defending the purity of Anglo-Saxonism. His biggest problem is that of paying more eloquent tribute to southern ancestors than do his opponents. This fact accounts for one of the sharp contrasts between political behavior in the South and the rest of the country. A politician pounding his chest and shouting the paens of Anglo-Saxonism in Boston would be digging his political grave, while in Georgia he would at least be pleasing an audience if not getting himself elected to office.

Again, the South was populated, white and Negro, by native people. There was no noticeable change in the ratio between native- and foreign-born in almost three-quarters of a century. A foreign-born person in many parts of the region was at once a rarity and a threat to the southern folk pattern. Highest in the scale of the southern states with foreign-born persons was Louisiana, with a native population of 98.4 per cent. Other southerners tended to regard the French-speaking natives of this state as foreigners themselves. This intensive native regional population generated deep satisfaction for southerners. To them this was a precious implication of racial purity.

Racial terms such as Scotch-Irish and Anglo-Saxon are highly revered in the South. They describe not only the vague and imprecise native origin of most of the people but also and, even more meaningful, a process of grueling pioneering, a homogeneous regional folk experience, a common history, full-blooded kinship, and a more or less fixed pattern of regional attitudes and loyalties. If there ever was something that could be called a solid South, it was to be found more in these human attachments and loyalties than in political and geographical harmony.

For the southern politician practicing his own peculiar type of campaigning, the folk pattern of nativism has long been an asset. An office-seeker has been in little danger of committing an unfortunate ethnic blunder which would insult a minority group of recently arrived immigrants. In fact southern campaigners could attack the immigrant bogie with ease of mind. Like a musician trained to play by ear, southern politicians know the ethnic strain without reference to a score. So long as they have made their popular approach within the framework of regional folk mores, politicians have maintained an emotional calm in other areas. Many a breast-pounding demagogue has held his audience spellbound by proclaiming the racial purity of native southerners. He has also avoided discussion of far more fundamental issues.

In the great mass of pro-segregation literature now being distributed in today's South, nativism is a central theme. Attacks are directed against foreign aid. Critics imply that money spent abroad is spent in fact to subsidize the Communist party and the enemies of the South. Internationalism is synonymous with communism, and there are bitter critics even of the United Nations.

Depression and the New Deal caught the South in an early period of transition from dependence on one-crop staple agriculture to the balancing of an old economy with a rising new industrialization. Despite the fact that the term New Deal long ago became anathema to many southerners, the 1930s were crucial for the history of the present South. The social and economic readjustment in the 1920s left it much more vulnerable to the ravages of depression than were some other sections of the country. Because by 1930 the South had fallen behind the nation in every positive statistical category, it received a lion's share of money spent on New Deal projects. Public labor forces, all the way from WPA "leaf-raking gangs" to corps of highly specialized TVA engineers, made a deep impact on southern economy before 1940. Agricultural legislation regulating crop production redirected farm interests from row crops to grazing and reforestation.

The South, Odum found in his studies made during the early 1930s, was short in every important asset category but people. Capital in sufficient amounts to hasten important regional changes was lacking, and the South had to seek outside assistance if it were to redirect its productive energies. Trained young southerners who moved away from the region had to be kept at home, soil and water resources had to be developed and conserved, and the old frontier concept of inexhaustible resources had to be abandoned. No one in the South in 1935 had any doubt about the fate of staple agriculture; already it faced ruin. The revolution begun in the cotton picking season of 1920 was in full swing by 1940, and a second world war saw a new southern way of life develop well beyond a point of return to the past.

III

The Burden Grows Lighter

The unacclimated whites on the sea coast and on the river and bayou banks of the low country, between which and the sea coast there is much inter-communication, suffer greatly from certain epidemic pestilences. This, however, only renders the fact that dense settlements of whites have been firmly established upon them, and that they are remarkably exempt from miasmatic disease, one of more value in evidence of the practicability of white occupation of the upper bottom lands. There are strong grounds for doubting the common opinion that the negroes at the South suffer less from local causes of disease than whites. They may be less subject to epidemic and infectious diseases, and yet be more liable to other fatal disorders than whites. The worst climate for unacclimated whites of any town in the United States is that of Charleston. (This, together with the whole rice coast, is clearly exceptional in respect to salubrity for whites.) It happens fortunately that the most trustworthy and complete vital statistics of the South are those of Charleston. Dr. Nott, commenting upon these, says that the average mortality, during six years, has been, of blacks alone, one in forty-four; of whites, alone, one in fifty-eight.

OLMSTED, A JOURNEY IN THE BACK COUNTRY, pp. 342–3

Southerners are not what they used to be. Pick one out at random and he is stronger and more virile than his grandfather was. By modern American military standards of physical, mental, and moral fitness, however, more than half of the Johnny Rebs who shelled the woods at Shiloh, Chancellorsville, and Gettysburg, or stood with Pemberton at Vicksburg, might have been kept at home as 4Fs. No one can say just how much pellagra and hookworm helped to sustain the Union. Certainly General Malaria fought on both sides.

Lean and lanky Johnny Rebs who hastened off to war armed with muskets to fight for Dixie also helped to spread hookworm, malaria, and tuberculosis.

Wherever southern land touched blue water, there was ever-present danger of yellow fever; malarial infection was almost a certainty. Mosquitoes responsible for yellow fever entered the region from the Caribbean and the Gulf of Mexico. They brought waves of death. "Yellow Jack" traveled as far upstream as Kentucky, and up the coast to Baltimore. Mobile, New Orleans, Savannah, Jacksonville, and Galveston frequently became sinkholes of death. Every summer season brought its dark threat of crisis. Even Memphis in the 1870s and '80s experienced yellow fever scourges which frightened away both human beings and industry. Railroads felt the shock of disease in loss of freight and passengers.

Visitors to the ante-bellum South were impressed with the listless victims of ague and chills. Perennially malaria took its toll of energy and life. Human beings were drained of life by diseases, leaving behind them human failures and heaps of clay as the only evidence that they had existed. Thousands of travelers were kept constantly aware of the liabilities to health in the South. An easier folk belief gave the region a bad reputation because of the presence of poisonous miasma. Rotting vegetable matter and marsh gases in the virgin southern woods and swamps, and an unusually heavy rainfall, with accompanying fogs that constantly beclouded the humid country, were all believed to be infectious. Seasonal outbreaks of sickness were an accepted price people paid for living in the South.

Persons who survived yellow and typhoid fevers in many areas still had excellent chances to become infested with hookworm. Those nameless Dutchmen who landed the first cargo of slaves in Virginia brought the South a bitter health problem. As the white population expanded, the incidence of hookworm became greater. Barefooted and carefree men of nature defecated on the ground, giving the bloodthirsty killer in their bowels the air and soil necessary to complete its life cycle. Pale, emaciated, tobacco-stained dirt-eaters became stock characters of the natural southern scene. Wherever warm weather and moist soils hatched hookworm, there were poor whites. So definitely a part of the population were they that historians, and even some sociologists, have discussed them as a mysterious genus that existed and multiplied especially to plague the South, or to sustain the ego of cotton snobs. These shambling human wrecks became standard southern folk characters in the first half of the nineteenth century, sometimes, it seemed, for the special benefit of amazed foreign travelers.

Each succeeding generation saw more southerners fall into the socially ignoble ranks of white trash. They became the original lazy men; illiterate, worthless, and debilitated. A myth grew in the ante-bellum South — and on the outside, too — that southerners generally lacked energy to accomplish anything. Where southerners boasted they could whip six or seven Yankees, Yankees believed by the same token they could crush a comparable number of southern starvelings.

As the barefooted population increased, the germ of laziness spread with enormous ferocity. No one, of course, knew that the cause was really a parasite. In the minds of hundreds of thousands of these people a privy was a symbol of false modesty on the part of women. Few of them regarded the garden house of nostalgic memory as more than an affectation of social climbing, a possible convenience on a rainy day, and a symbol of disappearing natural cover.

Those hard years, 1865–1910, saw great layers of southern population fall victims to the troublous regional ailments. People died largely of something else, but hookworm made their weakened systems more susceptible to other diseases. Nevertheless there was hookworm disease; ignorant doctors were unable to diagnose it. A complacent and long-suffering people reconciled their physical condition to the will of God and the illnesses of childhood. Poverty, ill-health, and economic backwardness were crosses which most southerners seemed born to carry.

In the first decade of the twentieth century, Walter Hines Page, the North Carolina gadfly, conducted an editorial and oratorical campaign in behalf of the New Yorker, Dr. Charles Wardell Stiles. As a biologist of long experience and precise training, Dr. Stiles had served the Bureau of Animal Husbandry of the Department of Agriculture with unusual professional fidelity. He had discovered that animals from the South carried hookworms in their intestines. From a study of parasitology he learned that Angelo Dupion had discovered hookworm in the entrails of workers who died while constructing the St. Gotthard Tunnel between Italy and Switzerland. He also knew that much of the southern population exhibited symptoms similar to those of the European victims; this meant that they too must be infected.

Since 1896 Dr. Stiles hammered away at the hookworm theory without getting anyone to listen to him seriously. Fortunately for southerners this was just the kind of an idea which set Walter Hines Page going. He needed ideas of this sort to use in his intermittent campaigns against southern ills. In the 1880s he had stirred lethargic Raleigh slightly out of its routine habits by attacking the Confederate myth in his noisy *State Chronicle*. But Raleigh was hardly ripe for a siege of tradition-smashing, and, although Page raised a lot of sand, he received little cash. Now in 1910 he was headed south with the double-barreled charge of illiteracy and hookworm infection.

Dr. Stiles's contention that southerners had hookworm was insulting to the South. Southern manhood was virile; if a hookworm could live through all that corn whiskey, said facetious commentators, then nothing would kill it. Southerners were just resting temporarily after a hard war. Page was an upstart, and Dr. Stiles was a Yankee mountebank.

Turnip greens, grits, sweet 'taters, sorghum molasses, catfish, and sow belly were treatment enough for even the worst case of laziness. Newspapers, orators, and even "statesmen" were loud in their angry shouts of defense of southern health. Yet a golden-tongued orator was hard-pressed to explain away the high incidence of worm eggs found in the stools of people in 35 Alabama counties in 1911–14. Georgia senators had a difficult time turning their backs on the facts of life among their people when they undertook to refute the libel committed upon them by a Yankee with a microscope. Besides, in 1902, Dr. Claude Smith of the Grady Hospital in Atlanta had first diagnosed a case of hookworm disease, and had reported on it at a meeting of the American Medical Association in Saratoga, New York. The facts remained that approximately 53.6 per cent of the people in some selected areas of Georgia were infected with hookworm, and one person out of thirty-five in particularly heavily infested zones was dying of exhaustion. Thousands of southerners were left suspended in a foggy and witless state of retarded animation.

Once news of the hookworm theory got abroad, cartoonists joined southern legislators in a field day at the expense of the Rockefeller Foundation and Dr. Stiles, and such garrulous wits as Irvin Cobb ridiculed both Dr. Stiles and his southern victims in the *New York Evening World*. The urbane Page fell victim to these wild shots of journalists who showed more wit than social tolerance and understanding.

Treatment was simple — so simple that even the most dense hookworm victim could pursue it. However, it was a sight easier to cram a dose of salts and thymol down his gullet than to put shoes on his feet and lead him into a sanitary privy to answer the call of nature — that, too, would have been a violation of an established southern tradition.

The battle against hookworm had to be won at legislative, editorial, and philanthropic levels. Page sought Rockefeller Foundation aid, but first he had to convince Dr. Frederick T. Gates and Dr. Simon Flexner of the devastation wrought by hookworm. Even these scientists were skeptical at first, but they were soon convinced. The Commission for Exterminating Hookworm was created on October 29, 1909, with a million dollars in its till. A year later, workers began a survey of Richmond County, Virginia. At the end of the five-year period for which the Commission was created over a million children were examined, and an incidence of infection of 30 per cent was found. Intelligence and physical tests were far more revealing and disturbing. Beyond a doubt large numbers of southerners were being sapped of their vitality by this insidious parasite.

Finding hookworm in many areas of the South dramatized further need for organized health services. If a microscopic worm could cause so much demonstrable havoc among the people, so could other diseases. Local health departments were organized, and existing state organizations were given more support. The region below the Potomac became health conscious, if not thoroughly active in combating diseases. Hookworm has not been completely eradicated, although rural electrification, new home water systems, and a more sanitary-minded rural society have accomplished much. No doubt hookworm will always exist in the South, but periodic surveys show an encouraging decrease in those areas where warm moist soils and primitive sanitary practices still prevail. The improved domestic economy of the South has further reduced hookworm infection because fewer people now go barefooted.

Southern public health officers have battled other diseases. Malaria once took an annual toll of lives and dissipated an enormous amount of regional energy. It is possible that the cost of malaria since the coming of the English to Jamestown would have built and supported an outstanding university in every southern state. Three preventive measures were obvious in 1920: screening of houses, drainage of marshes and bayous, and the destruction of mosquitoes themselves. Killing mosquitoes was not easy; the South had tremendous swamp and water areas. They existed everywhere, and outbreaks of malaria followed their ancient patterns. Introduction of dredging machinery with which to cut networks of drainage canals was a godsend. Reclamation of large areas of marshy lands not only helped to improve health but also aided regional agricultural economy. Hardware merchants did a thriving business in screens, but still there were people who trusted the Lord to preserve them from mosquito bites and malaria.

Economically malaria was no doubt the cause of one of the South's most fabulous human expenditures. In 1920 Dr. Henry Hanson of the Florida State Department of Health wrote that "this condition (hookworm) together with the prevalence of malaria constitute the most serious handicaps to our rural population. It is what holds the state back." Even though victims of malaria worked, they were seldom able to render full service because of their devitalized condition, and the characteristic recurrence of chills and fever.

The damage done by malaria in Georgia over the years makes General Sherman appear to have been a casual visitor. Dr. T. F. Abercrombie said: "Malaria was a major problem in Georgia. Although it was not the state's worst killer, 'chills and fevers' retarded the growth and economic development of sections of Georgia more than any other disease with which the health forces had to contend." A former public health director said, "The grave danger of malaria lay not in death alone but in the sickness rate." A single death often represented a background loss of 2000 to 4000 days of labor due to illness. A diseased victim was never able to perform at more than half capacity in a job.

Mosquito surveys were undertaken by many groups in the South, one of them led by Dr. L. Van Dine, who investigated malarial conditions on a Mississippi delta plantation. These studies were convincing evidence of the importance of ridding the South of malaria. A report of the National Emergency Council in 1934 said that the disease "is estimated to reduce the industrial output of the South one third."

Both urban and rural mosquito controls were exercised, with more headway being made around the towns and cities. Only *Anopheles quadrimaculatas* is said to carry the malaria parasite, but uninformed people came to believe that all mosquitoes spread the disease. For this reason they lacked faith in various preventive measures; nevertheless there was a significant reduction in outbreaks of malaria between 1917 and 1930. In the latter year of this period, however, hope of ridding the South of the disease still seemed remote indeed. Preventive measures against malaria were sure, but they were most difficult to apply universally. Both geography and prejudice born of ignorance reacted against complete destruction of the parasite and its mosquito host.

One of the most effective accomplishments in the field of mosquito control has been the Florida experiment. With 1221 miles of shore line and an incalculable amount of inland marsh and water surface, the state has had a long history of sickness and death from malaria. Florida was so great a mosquito haven that the insect's name was honored in at least one place name. The romance of sunshine and winter warmth ended in many places at sundown when swarms of mosquitoes whined out of hiding in search of blood. Summers were filled with dread of disease, and death from malaria was as natural as a rain storm. Between 1918 and 1925 various attempts were made at control in the worst areas. In the latter years the first mosquito control law was adopted, and since then it has been modified at least three times to meet changing conditions.

The Florida law permitted local taxes, and their use with matching state funds, to dredge, fill, and treat offending areas. In the 'thirties the federal public works agencies labored at the task of mosquito control. By 1939 the end was in sight. It remained for wartime D.D.T. to finish the job in Florida as well as all over the South. Mosquito bites would be expensive in Florida, for tourists who leave approximately a billion dollars annually below the St. Mary's River might stay away. Some Floridians have shown an unusual sensitivity toward the word mosquito. In 1951 the legislature abolished the name "Mosquito Lagoon."

In the upper South the Tennessee Valley Authority speeded up the fight against the mosquito. Creating as it did vast new areas of standing water, it brought a possible menace to health that might have destroyed the South. These facts were known, and a careful scheme of raising and lowering water levels was worked out to kill the larvae. Information made available by the Tennessee Valley studies was highly useful in the entire mosquito crusade.

Control of the mosquito in the South is one of the nation's greatest success health stories. What seemed all but hopeless in 1930 was a fact in 1950. No longer are the bodies of southerners wracked by the destructive drain on energy and by intermittent fevers caused by malaria. By 1947 Mississippi was offering a reward for a bona fide case of indigenous malaria, and in 1955 the State Health Department was somewhat concerned that local doctors might not be able to diagnose it. It has been said that microscopic slides should be distributed to younger doctors to enable them to diagnose malarial infection if a case should occur among their patients.

An ancient bit of race prejudice in the South revolves around venereal disease. Southern whites regarded the Negro almost from the beginning of slavery as host to syphilis and gonorrhea, even though syphilis was transmitted to him by white men. The Negro has been and still is a ready victim of venereal infections. For example of the 5331 cases of reported syphilis in Virginia in 1953–54, 4286 were Negro; the case incidence for whites per 100,000 was 45.8, for Negroes 253.2. In 1957–58 syphilitic infection in Virginia was 117.8 per cent per 100,000, and gonorrheal infection was 180.9. By races, Negroes showed a rate of 399.3 for syphilis, and 724.7 for gonorrhea as compared with a white infection of 40.6 and 29.8 per 100,000. In 1955 the North Carolina Department of Public Health estimated that approximately 80,000 cases of gonorrhea existed, but because of widespread self-medication only one out of five was believed to be reported. Virginia's infection rate was only half so high, or 40,000 cases, with a white incidence of 36.6, and a colored rate of infection of 874.6 per 100,000.

The story of venereal diseases in Georgia is a fantastic one. In 1939 the state had the third highest rate of infection in the nation. Of the first 2,000,000 selectees for blood tests 145 males out of every thousand were found to be infected. Whites showed an incidence of 34 and Negro males 275 per thousand when examined for selective service. The "Blood Wagon" in three Georgia counties in 1937 and 1938 revealed an incidence of almost one-third of the population. A heavy campaign of publicity smoothed the way for public health testing, and assistance from the Federal Government has made the fight against these diseases in Georgia more effective. Syphilis and gonorrhea have been staggered, but are not destroyed. Evidence of this is to be found in the public health report for 1959. The state had a total rate of previously untreated venereal cases of 4424 out of each 100,000 of population, or approximately 173,978 cases out of a total estimated population of 3,910,978.

In neighboring Mississippi, Negroes showed approximately 25 per cent venereal infection in 1948, while their white neighbors revealed only 2½ to 3 per cent in 1938. The reduction of Negro infection was indeed dramatic, coming down from 25 per cent in 1940 to 3 per cent in 1955. At present public health officials say that syphilitic infection of pregnant Negro mothers in Mississippi is a rarity, where a few years ago it was commonplace; in 1949 there were 4000 reported cases, in 1954 only 120 cases, while in 1955 the doctors saw almost no infection. Gonorrhea presents the same clouded picture in Mississippi as in North Carolina. A relatively large number of cases are reported, but vague knowledge of unreported cases indicates a much higher degree of infection.

In Alabama, tuberculosis and syphilis have struck a barrier in the Henderson Law. State Senator Bruce Henderson of Miller's Ferry is a man of good education, and the possessor of a good perspective in public affairs. His grandfather was a Union soldier who returned to Alabama after the Civil War and began the operation of a large plantation. His grandsons have remained on the land but have received good university training. Senator Henderson was able to get enacted in 1943 the so-called Henderson Law which requires that every Alabamian between the ages of 14 and 50 have a blood and tuberculin test. For a time after the passage of this law the Department of Public Health was running 20,000 blood tests a day, and in 1955 it made approximately 600,-000 tests; this was one of the most extensive examples of mass testing in the history of American public health. By these mass-search tests the State Health Department was able to detect both tuberculosis and syphilitic infections and to institute treatment.

It is too early to say what the final effect of venereal diseases may be in the South, for such control is most complex. The law, personal pride, fear, economics, and community attitudes are all involved. In some cases, laws have permitted testing to be mandatory. The biggest victory has been gained through breaking down of old Victorian taboos which kept mention of social diseases out of the press and public utterances. News releases, lectures, and use of movie films have been effective.

Scarcely an institution in the South has been left untouched by the crusade against venereal diseases. This is particularly true of those that serve Negroes. As venereal diseases are brought under control, the Negro becomes a much hardier individual and begins to offer much greater economic competition. He will also have far more money to spend on consumer goods hitherto denied him.

Malarial and venereal diseases have not always resulted in death in the South. Tuberculosis, however, has been a killer. In 1914 this disease sent 2490 Mississippians to their graves, and the incidence of infection was indeed high. In fact, no one could tell just how many people were victims of the disease. It was not until 1925 that it surrendered first position to heart ailments among fatal diseases. By 1954 tuberculosis was last on the list of the ten major causes of death, and in forty years the rate of death had declined by 2090 per 100,000 individuals.

Southern success in combating tuberculosis involves several factors. Accurate diagnosis and early hospitalization have been effective, but the war on poverty has shown equally important results. Tuberculosis has been a frightful companion of the poor — both white and Negro. In recent years the Negro has suffered a higher incidence of the disease and a higher death rate. He has been less able to afford healthful home surroundings, has been careless in matters of sanitation and taking care of his health, and, until the last few years, because of bi-racial practices in institutions, less able to secure hospitalization. Hospitals for Negroes have been the last to be built and placed in operation. Only now is the rather extensive hospital program, developed with federal assistance from Hill-Burton funds, getting into full operation. This public program permits both organizations and public agencies to secure federal funds to supply hospital needs in areas where such facilities are lacking. Likewise the mass search for the disease with mobile x-ray units has been effective in locating new victims, and largely accounts for the high rate of infection reported in Alabama.

Except in the state of North Carolina, tuberculosis still appears among the ten leading causes of death in the South. Better diagnosis, better trained doctors, larger state and local appropriations for public health work, and a growing sense of public responsibility for treating diseases have led to a significant destruction of the age-old prejudice of permitting tubercular infection to be known, and the creation of an awareness that tuberculosis can be cured. Another factor which has added greatly to the advances which the South has made in detecting tuberculosis is the realization of the economic worth of the individual to the region's new economy of industrialization.

When southerners moved over the vast stretch of pine lands from Virginia to Texas and from Kentucky to Florida in the early decades of the nineteenth century, they clung to certain fixed eating habits. For the most part they were backwoodsmen who had learned to live off the country. Cured pork, cornbread, syrups, and greasy white gravies were dietary staples. Moving across a land capable of producing prodigious quantities of fresh meat, southern pioneers still preferred salt meat. Three times a day they brought out the skillet and fried their meat. Burning grease was almost as much a regional aroma as that of the pines. Travelers were sated with the monotonous greasy fare. Everything from corn to okra was fried; eggs and meats were nearly always served from the skillet. Grease in foods was as characteristic of the South as cape jessamine blossoms. Vegetables which could be grown so plentifully were boiled beyond a state of recognition.

Every fiber had to be broken down and impregnated with grease before it was considered edible. It was possible to grow garden "sass" in unlimited quantities for most of the year. A little planning and a slight amount of work was all that was necessary to furnish the table with foods high in vitamins. But aside from black-eyed peas, sweet potatoes, cabbage and turnip greens, people ate few vegetables.

In those lean and barren years between the end of the Civil War and the beginning of World War I the dietary sins of the South are recorded in eloquent statistics in general store records. White corn meal, sow belly (white as an angel's wing), molasses, grits, and rice were basic foods. Corn meal, bolted to achieve a maximum whiteness, was robbed of its nutritional value. Grits, that humble dish which meant so much to southerners in many areas, was a subtle devitalizer on the breakfast table. "Sawmill" gravy, half grease and half flour, had the single virtue of sliding soggy biscuits down the gullet. When, in this period, a rural southerner was too ill to eat hot biscuits and white gravy he was indeed inching his way to the grave.

Spring and summer brought their outbreaks of curious ills. It was just as natural for some folks to have "risings" (boils) in hot weather as it was for plums to get ripe. Stomach trouble was nagging company for too many. Though it sapped them of their strength, they would not have felt normal without it. These ills came in summertime when vegetables were plentiful and fruit trees were loaded. To regard the curious red spots and characteristic gauntlets of discoloration about the hands and wrists as a dietary disease was sheer foolishness. If this were so, the disease would occur in the wintertime. Few or none knew that it took six months for a dietary deficiency to manifest itself. Failures of the winter diet showed up in summer.

Political caricatures of southern voters portrayed a lanky and scrawny man whose skeletal system worked with the uncertain mechanical co-ordination of the Scarecrow in *The Wizard of Oz*. His cheek bones were high, his eyes were buried in deep sockets, his Adam's apple worked up and down like a bucket on a rope, his skin was dry, his neck red, and his wit dull. This was the original "woolhat" boy who looked upon his physical condition as a manifestation of political oppression. He was the forgotten man whom

Walter Hines Page eulogized so fervently in 1897. Physically weak, perpetually hungry, chewing tobacco constantly, dipping snuff, drinking corn liquor, and sticking to traditional foods of the region, he could hardly be expected to support an objective opinion or to view the future with much hope.

Such a southerner was not uncommon. Pellagra actually has a long history in the South. At least one public health historian has been able to trace its symptoms back to 1828. Dr. Henry F. Harris of Georgia reported a combination hookworm-pellagra case in 1902, but the really significant discovery was that made in 1907 when the disease was located in the Negro wards of the Milledgeville State Hospital. It was not until twenty years had elapsed that this disease was isolated and proved to be confined largely to the geographical limits of the old southern cotton belt. One of the first scientific investigations of this regional disease was made by Dr. Joseph Goldenberger when he checked on diet and the prevalence of the disease in a South Carolina cotton mill village and in the State Hospital at Milledgeville, Georgia. Later he secured permission to run a controlled dietary check on a group of Mississippi convicts. He fed his charges biscuits, cornbread, grits, fried mush, rice, gravy, sugar, and coffee. In six months half a dozen of the group had developed pellagra, while none of those receiving a balanced diet contracted the disease.

Dr. Goldenberger's experiment should have set at rest bitter prejudice that no such regional disease existed, but it failed to do so. President Warren G. Harding felt the sting of southern wrath when he requested the United States Public Health Service to make a survey of the South to determine the condition that caused pellagra. Again editors and politicians raised a hue and cry. Tempers boiled. Even some public health officials rallied to the emotional cause by playing down the prevalence of pellagra. There was an argument as to whether or not pellagra was contagious, a fact disproved by Dr. Goldenberger. So objective a scientific body as the Georgia Senate adopted resolutions against the implications of the President's letter to the Surgeon General. Harding hardly expected to receive southern political support, but he did give in to pressures and called off the proposed survey.

Despite the great furor caused by the Harding letter, Mississippi faced the grim fact that pellagra was a third major cause of death in 1914 and ranked 10th in both 1925 and 1930. In 1923 Alabama reported 586 fatal cases in 1923, but by 1930 there were only 14 cases. North Carolina had 273 deaths from the disease in 1925, and in depression 1930 there were 1002 deaths, but in 1952 the rate had dropped to only 13 deaths. Tennessee had 408 deaths in 1929, and then the rate dropped to a negligible number. Pellagra does not now appear as a noticeable cause of death in any of the southern states. A number of factors have gone to make sturdier southerners. Yet no one knows what effect another depression would have.

Few aspects of southern life have undergone such fundamental changes as dietary habits have. One can still start a small war between Kentucky and Virginia over the merits of their respective country hams, with Tennessee chiming in with tones of hurt pride. It is doubtful, however, that one could get the feuding editors and politicians to eat with relish a mess of white sow belly, sawmill gravy, and unfortified grits topped off with hot cornbread sopped in sorghum. Occasionally a congressman or senator snatches at the headlines by ordering a mess of turnip greens and black-eyed peas, or a full baking of southern yams. Even these are not the same. The yams are so highly refined that they little resemble the old time starchy sweet 'taters, and plant breeders have even tampered with the peas.

A rising cattle industry in the South, rural electrification lines, and the generally improved economic conditions of southerners have changed their tastes in meats. An appreciable number of homes either own or have ready access to quick frozen-food facilities. Refrigeration has all but made salt meat a thing of the past. No longer does a southern farmer have to get the almanac, a drove of hogs, and the weatherman into agreement in order to butcher. The unpredictable changes of southern weather have no influence on the preparation of most meat today. No sudden warm spells destroy thousands of tons of it. In the face of all this progress a really good country ham becomes a true museum piece.

Fresh vegetables are no farther away any time of the year than the freezer, the locker plant, or the chain grocery. More southerners have been to school and have read in the health books that balanced diets are important. Agricultural extension services and public health nurses in all the states have made enormous strides in modifying old southern customs. The extension people are somewhat less eloquent than southern congressmen and folksy columnists on the subject of regional dishes, but they speak with far more conviction. New types of southern grains contain more nutrients. Corn breeders have produced a finer product, and southern millers have learned to compensate with chemicals for nature's failures. Fortified corn meal, grits, and flour have helped end the pellagra menace. Chronic alcoholics and food cranks make up most of its present victims.

Emphasis upon livestock production has for the first time in southern history popularized red meats. It may be a little more difficult to orate about fortified cornbread, fresh ground hamburger, and more nutritious potatoes, but these things are facts in the modern southern way of life. An important revolution has been an increased availability of dairy products. Fresh milk is in potentially abundant supply, despite the fact that family ownership of cows still shows a sharp discrepancy as to the numbers of cows and families.

It is still possible to die from many of the old natural causes in the South. The barriers of ignorance, prejudice, false pride, and failures of bi-racial institutionalism have only begun to be breached. Health officers still expend enormous energy selling ideas to people who ought to do better. Beds available in southern hospitals of all kinds are far too few for the need, but tremendously above what they were a decade ago. Of the old-time illnesses tuberculosis alone bites deep into medical budgets of the states. But a casual automobile drive across the region reveals the fact that this tough old killer is being licked in the new hospitals. Federal Hill-Burton aid, private philanthropy, and state and local appropriations have been used to build hospitals everywhere.

Not too many years ago to the average rural southerner hospitalization involved a long journey. Now the hospital is no farther away than the county seat. The meaning of this change to the nation is great indeed. Human stamina in the South no doubt has doubled in the last two decades. In terms of physical conditions the South has never in its history been in so favorable a position. Clearing away malaria and hookworm, and checking other diseases have gone far to unshackle the southerner.

In another way southerners have changed. Death comes to them in about the same form as to other Americans upon an adjusted age basis. Heart disease heads the list of causes of death, and is followed by cancer, pneumonia, accidents, tuberculosis, nephritis, congenital malformations, and senility. In Florida, cirrhosis of the liver is a greater threat than malaria, hookworm, and pellagra combined.

In a broad field of economic expansion improved health conditions ensure the fact that southern businesses today are less subject to absenteeism than was true in the past. And one of the reasons why southern communities can advertise so vigorously that their people are willing workers is because of the region's major health advances.

IV

Cotton's Going West

*There was something truly western in the direct, reckless way in which
the boat was loaded. A strong gang-plank being placed at right angles
to the slide way, a bale of cotton was let slide from the top, and, coming down with fearful velocity, on striking the gang-plank, it would
rebound up and out on the boat, against a barricade of bales previously
arranged to receive it. The moment it struck this barricade, it would be
dashed at by two or three men, and jerked out of the way, and others
would roll it to its place for the voyage, on tiers aft. The mate, standing
near the bottom of the slide, as soon as the men had removed one bale
to what he thought a safe distance, would shout to those aloft, and
down would come another. Not infrequently, a bale would not strike
on its end, and would rebound off, diagonally overboard; or would be
thrown up with such force as to go over the barricade, breaking
stanchions and railings, and scattering the passengers on the berth
deck. Negro hands were sent to the top of the bank to roll the bales to
the side, and Irishmen were kept below to remove them, and stow
them. On asking the mate (with some surmisings) the reason of this
arrangements, he said: "The niggers are worth too much to be risked
here; if the Paddies are knocked overboard, or get their backs broke,
nobody loses anything."*

OLMSTED, A JOURNEY IN THE SEABOARD SLAVE STATES, pp. 550–51

In 1784 a sailing vessel anchored in the Cooper River before
Charleston and took aboard three bags of sea island cotton for
Britain. This was the beginning of a rich cotton trade which has
endured to date. There are too many descriptions of the influence of the cotton gin and the expansion of the cotton belt
westward to make necessary a repetition of the history of cotton
in the early South. In its first century not only had the cotton belt

40

expanded westward to Texas, it had created its own peculiar social and economic systems.

Because of the enormous amount of hand labor necessary to produce cotton, this crop may have had greater bearing on human lives than any other grown in North America. Also, because it depended largely on intersectional and international markets, its fate was more intimately sensitive to the changing fortunes of world conditions.

In the middle of the nineteenth century the American Civil War was a vastly disrupting factor in cotton culture. Following the war southern farmers found that although the Negroes were freed from slavery the cotton planters were more enslaved to their crop. A lack of capital and stable markets for other farm products necessitated the development of a ruinous credit system which annually brought the South nearer to calamity.

By 1913 the coming of the boll weevil, a rising international competition, and sagging farm credits had brought the southern farmer to the brink of ruin. World War I disrupted the tragedy. But in the spring of 1920 farmers found themselves victims of short memories. For the preceding six years their eyes had been fixed on the furrow and the next harvest season instead of on the realities of the cotton market. They were incapable anyway of reading the signs of the time and of appraising them correctly.

The roll of credit failures, forced mortgage sales, bankruptcies, and heartless enslavement of men lengthened with each succeeding year. Tenantry became synonymous with peonage, and by 1920 the cotton South faced stark economic and social failure. From the shambles arose a grim poverty that caught the attention of reporter, novelist, and reformer alike. Exhausted and ignorance-blinded, cotton workers listened to soulful recitations of their woes by shrewd demagogues, and sent them to state capitals and to Congress to fight their battles against the undefined monster that held them in its stifling grip. A few years later, in the darkest days of the great depression, cotton land pride was so badly drugged by failure and economic exhaustion that it lacked the defensive energy necessary to strike back at the region's critics.

Cotton poverty was deep and stark enough, but there was still another ghostly manifestation. Rising on the very ground of cotton failure were chemically made synthetics. DuPont, Celanese Corporation of America, and other industrial chemists began converting plentiful chemicals into fabrics as fine as silk and as durable as cotton. This threat far outweighed abolition of slavery, or even competition from other cotton growers around the world. It knew no drouth, no insects, no ravaging plant diseases.

The invasion of King Cotton's private domain by synthetics was a reversal of ancient economic history. Wool and flax were limited competitors confined to an ancient code, but synthetics were bound only by the imaginations of an army of ingenious scientists under economic compunction to produce results. Synthetics had no long history, no social and economic pattern, no way of life, no social scars, and few human subjects. Trained chemists, a limitless amount of research capital, good rail connections, and an adequate supply of water and fuel were more important than warm climate, good soils, available fertilizer, labor, and a world market. The gauntlet of challenge was down — the fight was to be vigorous if cotton was to retain its position.

In keeping with the most fundamental contentions of the cotton conventions of the 1850s, the cost of cotton production had to be reduced while the quality of the product had to be greatly improved. Only science and invention could bring these revolutionary changes. In the 1930s the Rust Brothers near Memphis, Tennessee, tinkered with a new mechanical picker. This time there was promise. Not only the inventive brothers but the whole empire of farm machinery manufacturers was interested. Inevitably a mechanical harvester would one day succeed, or cotton would fail. The idea of picking cotton mechanically is not new. Since 1854 inventors have experimented with machines that would harvest cotton cheaply and quickly and thus permit a vast expansion of the industry. In 1904 George A. Lowery introduced a machine which seemed to take care of cotton picking. Lowery's machine was proclaimed by the conservative Latham, Alexander, and Company's cotton reports as a practical one. His invention, however, did not relieve human beings of the arduous task of cotton picking; it only gave them a chance to ride the picker and thereby increased their efficiency. But, like the dreams that had gone before, this one also failed. So complex was the cotton plant that planters everywhere reconciled themselves to the fact that the world's cotton supply rested after all on the availability of nimble human fingers to fight grass and to pull the locks from bursting bolls.

Cotton production showed an annual increase from the beginning of the industry in 1621 to 1929. In 1855, when David Christy published his famous book, *Cotton Is King*, the South supplied 2,982,634 bales to the international cotton market, and, in 1859, while the country was highly wrought up over the election, southern cotton farmers were driving themselves and slaves to the task of harvesting 4,861,292 bales. The size of this last ante-bellum crop goes far toward explaining the wrong guess which southerners made in believing the absence of a rising production of cotton would leave the world in a panic. The crop of 1923 passed the 10,000,000 bale mark for the first time, and since then American cotton production in one year has gone above 16,000,000 bales.

The history of cotton growing in the South, however, was highly charged with tragedy. Worms and wilt took their toll from the beginning. In the middle 1890s the boll weevil appeared in Texas cotton fields and quickly spread eastward, leaving a trail of bankruptcy and want. By 1908 the pest was east of the Mississippi in the big producing areas, and it spread across the land like an angry cloud. Economic survival of cotton farmers depended on several factors: new plant types, more efficient production methods, and more intelligent use of fertilizers and herbicides. Carelessness of production must be a thing of the past if cotton farmers were to prosper. The first shocks of weevil invasion drove hordes of traditional cotton laborers from the land to outside industrial centers and into southern towns. This was the beginning of a revolution in the cotton South that is still in high swing. For the first time in the history of the rising commercial cotton industry the economic-social pattern was broken. Not even an intersectional war and paralyzing economic panic had heretofore been able to alter the old pattern. Now Negroes left farms. Behind them gaping cabin doors and sagging window shutters stared vacantly into yards overgrown with jimson and hog weeds — symbols of poor people and poor lands. While cotton planters watched much of their cheap labor wander off in the face of the weevils' attacks, the shot that felled the Archduke Franz Ferdinand at Sarejevo was fired.

In many respects the shot at Sarejevo in 1914 was more important than the one fired at Charleston in 1861. Cotton prices had lagged well under fifteen cents since 1876, and there were several years when prices were below production costs. In August 1914 the cotton exchanges were closed, and the cotton industry was paralyzed. When the exchanges were opened again, prices went up with the growing intensity of war, but so did the cost of production. Never again were southerners to produce cotton by their ancient standards.

The war's demands for men and goods stimulated ruinous competition. For the first time foreign cotton growers passed the 10,000,000 bale mark, and the quality of much of their staple was high. Demands for war materials hastened the introduction of synthetics, a deadly and permanent form of competition.

No doubt since man picked the first boll of cotton two major objectives have been more fiber per plant and a stronger, finer product. While frontier American cotton planters slashed their way across two-thirds of the southern half of the continent, plant breeders were at work. Walter Burling of Natchez had become conscious in 1808 of the importance of Mexican cotton, and in a short time this type was introduced elsewhere in the expanding cotton belt. By the middle of the century H. W. Vick of Vicksburg and J. V. Jones of Georgia were experimenting with big boll types. In 1847 Boyd's Prolific was bred from a single plant. By the outbreak of the Civil War there was a consciousness of the importance of improved varieties of cotton. The sectional conflict, however, halted selective work, and the story of cotton breeding was not reopened until 1868 when new varieties appeared across the great southern belt.

Demands on plant breeders were many. Plants had to be fruitful, yield a good grade of fiber, be resistant to diseases, stormy weather, and insects, produce a high percentage of good oil, and ripen early enough to enable farmers to mature crops ahead of the boll weevil and to complete their harvests ahead of winter weather. These challenges have sent improvers to the cotton fields in surprisingly large numbers. For instance, there were many areas where cotton could not be grown because of the wilt, which now produce good crops with wilt-resistant varieties. The roll call of cotton types before 1940 is actually a recitation of frustrated hopes and ambitions in the industry. Many an old-time cotton farmer will recall with nostalgia the promise offered by such tantalizing varieties as Mexican, Jones' Improved, Peterkin, Southern Hope, Cleveland Big Boll, Half and Half, Pride of Georgia, and scores of others. In all there were at one time more than 500 varieties of cotton. All of these promised a new and more highly competitive advantage to their producers.

Everybody interested in cotton production realized that an almost complete revolution would have to occur in both plant type and cultivation practices if southern cotton was to remain a major staple crop. But revolutions in plant types come slowly. In the early years in the South there were no great scientific agricultural institutions where communities of highly trained scientists could attack the problems of cotton production on a prescribed plan. Experimentation was an individualistic matter. Often it amounted to no more than a selection of desirable plants and a follow-up of their yield with other selections. There were no geneticists who could hasten the breeding process with crosses and selections within the laws of heredity.

A pioneer in plant selection and breeding following the Civil War was John Griffin of Greenville, Mississippi. He experimented with a green seed sea island type in an effort to produce a practical plant bearing long fiber which could be produced on delta lands. In Lockhart, Texas, A. D. Mebane worked for eighteen years, 1882–1900, to improve upland cotton. He produced a satisfactory new type which was named Mebane's Triumph, and this plant proved to be a worthy parent stock for future experimentation.

On the Atlantic seaboard, Caleb Coker of Society Hill, South Carolina, interested himself in cotton improvement. He was a successful farmer in the sandy plains of his state, and his chief agricultural interest was growing cotton. When the war began, his son, James Lide Coker, left the family farm to become a major in the Confederate Army. Four years later he came home on crutches, a permanent cripple, to begin life anew. He had specialized in botany at Harvard under the tutelage of Asa Gray and in zoology under Louis Agassiz. Thus he was scientifically prepared to go far beyond Caleb Coker's accomplishments in the cotton field.

Combining a country-furnishing mercantile business with farming, the young Harvard-trained scientist was able to overcome the immediate handicaps of war and to establish a mercantile empire that was to have far-reaching influence in helping the region itself to surmount its handicaps. Like Caleb before him, James L. had four sons — James Lide, Jr., David Robert, William Chambers, and Charles Westfield. David R. became head of the family's farming and mercantile interests, while W. C. followed in his father's footsteps and became a trained botanist and a member of the University of North Carolina faculty. In 1901 the young Chapel Hill botanist and Dr. D. N. Shoemaker made the first selections of cotton plants in a field of Jones' Big Boll on the Coker farm. A year later D. R. Coker, recently graduated from the University of South Carolina, comprehending the enormous influence that improved seed stocks would have upon the South, organized the Coker's Pedigreed Seed Company.

It was one thing to say that the Pedigreed Seed Company wished to aid southern agriculture, but an altogether different matter to produce results. In a region notoriously lacking in scientific accomplishments, it was not easy to organize the necessary staff for a productive plant-breeding program. In addition to Dr. Coker the first breeders were Dr. George J. Wilds, S. Pressly Coker, Dr. Herbert J. Webber, and Dr. J. B. Norton. Cotton advances lay in two possible directions. The planters could follow the lead of the federal scientists who sought first to adapt Egyptian long staple types to the southern uplands and thereby produce a cotton that was equal to the sea island varieties, or they could select the upland types that lent themselves more readily to improvement and go forward with them. Egyptian cottons proved a failure, and were abandoned early in the history of scientific plant breeding. Interest was then centered on the upland types altogether.

Beginning a long and tedious process of selection by the "plant-to-row" process, thousands of choices were made for checking as to fidelity of type qualities, and these in turn were planted and replanted in plots of varying sizes until the best selections possible were made for planting in large controlled seed plots. Between 1907 and 1935 Coker's Pedigreed Seed Company offered southern farmers eleven new strains which went far toward revolutionizing production in the old cotton belt. As significant as these accomplishments were, the cotton industry still demanded more efficient types of plants. In 1934, 14,775 plant selections were made by the company's breeders, and the next year 3500 of these were used in a plant-to-row test from which 125 strains were selected, and from these have come the modern Coker types. North and South Carolina farmers now use Coker cotton almost altogether. Georgia and Florida planters use more of it than of other varieties, and Alabama growers plant 40 per cent of their crop with Coker seed.

At the Mississippi branch cotton experimental station in Stoneville, highly trained geneticists are working patiently with cotton plants which run the gamut of cotton plant history. Their greenhouses shelter fabulous parent stalks of both cultivated and wild types — both harboring in their genes highly desirable characteristics. Outside in hundreds of plots are cotton types that come under close scientific scrutiny. Ultimately these scientists hope to perfect a plant that can meet all the mechanical requirements and make cotton an indispensable fabric.

Not far away at Scott, Mississippi, the great Delta Pine Land Company rivals the Coker farms as a commercial breeding establishment. Here breeders strive to make nature meet a set of rigidly prescribed specifications. From this plantation have come the various Delta Pine Land varieties. These commercial varieties have changed both delta and hill cotton farming, and have even influenced international cotton growing. They have made a bale to the acre seem normal crop expectancy.

Cotton breeders everywhere are called upon to hasten their activities. No longer are genetics and cytology a leisurely scientific activity conducted within a university laboratory. Geneticists and cytologists in the great cotton breeding stations at Raleigh, North Carolina, and College Station, Texas, care little actually about the specific commercial possibilities of their handiwork. Their first concern is with plant types and characteristics. Wild and domestic types of cottons from all over the world crowd their greenhouses, and their book shelves are crammed with information on current trends in cotton demands. They go in search of certain desirable characteristics which might be established in a cotton plant to make it a better competitor to synthetic products.

If breeders ever produce a hybrid type which will be as successful as hybrid corn, cotton production will boom indeed. Although
hybrid cotton on a commercial scale has seemed an impossibility
because of the bi-sexual nature of the plant, there is hope that it
may be attained by the use of selective gametocides which could
render the male cotton flower sterile.

Mechanization of the cotton industry from seed-planting to the
weaving process makes exacting demands on the breeder. Again
he is tackling the old problem of adapting the best features obtainable by shaving the hairs off current varieties, dropping the
boll bracts, or producing a sturdy, quick maturing stalk that will
shed its leaves as quickly as possible, open its bolls just wide
enough for a whirling picker spindle to catch it, but not wide
enough to be injured by storm, with a boll lining tough enough
to crumple a boll weevil's snout, with fiber of sufficient staple
length and tensile strength to outlast synthetics, and with sheen
beautiful enough to robe an Oriental queen.

Even new methods of cultivation place wrinkles in the geneticist's brow. His cotton plant has to produce many and sturdier
branches, but the first ones have to grow high enough off the
ground to be above the hot breath of flame throwers used to destroy grass, yet not high enough to prevent the setting of a full-
fruited crop. The plant needs to be sturdy enough to resist rude
brushes with the cultivator, but not high enough to become en-
tangled in the bridging of the machines. When the plant sets its
bolls they should be far enough out on the limbs to enable the
mechanical pickers to reach them without crushing the plant and
injuring a secondary crop, or without missing an appreciable
number of bolls.

While cotton geneticists and breeders are checking their
guesses and hopes in the fields, millmasters keep their eyes on the
manufacturers of synthetic fibers. In order to meet competition,
the cotton growers are called upon to deliver longer staple with
more uniform tensile strength and fiber diameter. By micronaire
measurements, textile manufacturers are able to make a detailed
material check on the kind of cotton that reaches them from the
southern growers. This has resulted in the reduction of varieties
of cotton from more than 500 to less than ten.

Never in his wildest speculation on cotton did the ante-bellum plantation owner give thought to the diameter of his staple, and it is doubtful that many of them gave much thought even to the elementary matter of its length. So far as they were concerned cotton had three basic qualities: it was clean and white, it was fruitful, and the relationship between seed and lint was satisfactory by pre-conceived standards. Few of them knew anything about quality and quite possibly cared less.

From the beginning of the ancient Egyptian cotton industry to 1902 there was little improvement in the cotton plant. Where plant selections were made, improvements might or might not result; at any rate the grower had little more than his eye and his judgment to guide him. The only scientific instruments at his command were the clumsy scales he used to gauge the return of the land in pounds produced. The modern cotton geneticist and commercial breeder must hurry to keep up with cotton's competitors. Breeding establishments work fast to crowd in three crops in two years. Cotton grown on southern breeding farms during the summer is hastened to Mexican plantations for fall plantings so that a third planting in twenty-four months can be made in the South the following spring.

A quarter of a century ago cotton farmers did not dream of the current changes in their crop. For instance, the term "close to the breeder" would have been absolutely meaningless. Today manufacturers are well informed on the precise mill performance of the various new varieties, and many of them buy on that basis. Several of the breeders carry through their operations from row to mill, and even check finished garments through a normal period of wear. Every step of processing is checked, and the end performance serves as a guide as to whether or not a new variety is ready for the market. Thus far southern cotton growers have not accepted generally the single variety and gin certification plan. San Joaquin Valley cotton farmers in California have selected a single variety and have outlawed all others. There is no indication that there will be restriction of this kind in other areas.

There prevails an argument of some intensity as to whether or not the mule and the little farmer can survive this age of mechanization. The mule has practically lost the race, but there is some uncertainty about the little farmer. While his cost of production can be reckoned in the barest minimum terms of mere subsistence, and fixed costs for him are not so arbitrary as for the big farmers, he still faces a struggle to survive. Certainly, economics and technology of production favor the bigger farmer who can afford the machines necessary to cut costs of production by cultivating enough acreage by scientific methods to reduce expenses appreciably.

One cotton research worker has said without reservation that "the survival of cotton production in the United States depends upon a complete mechanization of the planting, cultivation, and harvesting processes. The efficiency of every step of growing and processing a cotton crop must be increased by the use of equipment, herbicides, cultural practices, and adapted varieties."

Geographical statistics bear out this scientist's statement. The cotton belt is moving rapidly away from those areas which are not ideally adaptable to machine use to areas where conditions are conducive to maximum mechanization and production. Precisely, cotton is coming down off the hills to the river and creek bottoms.

Cotton is still moving westward. Geographically it is by no means restricted to a single area. Tradition means little in the location of the modern cotton fields. Confined for three centuries to the South, the staple in recent years has demonstrated a tremendous mobility. Since 1929 cotton acreage in the South dropped 43 per cent, from 44,448,000 acres to 25,244,000 in 1955. Every major cotton growing southern state by 1955 showed a sharp decrease in acreage in the low-production areas. Only two states, Texas and Arkansas, recorded increases in the high production sections. Decreased acreage in the poorer southern lands ranged from 79 per cent in Texas to 46 per cent in Mississippi. Losses are more adequately reflected in a 60 per cent decrease in Georgia, 55 per cent in Alabama, 53 per cent in North Carolina, and 51 per cent in Louisiana. From 1931 to 1956 the number of southern cotton farms dropped from approximately 2,000,000 to about 864,000. In 1958 all the traditional cotton states east of the Mississippi River showed a material reduction in acreage, even below that allotted under crop control regulations. A vast area of cotton lands was placed in the soil bank program, which no doubt means that it has been permanently withdrawn from production.

In 1956, eight of the major southern cotton states, excluding Texas, planted 6,991,000 acres and produced 5,650,000 bales.

These same states in 1920 planted 20,349,000 acres and gathered 7,448,141 bales. The 1920 acreage was almost three times greater than that of 1956, but the yield was only 30 per cent higher. Translated into broader human terms, a greater amount of energy went into the cultivation of an acre of cotton in 1920 than in 1956, when machines had come to perform most of the tedious labor of cultivating and gathering cotton. As important as the relative cash income from these two crop years may be, it is of little significance compared with the acreage differential and the heavy demand on human efforts.

California, New Mexico, Arizona, and West Texas are the new and booming cotton states. California plants almost 2,000,000 acres on irrigated lands, and cotton yields a bigger income in that state than do all other crops combined. Westerners are planting almost their entire acreage allotments. Even though the western farmers have to irrigate, cotton is grown at lower cost than in the old grass-ridden southern fields. Grass does not grow and the boll weevil is unknown in arid western lands. Also, the topography permits a maximum use of machinery, reducing sharply the need for expensive human labor.

California, Arizona, and West Texas offer the southern cotton farmers ruinous competition. Since 1938 the Far West has gained 84 per cent in cotton acreage, and the South has lost 40 per cent.

In 1910 approximately 20 per cent of all the cultivated farm land in South Carolina was planted to cotton, but forty-five years later less than 10 per cent grew the staple. Neighboring North Carolina and Georgia are also falling behind. Certainly King Cotton's crown rests uneasily in these ancient foothold states.

No general statement could adequately describe changes which have occurred in cotton production since 1929. The New Deal hastened the dawn of another era in the cotton patch. Depression closed the old style ledger on the industry. A phase of history dating back to Whitney's invention of the gin was ended. A bizarre incident made a sharp cleavage in cotton history. Farmers were required to plow up a fourth of their crop in 1933 or suffer a penalty at market time. Sweaty plowmen cudgeled stubborn mules into breaking centuries of training by walking atop rows. They were in fact plowing under an old way of life.

Cotton planters pondering world conditions that called for such a drastic remedy found their answer in a surplus of 25,000,000 bales. Consumption of American cotton, at the rate of 14,600,000 bales a year, was losing ground to foreign growers. After one fourth of a promising crop was destroyed in those perplexing early days of the Roosevelt Administration, there was still a surplus. Bonded warehouses were crammed with millions of bales which millmasters could not use.

Never again after 1933 was southern cotton farming to assume its historic role of enslaving so vast an army of southerners. Tenant farmers, white and black, had reached the end of an era. Either government and industry had to provide new economic opportunity or the people stood fair to perish. Exhausted lands, glutted markets, bankrupt landlords, and the appearance of competitive synthetics were all a part of the weakening of cotton as a staple crop. Abroad, foreign cotton growers were competing effectively for overseas customers.

Troubled world conditions created a greater demand for industrial goods than for cotton. Cotton-field workers were needed more than ever in industry. Meat, lumber, and grain were basic to a quickening war effort. Fields which had grown cotton for a century now burgeoned with grass and white-faced cattle. Farmers squatting about county courthouses on Saturday afternoon talked of cattle breeding rather than the grass menace and scarcity of hoe hands. New soil conservation practices created a fantastic modern design of terrace whorls on red hills. Lands that were worn to bed clay for so many years that no one recalled their virgin state now turned green. Cabins whose gaunt rock chimneys had stood as beacons amidst cotton fields became heaps of decaying rubble.

Thousands of cotton patches carved out of the woods by generations long dead were reseeded to pines. Rising acres of fresh young trees crowded themselves in amongst older woodlands like fresh greens crammed into giant natural salad baskets. For the first time the term "non-row" crops became a part of southern planter vocabulary. Farmers reaped their profits from crop benefits and conservation payments. They hastened their tenants off the lands so as to monopolize these payments.

If the scene in the cotton field has changed, so has processing of the crop. Since the days of Eli Whitney, ginning cotton has been a traditional southern industry. In the history of the South, ginners have nearly always been a tribe of irascible human beings capable of great explosive qualities in the harvest seasons. Like steamboat captains, they were once lords of important domains. But engage one in conversation today and his tale of woe is heart-rending. The whir of a gin is music to his ears, but crops are so slender that there is hardly enough cotton to pay, yet there is too much to ignore. Once the cotton gin was as much a landmark in a southern town as the Confederate Monument. Surrounded by rows of freshly ginned bales smelling highly of their tarred metal bindings, they were centers of feverish activity. Even the most casual observer could gauge fairly accurately the promise of local prosperity by the number of cotton bales about a gin. There was once an old folk saying that the way to try a man's patience was to sell him a second-hand gin. Whether or not this was true there are now plenty of second-hand gins for sale in the old cotton South.

No longer are there big leather-bound ledgers bearing their burdens of charges for fat meat, meal, lard, molasses, and patent medicines. Even fertilizer dealers have had to develop new techniques in selling cotton farmers. Both farmer and merchant must now know another kind of record; they want to be told in modern economic terms the precise cost of production. This troublous factor has become as great a specter as boll weevils and grass. To survive cost of production, methods of cultivation and harvest have to be made far more efficient. Old masters of the tenant system were never unconscious of the fact that their methods were unprofitable. Their margin of economic survival was so thin that literally hundreds of thousands of southerners depended on the troubled cotton system long after it was exhausted.

In 1939 the day of judgment was at hand. It hardly seemed possible that the old cotton industry would survive. That year the National Cotton Council was organized, not to save a way of life in the region, or to save armies of displaced persons moving away from the land and the South, but to save an industry. Foreign growers had equaled American production of fiber, and northwestern dairy farmers were producing both surplus butter and local laws to protect its sale in competition with cottonseed oil. In Congress the dairy interest found a sympathetic hearing in its fight against oleomargarine. Synthetic manufacturers made available attractive fabrics and promised cheaper and more exciting ones for the future. Even the southern pines which had kept constant vigil with cotton fields for centuries now promised paper and bags in competition. Cotton states newspapers published fantastic filler stories of the prospects of the paper industry; in time, they said, even paper clothing would be available. Already the cotton farmer's newborn infant was clad in absorbent paper diapers, and the father might expect disposable paper shirts at some early date. Automobile and tractor tires used by cotton growers contained nylon, and robbed the farmer of one of his richest market outlets. Lobbying dairy farmers ran cotton oil and its end-product, oleomargarine, into a tight legislative pocket with all sorts of trick provisions.

With each succeeding year farm implement dealers crowd their display yards with bright and gaudily painted machines. Mechanical pickers with their grasping spindles and deep net wire maws await each new harvest to displace armies of human cotton pickers. There were 12,000 of these in 1954, and more than 19,000 in 1955, plus 23,000 mechanical strippers. On a fair fall day these machines can do the work of a million human beings. They help account for the fact that from 1939 to 1954 at least 8,700,000 people left southern farms.

As vast as is the human revolution in southern cotton since 1939, it has not been so important, perhaps, as the revolution in cotton management. The National Cotton Council has had enormous political influence at state and national levels in protecting the interests of the industry, but even more important has been its market research. Until 1933 cotton was perhaps the most carelessly handled of any major American agricultural crop. Cotton economics consisted largely of speculative researches and guesses. Consumer research was limited. How many bales of cotton went into specific end-uses was at best a wild guess, and nobody really seemed to care. So thoroughly was the idea implanted in the minds of farmers, speculators, and manufacturers that cotton goods were indispensable that they never took the trouble to analyze their market. Rayon made the difference. The synthetics industry had almost unlimited capital resources behind it. In 1954 Du Pont alone spent $61,000,000 in research.

A decision made in a cotton manufacturer's conference room to add even a fractional part of synthetic fiber to a new fabric can have fantastic social and economic bearing on the cotton-growing South. Addition of 25 per cent of synthetic fiber to dress goods alone is enough to create serious economic displacement in the cotton fields, not only by lowering the demands for raw cotton at the moment but for all the foreseeable future. Such changes in cotton consumption further reduce the margin by which farmers can maintain themselves in business and still meet the costs of production. This reality is reflected in the fact that, proportionately, the American people are using less cotton every year.

The National Cotton Council's market research follows every end-use of cotton, and an aggressive corps of economists is constantly hunting new outlets for the staple. That cotton is an uneasy king in the world of fabrics is a basic assumption of the managers of the industry. Year by year grower and manufacturer alike are told where their market sagged and where it expanded. Cotton growing and marketing is fiercely competitive in modern America, at the moment one of the most competitive of agricultural industries. Yet orthodox applications of economic principles hardly describe the problems of the southern cotton farmer. Acreage reduction has proved a virtual failure in controlling production. In 1935 farmers gathered 240 pounds of lint cotton per acre; they produced the phenomenal crop of 341 pounds of lint per acre in 1954; they harvested 466 pounds in 1955. The estimated 1959 crop was 15,000,000 bales, or about four-fifths of a bale per acre. Scientific applications of fertilizers, herbicides, grass control with new machines, and the planting of newer varieties of cotton have produced explosive results.

As the human army has deserted the cotton fields and the acreage has dropped cataclysmically, the rate of production has climbed. Farmers have poured 11,000,000 bales per year into the government pools. At the same time millmasters have operated on short inventories, the international market for American cotton is giving way to rising production in low cost areas of the world. The old kingdom is changed. Today it is supported by an army of roaring machines, a battery of bright young economists, a clever advertising campaign that sends forth a beautiful Maid of Cotton annually to entice American women to wear cotton, and an active political lobby which keeps a watch on unpromising legislation. The industry is becoming mechanized and dehumanized. Better varieties and prodigal fertilization, coupled with selections of choice cotton lands, make the difference. The ancient marriage bond between the old cotton-growing South and King Cotton has been renegotiated as a common law agreement by which either can make promiscuous adventures without seriously compromising the other.

V

So Runs the Land

So while multitudes abandoned their ancestral acres in despair, or were driven from them by the recoil of their fathers' inconsiderate expenditures, they were taken possession of by "new men," endowed with more hopefulness and energy, if not more intelligence than the old. Movement, though it be apparently downward, is evidence of life, and is stimulating to the mind. Every man who thought about it, saw that either tobacco must be given up, or its method of culture essentially modified, or that his land must continue to decrease in productive value.

OLMSTED, A JOURNEY IN THE SEABOARD SLAVE STATES, p. 276

Three and a half centuries of farming fastened a strong agrarian tradition upon the South. So strong is this tradition that changes in conditions of farming upset the equilibrium of southern life. Since Jamestown, southern economic foundations have been anchored in field and furrow. Like all such traditions, regional economy was cast in a rigidly conservative mold. A monotonous succession of staple crops sustained a society that was often forced into a strait jacket of ignorance, prejudice, defeatism, and fear. Long before the Declaration of Independence, southern farmers faced troubles. Tidewater planters floundered in debt and frustration, largely because they failed to conserve their lands, to develop markets, and to diversify their crops. Historically the South's emotional response has always been based on its agricultural fortunes. Staple agriculture has been sensitive to competition, political conditions, and criticism.

After the Civil War, farmers faced the problem of beginning anew their operations. Their lands were injured by years of neglect; fields were overgrown; and implements were destroyed. Credit was almost unobtainable, and normal production impossible.

Post-Civil War farming in much of the South was synonymous with poverty, yet there was an abundance of fresh lands, a good labor supply, and a will to work. Despite high-priced cotton in the immediate postwar years, the future of southern agriculture was clouded. Landowners had land but no money with which to employ labor; laborers often had neither land nor money. The ensuing barter between the two inevitably produced a practice of tenant farming, with its peculiar arrangements. Pressure of debt and threat of economic collapse were so great that a southern farmer had little room within which to maneuver. Actually thousands of southerners trampled hard on the treadmill of staple economy every year just to stay in the same place. Colonel L. L. Polk, founder of the *Progressive Farmer,* said that Georgia farmers in 1866 owned 72 per cent of that state's wealth, but only 24 per cent twenty years later. In 1870 a farmer could have paid a thousand dollar mortgage with ten bales of cotton, but it took twenty bales to pay the same debt in 1886.

After 1865, white and Negro alike settled down to the grind of producing tobacco, cotton, sugar cane, and rice. They grew these crops on land incapable of continuous production without heavy application of fertilizers high in nitrogen, phosphate, and lime. There was a serious soil deficiency which demanded scientific knowledge and treatment which were non-existent before World War I. Whatever pressure political and social forces exerted in producing living conditions in the South, the qualities of the soil exerted an equal one. This fact was recognized in the South's earlier years.

Until 1945, cotton was the great common denominator for vast areas of the South. Almost every state south of Kentucky, Virginia, and a part of North Carolina reckoned its major income by the cotton yield. The sharp decline of the staple economy after 1890 made the farmer adopt, almost of economic necessity, conservative points of view in religion, social affairs, politics, and economics. The creeping paralysis of agrarian failure closed men's minds to new ideas. Progress was slow in a land of low fertility, mounting debts, deepening gullies, and sand-gorged streams.

In 1936, Howard Odum viewed the history of southern agriculture along with that of the South in general in *Southern Regions* as consisting of a series of crises. He wrote, "There was and is the crisis of the agrarian struggle for survival against the overwhelming handicaps of poverty, inefficiency, and the aftermath of the plantation system; and the later rise and sweep of the industrial movement and its creation of new classes and labor relations."

Agricultural progress in the South has been slowed by crises in every aspect of farming. Some parts of the region have thrived while others have failed. The rural South comes off badly in a statistical comparison. Deep in the middle of the region, the Appalachian Highlands form an economic world of their own. No modern comparison of conditions of this area with the rest of the agricultural United States is remotely encouraging. Landlocked, agriculturally the highland South remains in a state of economic suspension dating back to the mid-eighteenth century. This is a land of much natural beauty, rich mineral deposits, and many islands of high productivity. But on the whole it is victimized by thin soils, rough terrain, and limited agrarian promise. Fundamentally, it is a timber-growing region which has been grossly abused by patch farmers.

Among the pine hills, in river delta, and along coastal plain, earlier, farmers were stuck so deep in the mire of primitive roads on a rugged frontier that they had little opportunity to receive and absorb new ideas. They had little comparative insight with which to assess their own failures. After 1886, experiment stations and, later, extension workers were rebuffed when they appeared on the scene. Sometimes, as in the dipping vat campaign against Texas fever ticks, the extension workers were even faced with occasional outbreaks of violence. There was a saying that it took at least fifteen years to establish a new agricultural idea. Whether or not this was true, the southern farm was for seventy years the scene of the greatest economic struggle in the country.

War also hastened the day when farmers would use complete fertilizers. In times of national emergency they learned that lands could be cropped continuously only by adequate fertilization. In supplying farm products during two world wars an increasing use of fertilizers had made the difference between success and failure for southern farmers.

Farmers were caught up in the tightening web of a usurious credit system. Furnishing merchants supplied, or rejected, capital support to tillers of the soil, not on a recognized dollars and cents banking basis but on a peculiar system of guesses, discriminations, and faltering optimism. Thousands of customers of southern furnishing merchants were seldom capable of securing outright cash loans. Their collateral resources were so severely limited that they had only their uncertain honor and brawn with which to guarantee such loans. A form of colonial capitalism gripped the economically handicapped agricultural South. Its highly discriminatory methods of farm financing, aided by rising freight rates, produced a form of peonage, and it expedited some of the worst extra-regional exploitation in American history. More detrimental, however, was the fact that this financing system closed the southern agrarian mind to progress.

While much of the nation was making industrial and agricultural progress, the South was wasting manpower and natural resources. For much of the southern farming population, life was at best a fleeting adventure which encouraged wholesale waste and neglect. Except for certain favored regions, such as the Carolina piedmont, the South remained overwhelmingly rural and agrarian.

Several factors in American economic growth shattered the mores of southern staple farming. These were the growth of international competition in cotton and sugar, the artificial stimulus of World War I, a rising tide of Negro migration out of the South, and the arrival of the boll weevil. Of these factors, World War I probably had the greatest bearing on agricultural change. Never before, except during the Civil War, had the southern farmer been called upon to produce more with less labor. Rising prices for all farm products completely changed the economic picture for the region. War reduced the labor supply and increased the demand for labor-saving implements and fertilizers. Motorization of transportation was followed by use of the tractor, and better markets for a wider diversity of products came into existence.

Between World War I and II the number of tractors increased appreciably. Where the land was level and could be cultivated in large tracts the tractor proved satisfactory. In the upland South, however, it remained only a seductive advertisement in farm journals. The early tractors and hillside land were unsuited to each other. Hill farm units were small, the ground surface was slanting and irregular, and the proportion of men and mules to land was possibly greater than in the lowland areas. Too, the cost of tractors, implements, and fuel was prohibitive. Manufacturers, however, adjusted their machines to southern pocketbooks, and the region has become a highly profitable implement market. In 1955, presidents of the major tractor manufacturing companies expressed in the *Progressive Farmer* a keen desire to adapt their machines to all types of southern farming.

It can hardly be said that motorized farming now predominates in the modern South. Yet this is rapidly becoming true. The yearly growth of power farming is almost phenomenal. In Alabama, for instance, the farming picture is changing radically. When Hitler's troops marched into Poland the mule was still in his glory in that cotton state. The roar of only 7,638 tractors disturbed the relatively silent countryside. Five years later more than twice that number of machines rumbled across the fields; in 1950 farming had experienced a mechanized revolution with 45,751 tractors in operation; in 1954 there were 65,175, and the number is still growing.

Mississippi, the traditional and hospitable home of the cotton mule and the one-gallused farmer, showed an even greater increase in mechanization. At the depth of the great depression in 1932, Mississippians still thought of farming in terms of mule power. They possessed only 5,542 tractors, and most of these operated on flat delta lands. Fifteen years later the number had quadrupled, and in 1954 there were 81,621 tractors, many of which were equipped with canopies and parasols to prevent the traditional reddening of plowmen's necks.

Tennessee, Missouri, and Kentucky mule breeders are forgotten men. Kentucky's State Fair now exhibits only a token number of jacks and jennets, and were it not for a strong tradition possibly none would be shown. In equipping its new Eden Shale Belt Farm, the University of Kentucky Experiment Station made no provisions for mule barns. There were fewer than 200,000 mules in Mississippi in 1956, as compared with 358,000 in 1930. At the same time the value of mules in that state shrunk from $31,934,000 to $9,417,000. Eleven southern states lost 293,000 horses and mules between 1954 and January 1, 1957, a drop from 1,851,000 to 1,558,000.

In 1955, the Mississippi sub-experiment station at Stoneville razed its mule barn; its cotton operation was completely mechanized. Surrounding the station, delta planters have turned largely to use of machines. Even where the Negro-mule combination has persisted, the tractor is used for heavy plowing. This step toward mechanization has far-reaching importance in destroying the old economic-social pattern.

Mechanization of farming has an important bearing on the South's general outlook. Now it is not possible for a southern farmer to employ ancient credit methods and survive. At the same time he is unable to think of farming apart from the necessity of providing a sizable capital outlay. Margins of profit on the average southern farm are so small that operators cannot afford to buy machinery on a time-payment plan and pay carrying charges. Unless they can get low-interest loans the cost of equipment is too great to permit operation.

One of the sharpest breaks with the past is the virtual end of opportunity for a young man to begin farming with no other assets than his physical vigor and will power. It would be most difficult, if not impossible, for a young couple who has nothing more than an enduring affection for each other and a pair of healthy bodies to become successful farm owners in the modern South with its restricted acreages. Some close observers of southern change say that unless a young southerner inherits land and then marries a considerable amount of money it is doubtful that he can succeed as a competitive farmer.

At all times in the region's history southern farm conditions have been good subjects for pamphlets and books. But few such publications have carried so penetrating an insight as a report on the conditions of human resources on low-income farms published by the United States Department of Agriculture in April 1955. Of nine problem areas in the United States, six were in the South. A graphic chart portrays areas in twelve southern states as critical, or having less than $1000 a year in farm income. Among the problem areas, only the delta of Mississippi exceeded $1000.

The level of living standard index for this whole region was within the lowest fifth of the nation; and the region contains more than half of the farms classified as "low production."

This federal study presents the South against the general economic condition of farming in the country. Its picture is gloomy, despite the location of non-critical areas in all of the states except Mississippi and South Carolina. The report offers little hope for marginal farmers in the South. In a brave effort to represent farming in a more attractive light, President Dwight D. Eisenhower, Secretary of Agriculture Ezra Taft Benson, and the specialists who prepared the report, seek remedy beyond the farm gate. "Any substantial reorganization in the areas of limited job opportunity is bound to be a long-term process," the report says. "The job is a large one and is to be undertaken with a sense of persistent effort of necessary continuity. As an example, the Mississippi Agricultural Experiment Station recently estimated that an efficient reshaping of farm resources in the Mississippi uplands would mean larger farms and probably double the amount of capital. It also would involve a 60 per cent reduction in the number of farm workers. Such changes would take time. The challenge is how to permit the speeding up of solutions already under way by education and by the practical application of credit, employment services, and other facilities which may be brought to bear by official or private agencies."

Southern landholding has been tending in the direction indicated in this report. Despite the fact that the Farm Security and the Farm Home Administration and other Federal and state agencies have attempted to place tenants on land of their own, the number of southern farms has declined. A look at seven southeastern states — Virginia, the Carolinas, Tennessee, Georgia, Alabama, and Florida — shows in a dramatic way the changing patterns on the land. The number of farms in this region declined by some 300,000 from 1930 to 1950, while the size of the farms increased by 30 per cent. In Georgia, specifically, the number was cut in half between 1920 and 1957. At the present time only 36 per cent of the total southeastern landed area is in cultivation. There are at present sufficient lands to support a much larger population, but it would have to be cultivated in considerably larger units to yield maximum production. Despite the fact that corporate ownership is increasing in terms of acreage, the Southeast remains decidedly a region of individual ownership. More than 96 per cent of the land is still in private possession.

In 1900, the proportion of landowners in the Southeast possessing 200 acres or more was 15.8 per cent; in 1946 it was 24 per cent. In 1900 3.8 per cent of the owners held more than 500 acres; in 1956 this number had increased to 7.2 per cent. In the smaller ownership group, comprising about one-quarter of the farmers, 2.4 per cent of the land was owned by farmers possessing thirty acres or less. At the same time 28.4 per cent of southern land was owned by the 2.8 per cent of farmers possessing 500 acres or more.

Even more basic to the situation of agriculture in the modern South, though, is the question of the soil itself. Since colonial beginnings in Virginia, farmers have been aware that sandy soils are quickly eroded and exhausted. In the nineteenth century, Edmund Ruffin, a pioneer in soil analysis and management, found it was difficult to convince farmers to conserve the soil so long as vast areas of fresh lands were available. The practice of exhausting lands and constant removal of farmers long characterized much southern land use. In the first half of this century population increases and the exhaustion of available public lands have finally caught up with farmers.

Extension workers, soil conservationists, and even private individuals have crusaded for terracing and contour plowing. It hardly seems possible that it was necessary to campaign for contour plowing and adequate fertilization in a land where farmers took pride in their horse sense. Yet a lack of interest and common judgment kept many farmers from changing their traditional habits of land management.

By 1930, soil exhaustion was about as basic to the South's economic and social stalemate as was the great depression. The wasteful gutting of land had done its work. Everywhere sheet erosion and exhaustion of plant nutrients were in evidence. Even the highly prized and presumably inexhaustible bluegrass lands of Tennessee and Kentucky and the deep loams of the river delta showed signs of wear and nutrient deficiencies.

Today conditions have changed radically. An air traveler flying low over the southern states is impressed by the modern land patterns below him, created by contour terracing. Great banks of earth lie athwart gullies to stop the wash of land. Even wide bands of fallow land bound by turf fortify the soil against wind and water erosion. Most farmers give much thought to preventing scars appearing on their lands which in time would deepen into gullies.

Never in the South's agricultural history have farmers shown a greater willingness to apply fertilizers in amounts necessary to bring their lands into maximum production. Yet, in April 1945, M. J. Peterson and G. H. Aull of the South Carolina Experiment Station wrote of their state that *"proper fertilization has not been followed by a sufficient number of farmers to promote noteworthy results."* (italics added) This could no doubt be said of the whole South. Acreage control of at least two major crops, however, has given great impetus to more abundant use of fertilizers.

Before 1930, too few southern farmers had a clear understanding of the importance of the chemical constituency of their soils. They relied largely on clumsy visual judgments and sketchy production histories to guide them in land use. It was not until the considerable worth of soil analysis was demonstrated that new ideas of management became acceptable. Farmers in the Tennessee Valley were convinced through the use of demonstration test farms of the importance of land-use based on knowledge of soil chemistry and analysis.

At the University of Kentucky, George Roberts, a mountaineer himself, crusaded for more adequate care of the soils. In many respects he may be considered a pioneer spokesman for adequate fertilization. It was he who advocated a combination of lime and phosphate to bring soils up to maximum production. When the Tennessee Valley Authority made phosphates available to eight southern states, Kentucky farmers purchased approximately 70 per cent of the available stock. Roberts had done his work, and farmers were ready to profit from his ideas.

To the south of Kentucky, Harcourt A. Morgan had preached good soil management for a generation as Dean of the Tennessee College of Agriculture. When he became a member of the Board of Commissioners of the Tennessee Valley Authority he was in an even better position to spread his ideas. Farmers in the area were shown that a good scientific practice of land-use and adequate fertilization yielded profits.

Since the early decades of the nineteenth century, when literate gentlemen farmers concerned themselves with writing learned papers on the use of manures and marls, southerners have made a gesture at fertilization. During the post-Civil War cotton era, chemical fertilizers of low analysis were applied in such meager quantities that they did little good. Their purchase and freight costs only put cotton growers hopelessly into debt. Politicians and farm furnishing merchants were allied with fertilizer manufacturers and railroads in enslaving farmers. Tradition prevails in the South, and it is still difficult to persuade farmers to forsake the past and make adequate investments in fertilizers.

The modern fertilizer industry has been aided by the Tennessee Valley Authority and commercial chemical companies, which have made available highly concentrated phosphates, nitrates, and potash. At the same time these chemical products are more reliable in quality than were the older ones. In the Tennessee Valley there has been an intimate association between the production of nitrogen and phosphorous for war purposes and for agriculture. For fifteen years the Muscle Shoals nitrate plant stood idle until it was turned over to the T.V.A., and that agency began production of highly concentrated phosphates and nitrates. Indeed, T.V.A. fertilizer production has had almost as significant an effect on agriculture as its power program. Increased nutrient contents reduced weight and cut freight rates in half. New types of fertilizers were introduced in super-phosphates, calcium meta-phosphates, ammonium nitrates, and tri-calcium phosphates. These new fertilizers were sold to the Agricultural Adjustment Administration and other agricultural agencies, which distributed them to farmers in lieu of crop payments. Some of the credit for the revolution must go to private companies for introducing the farmers to new types of concentrated fertilizers.

By addition of fertilizer alone, southern tobacco, cotton, cane, and rice growers greatly exceed the old unlimited-acre production figures. Reduced acreage, in the aggregate, has actually meant little in total production. A new knowledge of soil chemistry is for the first time bringing about intelligent diversification of crops, thus answering at long last one of the longest and most fervently sustained rural editorial pleas.

An age-old question in regional history and economics was whether or not the South produced sufficient food crops to sustain itself. Several states showed "crop deficits" because they failed to produce necessary supplies of grain and forage for regional consumption. The problem has been met to a remarkable extent by the success of plant breeding.

From frontier beginnings an argument has persisted over both the quality and quantity of southern white corn, a major southern crop. No other staple of diet has approached its universal popularity and use. Lack of corn has sometimes contributed to faulty food habits, and improper use of it has also propagated ill health. Since the days of Uncle Tom and Little Eva, the myth has persisted that southern white corn was inferior to the northern yellow corn. It was too soft and lacked nutrients, said its critics. Unquestionably one of its most serious drawbacks was the poor yield per acre. Ironically, South Carolina early in this century held the record for the largest amount of corn produced on a single acre, and at the same time it sustained one of the lowest average yields per acre. Approximately the same story could be told in the other southern states. Average yields ranged from ten to twenty bushels per acre.

Southern corn production history has been reversed in the last decade. Higher fertilization and hybrid seed stock have revolutionized this important crop. Hybrids made a poor beginning in much of the South because breeders from other sections dumped unadapted seed stock onto the southern market. Farmers were disappointed in the performance of the new corn, and not until hybrids were bred specifically for southern conditions did they become acceptable. Even then, it took an extraordinary selling effort to establish confidence in the new seed stocks. Once regional breeders met the challenge of new types adapted to varying soil and climatic conditions, southern corn production made encouraging advances.

Hybrid corn has not only refuted the ancient contention of inferiority of the southern crop, but it has brought about phenomenally changed production figures. Alabama and Mississippi in 1940 produced twelve to fifteen bushels of corn per acre. In 1955 their average was thirty bushels, with 65 per cent of the crop planted to hybrid stock. In the last decade southern corn acreage has dropped 40 per cent, but total production has increased. Two large feed mills in Decatur, Alabama, alone reflect the change in southern grain growing. One of these mills was moved from Nebraska to the banks of the Tennessee River to supply northwestern grains to the great broiler-chicken industry. It now depends altogether on local grain, which equals in quality that grown in the Midwest.

Hybrid corn and greater use of fertilizers have not only revolutionized southern grain production and reversed an abiding southern tradition, but they have hastened mechanization of the southern farm. Plants are now bred to facilitate machine cultivation and harvesting. While breeders keep their eyes on rising mechanization, they also take note of the southern climate. Hybrid corns are more drouth-resistant, and heavy yields are possible even when weather fails to co-operate.

Almost every other southern field crop has felt the hand of the plant breeder. From the experiment stations and private establishments have come new seed stocks. Improved varieties of tobacco have partly met the challenge of disease and the demands for lower nicotine content, better coloring, and increased production. By 1935 the southern tobacco industry faced a serious threat of greatly reduced production. Disease was rampant, and the traditional varieties succumbed to increasing infection by nematodes, fungi, bacteria, and virus.

Historically the plea for brighter and lighter tobacco was basic to tobacco production. In fact it was John Rolfe, of Pocahontas fame, and his associates at Jamestown who started the trend for milder, better-flavored tobacco when they imported "Sweet Orinoco" seeds from the Orinoco river valley in Venezuela. The search has gone on ever since. In Virginia, North Carolina, Kentucky, and Maryland farmers have sought new and better plants. "Sweet Orinoco" was succeeded by better types until the end of the Civil War, when the bright leaf varieties in the older eastern belts supplanted the old stand-bys.

George Webb of Brown County, Ohio, bought a parcel of seed in 1867 from G. W. Barkley of Bracken County, Kentucky. There appeared among Webb's plants some light-green and broad-leafed variations with exceptionally light mid-veins and stalks. The first plants were destroyed as defective, but the next year some light-colored seedlings again appeared in the seed bed. This time the Ohio farmer set approximately a thousand plants, and from these came the great burley industry of Kentucky and Tennessee.

In the late nineteenth century, smoking habits changed. Men gave up pipes and began to smoke cigarettes. As cigarette smoking grew, there was even greater demand for milder tobaccos. Burley farmers focused their attention on the new market, and plant breeders struggled to supply a more acceptable raw leaf. White burley was perhaps derived from a Maryland tobacco. Whatever the origin, it changed tobacco history along the Ohio. The dark leaf types gave way quickly to the luscious, light-colored, broadleaf variety, and in time this new tobacco was to bolster a faltering Kentucky farm economy, formerly devoted to hemp culture. Kentucky burley history was to be colored by all the difficulties and uncertainties which made tobacco farming at best a gambler's choice.

From the beginning three ills have beset southern tobacco farming. These are soil exhaustion, disease, and an imperfectly organized marketing system. The depression of 1921 gave the industry a serious setback, and the accumulation of disease on overcropped land reduced production below a level where normal tobacco demands could be supplied in the future. By 1935 tobacco breeders faced the challenge of restoring the crop to full productivity. The problem was not new. Pioneer breeders had worked hard to produce a better tobacco, but disease was the spur which drove them on frantically. The best tobacco soils had become heavily contaminated, and inefficient management further aggravated conditions.

Blackroot rot, mosaic, black shank, bluemold, Granville wilt, nematodes, and other infections were among the vandals of the tobacco patch. There was no known chemical preventative for most of these diseases. Salvation of the tobacco industry lay, to a great extent, in the development of disease-resistant varieties. Endless breeding experiments marked the history of the scientific battle against the looters of this crop. Had it not been for this continuing struggle southern tobacco farmers would have faced ruin and the nation's smokers would have suffered a shortage of cigarettes during World War II.

In both the flue-cured and burley belts the story was much the same. Old varieties had succumbed to disease. East of the mountains both experiment station and private breeder struck back at the viruses. The North Carolina Experiment Station and the Coker Pedigreed Seed Company in Hartsville, South Carolina, produced new types of disease-resistant plants. Bluegrass breeders improved George Webb's rangy burley and introduced varieties resistant to blackroot rot, mosaic, and fusarin wilt.

By conservative estimate, plant breeders in Kentucky alone have added at least $30,000,000 a year to tobacco income, and may have saved the burley crop. Varieties of burley resistant to blackroot rot made it possible for farmers after 1945 to grow succeeding crops in highly fertilized fields. As a result, the quantity of tobacco has been much greater, and the nicotine content has been increased. By 1956 the tobacco manufacturing situation had changed radically. In September of that year the *New York Times* carried a news story that the increasing use of filter-tip cigarettes made the heavier and darker tobaccos more desirable. This fact reverses a long-standing desirability of light leaf tobaccos.

Whether or not cigarette smoking causes cancer is a controversial point which affects southern agriculture. There was concern on the part of tobacco producers earlier over this issue. It is true that much more research will be necessary before anybody can be sure of the relationship between tobacco usage and health. The health issue is one of tobacco's oldest stumbling blocks.

At first tobacco manufacturers were conservative about accepting the newer disease-resistant leaf, but in recent years in their advertising they have proclaimed the new varieties. If any smoker is influenced by the extravagant advertising about the superior quality of new cigarettes, he might examine the fact that there has been an almost complete varietal change in southern tobacco since 1935.

Tobacco farming, like cotton raising, has undergone an ecomic and social revolution. Acreage control has reduced materially the need for farm labor, and tobacco tenants have left the land for lack of crop. Even small farmers who poured appreciable quantities of leaf onto the market from fractional acre plots now feel the pinch of crop reduction, and many of them seek income from other sources. Much southern tobacco land has reverted to grain and grazing sod, and an older pattern of agriculture has experienced great change.

Today southern farmers are producing greater quantities of grain. Here again, soil analysts and geneticists have helped destroy a lingering regional myth. Although the South is not in a position seriously to challenge grain growers of the Midwest and Northwest and the great plains, they are able to offer competition. Oats, wheat, barley, and rye have been adapted to soils and climate, and the old story of these grains not reproducing their planting seed is largely ended in the South.

One historic southern grain crop has followed the path of the pioneers who came out from the Carolinas to plant a civilization in the vast pine barrens of the old Southwest. In 1854 Olmsted visited the great tidewater rice fields of South Carolina. Here slave and master struggled to wrest life and fortune from steaming low country marshland, though white men had to remove themselves during the summer to escape malaria. In a graphic description, the northern traveler recounted the hardships of rice production under tideland conditions. Because tragedy pervaded the rice bogs of the old belt, there was a certain amount of romance associated with rice planting. Rice-laden ships sailed out of Carolina ports to deliver their white "gold" cargo to northern and European consumers. But malaria and heavy demands for cheap labor defeated the old rice planters.

No longer do summertime swarms of mosquitoes swirl up from the rice bogs, and the slaves are gone. Old Carolina fields are reed-grown hunting preserves for eastern millionaires; rice itself has gone west. Louisiana, Mississippi, Arkansas, and Texas planters supplement cotton income with rice. After the Civil War, planters in Louisiana learned that rice would thrive on some of the state's lowland soils. Arkansas and Texas growers followed suit, and in the last two decades Mississippians have turned to rice culture.

During World War II southern rice production more than doubled. Not only was it sold domestically, but it was sent around the world. Wherever starving human beings existed, rice was sent to alleviate hunger. Following the war, American rice and crop specialists were important in suggesting methods of rehabilitating the East and Near East. This crop was basic in operating the Point Four Program in areas of perennial food shortages.

Although America is not a prime rice-consuming nation, this traditional southern crop finds its way onto a reasonably good home market. Few southern field crops lend themselves so completely to mechanization. The great armies of slave labor which Olmsted saw sloshing around in tidewater Carolina bogs would be useless on the present southern rice plantation. Land is broken by tractor, some seeds are sown from airplanes, and harvesting is done by automatic machinery, with the result that the manual labor in rice production is greatly reduced.

Just as rice has crept into the older cotton lands, so has the soybean. This plant was first introduced into North Carolina from China, but the big pioneer commercial crops were grown along the Mississippi and the Ohio River in Illinois and Indiana. Today delta and blackbelt cotton plantations are planting surplus cotton lands to beans, and, where once Negro and mule combated grass, tractor-drawn cultivators and harvesters produce a yellow stream of beans for thriving oil, feed, and plastic markets.

Agricultural change in southern row crops has been enormous, but it has been even greater in turning away from row and cultivator. For the first time in southern history the southern farmer can take deep satisfaction in letting grass grow under his feet. Cotton farmers of the Old South dreamed of an after-life where there would be no grass. They even hoped to be buried on barren hillsides. A lifetime of lingering rains strangled their crops with thickening carpets of green. Hoe-hand backache was a form of purgatorial torture for southerners' enslavement to row crops. Waggish farmers in moments of frustration warned strangers to stay off the grass because they had cotton planted under it. Grass persisted even on the poorest soils. In fact one of the greatest mysteries of the farm was where did all the seeds come from that perennially pushed up countless shoots?

Modern southerners have reversed their feeling for these progeny of persistent nature. Today a sea of green obliterates the ancient corrugation of cotton rows and is a vital factor in regional economy. From the air an observer can virtually trace the route of progress by the waves of green. The traditional red splotches which once ran from farm to farm in leprous patterns are disappearing.

Varieties of southern grasses stretch out into a multitudinous roll of names reminiscent of those buoyant days of early cotton culture. Dallisgrass, Sudan, Bahia, coastal bermuda, Kentucky 31 fescue, and others account for the rolling green binders that knit southern hillsides together. Grazing has relieved much of the arduous labor on the southern farm. A North Carolina experiment demonstrated that the return per man-hour of labor in digestible livestock nutrients was: grass, $23.09; wheat, $5.81; corn, $3.69; and oats, $2.79. As row crop acreage is restricted, constantly widening meadows and hayfields take their places. There is still an urgent need for new types of grasses adapted to new regional demands.

Southern farmers have taken a century and a half to complete a cycle and revert to pioneer grazing activities. This reversion might have been faster except for the concentration of population on small farms. But even small farms feel the influence of industrialization and abandonment of row crops and are returning modest acreages to grasslands. Hay deficits have been reduced in areas where forage bills historically nicked farm incomes.

The world-wide search for grasses has a close relation to the southern agrarian revolution. From four plant introduction centers south of the Potomac, new plants arrive on southern farms. The pioneer Miami station and the new one at Coconut Grove Gardens feed a succession of new plants into the South. Near Savannah the Barbour Lathrop Garden memorializes a pioneer in plant importation. Both its grasses and fiber-bearing bamboo promise new crops. Through the co-operative southern introduction station near Griffin, Georgia, southern farmers receive new grasses. Experiment stations and plant breeders alike search for plants to smooth the way for a growing horde of non-row farmers.

Grass growing in the South has promoted a whole new concept of land care. To have fertilized a grass crop a half-century ago might have subjected a southern farmer to a question about his sanity. Today grasslands absorb a large proportion of the South's chemical fertilizers. Deep sods have gone far toward erasing the scars of cotton and tobacco exhaustion. Grass farming involves less uncertainty than any other type of southern agriculture. Even some of the famous row crop vagrants like Johnson grass promise profitable use. Already a cross between it and sorghum has occurred, and in time this historic nuisance may become an inexhaustible source of forage. When this happens, production of prime beef on a sandy southern hillside will be as devoid of arduous labor as jug fishing.

Today a considerably larger proportion of land is being converted to pasturage and hay production. In 1944, within a period of seven years, eleven southern states, excluding Maryland and Texas, had rescued 13,964,000 acres from the plow, and five years later this area had been increased to 20,600,000 acres. This latter acreage was just slightly less than the entire farming area of Mississippi.

Four states, Mississippi, Alabama, Georgia, and Tennessee, devoted 37 per cent of their farm lands in 1950 to pasturage, and in 1956 this percentage was approximately 41 per cent. The eleven states mentioned above devoted 9,881,000 acres specifically to hay production, further reducing the area devoted to row crops. It is not enough, however, to cite statistics to show a change in land utilization. The quality of southern hay has risen steadily since 1940. Use of legumes, vastly improved grasses, and more complete fertilization have resulted in a more nutritive forage. Much of the land now devoted to cultivated crops produces corn, grain, sorghum, oats, peas, and beans for feed purposes. Southern farmers historically have faced almost the same problems in curing hay as in curing meats. Heavy rainfall in much of the region during haying seasons has often discouraged the raising of this crop. An improvement of plant types and methods of handling green hay in barn curing has done much to reduce the hay deficits in most of the southern states. There is, however, in many of the states still a considerable deficit.

Crop types in much of the modern South more nearly reflect the changing economic and social organization of the country than in most of the older farming areas in the nation. An increasing national population has created a demand for foods in excess of that for cotton fiber, and much southern agricultural energy is going into the production of fruits, vegetables, oils, and meats. No agricultural changes in the South have surpassed those relating to production, marketing, and capitalization. These three aspects of regional economics have undergone a complete revolution. Aside from better types of plants, the farmer has taken other production factors into consideration. Pre-emergent and flame control of weeds and grass and chemical control of insects have made farming a capital undertaking. Chemical factors in southern farming alone have greatly increased capital demands on farmers. Controlled acreage of major crops has enforced a more careful consideration of means to promote maximum production. The only way this could be accomplished was by use of chemicals both as fertilizers and as insecticides and herbicides.

Diversification of crops has given greater impetus to scientific management in farming. The growing of increasing quantities of fruits, melons, and vegetables has enforced more precise methods of care and cultivation than was ever true with cotton, tobacco, and corn. No changes have ever been so complete as in this area of commercial farming.

Just as diversification brought more efficient methods of production, it encouraged the development of more adequate local markets. Since the beginning of farming in the region, the South has suffered a lack of dependable markets. In fact, diversification was nothing short of a wild dream when there was no place to sell the new and perishable types of farm produce. One of the major reasons cotton has held on so long as a staple is its imperishability and the existence of an established scheme of production; so long as there were no markets, the liability was entirely too great to encourage the growing of newer crops.

A realistic economic factor agitates the modern southern agrarian mind. For the first time in the South's history, industrial income surpasses that from farming. In some states the proprietary agricultural income has dropped below 10 per cent. A constantly expanding industry has offered new hope to the agrarian South on the one hand and serious competition on the other. To hold their labor farmers in industrial areas have to pay wages approximating those of industry. Likewise they have to adopt industrial hours in measuring a day's work. In some of the old farming areas, like the Bluegrass of Kentucky, the delta country, and the blackbelt, there exists much open hostility to the coming of industry because of its competitive aspects.

Capitalization of southern farming has experienced at least two distinct periods in its financial history. The old factorage and farm furnishing systems were geared specifically to the staple type of agricultural production in the ante-bellum and post-Civil War South. Whatever wastefulness they forced upon individual and region, they profited bankers, storekeepers, and wholesalers. Changes following World War I and the great depression in 1929 dealt a mortal blow to the agricultural lien law. What New Deal surveyors of southern agriculture reported in their numerous publications was the collapse of a credit system which had crushed hundreds of thousands of people. By their own pig-headedness and conservatism, manipulators of this credit scheme destroyed the source of their profits and involved a sizable portion of the nation's farmers in near economic suicide.

In recent years many observers of the changing southern scene have had time to look about them and to arrive at some conclusions. In many respects farming as a way of life has apparently come back into its own in the South. But on the other hand telltale statistics refute this. Subsistence farming is being replaced by commercial agriculture. Farmers living in a world of big business have for the first time had to trim their own operations to something approaching efficient capital management. Regional capitalization in a period of inflation calls for long-range planning and sensitivity to national and international economic currents. Although changes have come fast, southern farmers are still the first to experience economic shocks, and the last to recover from them.

Scientists and machines have brought a new southern agrarian world into being. Sagging cabin doors and tumble-down chimneys in old plantation areas linger as reminders of another age. For every three farmers left behind to struggle with the new agriculture, two of them could leave for the city and never be missed, regional economists say. Measured by the standards of nineteenth-century agricultural aspirations, southern farming has reached goals of efficiency and productivity sufficient to sustain both a reasonably happy agrarian and industrial society. But this achievement cannot obliterate the fact that a diminishing army of farmers has survived to enjoy the victory. Crusaders for farm progress never realized that their goal would be achieved in a condition of stifling competition, complex capitalization, and scientific advances.

Changing patterns in southern agriculture are not to be gauged in production tables and machine sheds or at credit-granting desks in banks. They are to be more accurately appraised in the political headlines of the national press. Often headline stories of social emotions and confusion of race relations and the dawdling with farm problems in Washington, reflect changes which have occurred in southern fields and pastures. Rising southern urbanism is not a reflection of increasing industrialization alone. Sometimes it may reflect more accurately the displacement now taking place on southern farms.

Stabilization of many of the South's social changes will have to await the results of further advance of the revolution in agriculture. Not until the new place of the farm in southern society in relationship to the new industry is fully established can there be much social calm in the region. Eventually, idealists, romanticists, rear-guard warriors, and the old way of life will be ground underfoot by the juggernaut of change. Farming will continue to be of major importance in the region, but there is every indication that it will conform more and more to the national rather than regional pattern.

VI

Cattle's Coming East

The range was much poorer than formerly. It was crowded, and peo-
ple would have to take their stock somewhere else in four or five years
more, or they would starve. He [a Louisiana farmer] didn't know what
was going to become of poor folks, rich people were taking up public
land so fast, induced by the proposed railroad to New Orleans.

More or less stock was always starved in winter. The worst time for
them was when a black gnat, called the 'eye breaker,' comes out. This
insect breeds in the woodlands, and when a freshet occurs in winter is
driven out in swarms upon the prairies, attacking cattle terribly. They
were worse than all manner of mosquitoes, flies, or other insects. Cattle
would herd together then, and wander wildly about, not looking for
the best feed, and many would get killed. But this did not often
happen.

Horses and cattle had degenerated much within his recollection.
No pains were taken to improve breeds. . . .

OLMSTED, A JOURNEY THROUGH TEXAS, p. 404

In 1855, Governor Henry A. Wise of Virginia took stock of what
had happened to his state in the preceding half-century. Much of
the forest had been cleared, and the soils lay in exhaustion.
"Commerce," the Governor warned, "has long ago spread her
sails, and sailed away from you." Then turning his attention to
agriculture he said, "Your sedge patches outshine the sun. Your
inattention to the only source of wealth has seared the bosom of
mother earth. Instead of having to feed cattle on a thousand hills,
you have had to chase a stub-tailed steer through the sedge
patches to procure a tough beefsteak."

In the opening decades of the nineteenth century the South

was an important grazing ground. Visitors to the region made frequent comment about the grazing herds they saw along the way, and pioneer records reflect the importance of the range in the expansion of the area. However, by the middle of the century, regional statistics were dropping behind the rest of the country. More important, however, was the fact that statistics did not reveal the conditions of livestock culture in the South. There was indeed a wide gap between the numbers of animals reported and their quality. The cattle grazing on the richer grass carpets in a cooler northern climate were superior to those in the South which foraged for provender on limited sustenance. Kentucky breeders improved types of cattle and sheep, but farther south efforts of the serious breeder were thwarted by the open range. The stray bull, ram, and boar wandered through the woods at will begetting progeny which grew progressively more inferior with succeeding generations.

In its virginal state the land of the South gave great promise for livestock development. A lack of population and market places in the early years, however, curbed expansion of the industry and, later, devotion to the routine of staple crops left little room or time for grazing. Only animals able to make their way to market afoot were bred — for example, hogs and cattle. Natural grasses in savannas and swampy pine woods fattened cattle, while an abundance of grass and the heavy annual falls of mast produced hogs in large numbers.

Following the Civil War the South had virtually no breeding stock with which to build a future industry. Starving natives and foraging invader alike had cut herds below safe levels for replenishment. A lack of money during the reconstruction era further aggravated the South's plight in developing its livestock industry. The farmer was again berated for his failures to diversify his farming operations. Legislative halls, newspaper columns, and roadside conversations rang with bitter arguments over the issue of building fences in the post-Civil War South. Fences had never existed in most of the region, and now the question had to be faced of whether crops would be fenced in and animals left on the open range, or whether the animals would be fenced in. While legislators, farmers, and editors debated the issue, the scrub bull and boar continued to degrade the quality of southern herds. Before the South could be brought under fence a revolutionary change had to be made in folkways. The free range was part of the frontier heritage, and to close it meant curbing a certain amount of American freedom.

A less debatable issue was the ravage of livestock by southern climate and soil conditions. Parasite and disease alike thrived in the warm and moist areas of the pine barrens. Texas fever ticks had spread the bloody murrain east of the Mississippi and had virtually checked, if not destroyed, cattle grazing in most of the gulf coastal counties. What the tick had begun, the spreading lumber industry almost finished. Free ranges were laid waste, and the promise of returns from cattle hardly justified the expenditures necessary for planned development of new grazing facilities.

In the opening decades of this century there began an effective crusade to destroy the lethal tick. To accomplish this it was necessary to use concrete vats charged with strong smelling chemicals. Actual knowledge of the tick and its deadly threat upon cattle herds dated from the early days of trail-driving in the western plains, but southerners either did not know of this or they were just reluctant to use the knowledge. When the dipping vat was introduced in 1900 it brought with it a strong element of discord in many communities. The campaign against ticks went on with varying degrees of success for thirty years before they were brought under control. As important as this battle was for economic returns to the South, it possibly had a wider implication in its human meanings.

Somehow free-ranging cattle symbolized for the countryman a notion of personal freedom, however ill-conceived. The milk cow, no matter how poor her return, was as much a badge of domesticity as the housewife. To require a man to shove the family cow into a crude concrete vat filled with poisonous-smelling chemicals was a denial of personal freedom. All sorts of legends were set afloat: dipping was a machination of Washington and the government expert to poison the people; the chemical bath caused the family cow to go dry, and denied the baby its milk; it caused animals to go blind, or they were injured in the rough handling necessary to force them into the vats. In many instances cattle owners looked upon fancied mistreatments of their animals as personal affronts and often started community quarrels which lasted for a generation. Some southerners resisted this infernal invasion by dynamiting the menacing vats out of the ground and threatening tick inspectors with leaden sprays from family shotguns.

Characteristically, local politics became involved in the explosive dipping-vat issue; about as much time was spent in corraling politicians as in bringing fugitive range cattle to the vats. Fortunately the tick crusade, like that against the hookworm, moved ahead despite aroused emotions, and eventually the murrain scourge was brought under control.

The progress of the southern livestock industry was also blocked by lack of local markets where farmers could sell their products. The average farmer in most of the cotton counties was wholly dependent either on local hog and cattle buyers who paid low, non-competitive head prices, or on local butchers who quickly saturated their market in local, non-refrigerated trade. Added to this were inefficient transportation facilities. Most southern railroads were unequipped to handle livestock shipments. Few had loading pens and chutes or facilities for feeding and watering animals en route. Markets were located in distant cities, and freight costs consumed profits for the most part. Farmers themselves made only minimum efforts to supplement nature's bounty by cultivating pastures. Long sieges of drouth limited both pasture and water resources, with the result that livestock growing was replaced by the traditional row crops.

In 1936 Howard W. Odum revealed that the southeastern states had the lowest per capita income from livestock production in the nation. This meant a low ratio of pasturage as well. The Carolinas had a pasture ratio of less than 20 per cent of the total acreage of land in agricultural use, and much of this had a severely limited grazing capacity.

Southern tenant farming and the ruinous credit practice placed almost no emphasis on home production of meats and dairy products. During the decade 1920–30, livestock production continued to decline, and, in the depression years that followed, it reached its lowest ebb. In fact, one of the most widely publicized sins of southern agriculture was its failure to meet the region's dietary needs in one of the staple products of farming. In 1930 the South had an annual billion gallon deficit of milk, if the standard of a quart a day per capita was accepted as a desirable measure of consumption. Odum wrote in *Southern Regions:* "The spectacle of carload shipments of milk from the middle states' territory to Florida at a loss to the producers while the prevailing condition of South Georgia and Florida farm families is one of poverty, poor use of lands and time, the people mal-nurtured for lack of dairy products, working on depleted soil for cash crops that they must produce at a loss, is one to challenge somebody somewhere and somehow to attempt some planning." The region failed to produce enough meat and dairy products to sustain its needs.

One of the most readily noticeable changes in the South today is to be seen on the highways. Cattle trucks are almost as numer-ous as lumber and crosstie wagons in earlier decades. There are thousands of pick-up trucks and stake-body vehicles which de-liver hundreds of thousands of cattle and hogs to local markets. From the markets go towering double-decked freighters roaring along with their herds of animals headed for packing houses, which themselves have gradually moved closer to southern pas-tures.

Every significant farming community has its local livestock sales barns. Where once, in trading lots and livery stables of old cotton towns, shifty characters haggled and bargained over mules with tobacco-stained farmers each spring, there are now cattle auctions. Sale days at the new southern livestock markets have been substituted for the famous court days of earlier times. Knots of trucks and automobiles are gathered about the new market places as they would be around circuses. Shabby and commonplace though these places may appear, these sales barns actually symbolize a major part of the agricultural revolution in the New South. At the end of almost two centuries the South has developed a dependable market for its livestock.

Not only do sprawling sales barns dot the southern landscape, so do animal clinics. Where once southerners resisted efforts to eradicate the tick, they are now dependent upon the services of professional veterinarians. Killing a scrawny piney-woods cow in a dipping vat accident in 1910 involved a loss of ten dollars, but to endanger the life of a registered white-face bull or a

Guernsey herd sire today would entail a greater loss than the income from a fairly good-sized cotton crop.

Before 1935 the profession of veterinarian in most southern cotton counties was about the most unpromising imaginable for a youth. Except in the Bluegrass areas of Kentucky and Tennessee and the limited horse-breeding communities of Virginia and South Carolina, the southern veterinarian could expect to earn only a modest income and that from treating sick cotton mules and bird dogs. Veterinary science was neglected in the southern agricultural colleges. It was one of the main fields to receive co-operative support from the Southern Regional Education Board when its program went into effect.

Veterinary science was greatly popularized by the introduction of artificial insemination. By 1954 this type of breeding had a vital role in improving the quality of southern cattle herds. An estimated 471,704 cows were artificially bred, and it was estimated that their offspring would yield a return of $16,000,000. By freezing semen it is possible for a single bull to impregnate 100,000 cows annually. Freezing also allows storage of semen from two to three years. Kentucky led the South in 1954 with 65,518 artificially bred cows. Co-operative syndicates have purchased bulls of extraordinary quality and placed them in artificial insemination plants so that their semen could supply numbers of herds which otherwise would be denied their services. Mississippi dairymen are able to purchase semen from prize herds in Illinois and Michigan and thus make phenomenal progress with their own herds. But artificial breeding requires far greater care on the part of the farmer than was required in the period when nature was given free range.

Conversion of southern lands from row cultivation to pasturage put strong emphasis on the need to conserve water resources. Fertilization brought grass up to the grazing stage, but abundant moisture was needed to maintain it through the hot summer months. Earlier, farmers had argued that grazing was impossible during the hottest summer months, but they were thinking about native grasses which were quickly exhausted on dry land and in searing heat. New grasses and better pasture care helped make summer grazing possible, as did more careful conservation of water resources. In 1954 there were almost a half million stock water ponds on the face of the land in twelve southern states, and in the years following this number has been multiplied at a phenomenal rate. In many instances these ponds are large enough to sustain a considerable amount of pasturage irrigation.

Rural electrification has not only permitted a much more effective use of water resources but has also facilitated the processing of meat and dairy products. Since 1954 many areas of the South have overcome the serious milk deficit of the 1930s. Alabama ranked twenty-fifth in the nation in 1953. Across the line, Mississippi farmers produced 1,529,000,000 pounds of dairy products; there were 1,008,672 head of cattle in that state in 1930, and 2,319,590 in 1955. Louisiana in 1951 had 1,569,000 cattle, and dairying and livestock yielded a cash return of $175,000,000.

A growing urban southern population stimulated the demand for beef and dairy products. Farmers, whose interest in cotton at the time of the depression had made them antagonistic toward milk cows, now give full time to dairying. The economic implications of this change are no greater than the psychological changes within the people themselves. Old-line cotton farmers looked upon milking a cow as a mark of femininity. No matter how nostalgic they could become over a jug of buttermilk hauled up from a cool spring of water, many of them were unwilling to keep milk cows.

Once the columns of country papers were filled with pleas to farmers to grow their own meat and to stop paying high annual tribute to packing houses and railroads. But this was only half the story, for the uncertainties of climate made home butchering a gamble. One of the soundest accomplishments of rural electrification has been its contribution to the preservation of home-grown meats, and as a result the processing of meats in the South has increased phenomenally. Regional stores carry larger stocks of locally produced fresh meats. Both local butchers and national packing houses are using southern-grown animals. This fact is reflected in the comparative agricultural incomes between crops and livestock and dairy products in eleven states in 1954. Crops yielded a cash return of $3,605,000,000, while livestock returned $2,013,200,000.

Large numbers of southerners have become interested in the development of herds of pure-bred cattle, sheep, and hogs.

Scarcely an important sale of pure-bred cattle takes place in the country without southern representatives being on hand. Shorthorn, Angus, Hereford, Santa Gertrudis, and Brahma all have their partisans among the beef-cattle growers. Cattle shows are held all over the region. That held in the elaborate arena of the Louisiana State University is little short of a parade of southern cattle aristocracy, as are the annual shows in the University of Kentucky.

Dairy breeds are as popular in their way as beef types. Today a good herd sire with noble pedigree will bring as much money as a herd of tick-infested southern cattle would have brought in 1900. Not only have southerners gone a long way in their attitudes toward pure-bred cattle, they have developed a professional cult among themselves. Apparently the ownership of a registered Hereford bull and a small herd of grade heifers entitles an owner to sport a broad-brim stetson hat, to wear tight-legged levis and a pair of sharp-toed western shoes (made in Clarksville, Tennessee), and to imagine himself riding up the Chisholm Trail to glory. In recent years the uninitiated visitor to the South would have to look around a sales barn carefully to tell whether he was among the woolhat boys of Texas or of the old cotton belt.

The modern South is fortunate in having enough land, grass, and water to maintain a profitable livestock industry. Now that industry is increasing southern incomes, the demand for meat is good enough to sustain a thriving grazing industry. Already the South is offering competition to the western grazing ranges. A new balance is being established between the two sections. The arid West is gradually attracting cotton westward, and extended drouths are forcing cattle eastward. The South will continue to increase its income from grazing. The cow-land grazing ratio in most parts of the region is now too high to suffer materially from western competition. Most important of all, there is an abundant water resource.

A return of the cattle grazer to the South has brought back the rustler. Modern country papers contain a strong touch of the Old West. There is a difference, however; the modern rustler east of the Sabine moves about in a pick-up truck and snares his loot from docile and truck-broken herds. Good roads are a boon to the cattle thief. There can be no more of the hard-riding, pistol-packing dramas of the Old West where there are modern asphalt and concrete getaway trails. Under these conditions the brand book has been restored to its former place of honor among court records in many parts of the South.

It is true that many changes in pasturage management have occurred, disease has been brought under control, and new live-stock markets established, but the industry itself is still a traditional one. The boll weevil and depression combined forces to bring to the Appalachian highlands and Arkansas an industry which had little or no traditional background. Since the beginning of English settlement in Virginia, southerners have been loud in their praises of fried chicken. It is doubtful that there was ever a "big dinner-on-the-ground" or a fancy company dinner at home when fried chicken was not an important part of the meal. Southerners ate it for breakfast, dinner, and supper, and then ate it cold between meals. But the trouble was that frying-sized chickens were about as seasonal as watermelons, figs, and scuppernongs. Southerners were dependent upon flocks of scrub hens to lead enough of their broods safely away from marauding rats, hawks, and foxes to supply family tables with their favorite viand.

In the Arkansas hills, cotton farmers victimized by the depression discovered that chickens could be grown in concrete block and frame sheds throughout the year. At the same time, Marylanders were producing broilers for the metropolitan markets along the eastern seaboard. As the depression deepened its inroads in the South, other regions began to grow chickens for the commercial broiler market. Where farmers had supplied an uncertain local demand with a slender supply of poor quality dung-hill fowls, they now began selling co-operative carloads of battery-fed chickens to midwestern and northern consumers. In northern Georgia the spread of the boll weevil in the poor hill country wiped out the margin between the price of production and meager profit for cotton growers. Farmers were left stranded. They were able to find only a limited amount of wage labor to supplement their flagging crop incomes, and their land became well-nigh valueless. Not only were farmers in hard financial straits, so were town and country merchants. As early as 1918 Professor

J. H. Woods of the University of Georgia made the critical observation that "Georgia is an ideal state for poultry, yet we are importing 60 to 75 per cent of the poultry and products we consume. It is almost impossible, at the present time, to buy fresh eggs in Georgia."

It was in this troubled time that many farmers deserted the cotton patch for the chicken house. A few crude brooder sheds were constructed, and wood was dragged in from the hillsides to keep them warm. Within a reasonably short time the first small batches of broilers were ready for sale, and despite depressed conditions the early growers made a profit. When one farmer succeeded the fact became general knowledge among his neighbors and they too turned to chicken raising.

From 1930 to 1937 the broiler industry in Georgia and its neighboring states in the Appalachian foothills made a rapid growth. In early May 1955 the editor of the *Georgia Poultry Times* boasted that "Georgia's biggest agricultural industry — homegrown and hustling — was cackling, crowing, and flapping its wings." His enthusiasm was not inconsistent with the facts, for the year before broilers yielded $101,487,000, and the total income from poultry was almost $150,000,000, as compared with an income from cotton of $132,029,000. This was a far cry from 1930, when 41,780 Georgia farmers had no chickens at all.

The rise of the broiler industry in the South brought with it enormous changes in many aspects of local economy. The base of change was indeed broad and really extended more into the field of industrialization than into that of traditional agriculture. But no change was greater than that affecting the sources of capital support. If a hill farmer had approached a merchant or banker in 1914 with a request for a loan to enable him to grow several thousand frying chickens every three or four months, he would have been laughed at.

Never before had southern hill farmers needed to rely so heavily upon the services and advice of experiment stations and extension experts. Research in the field of battery production and sale of broilers was a necessity. From the beginning it was obvious that careless handling of chickens would result in disaster. Whether individualistic farmers liked to be bound by precise practices of management or not, they were without choice. Within a single decade the broiler industry wrought changes which earlier agricultural crusaders sought to accomplish within a half-century.

Once southerners advanced their broiler industry beyond its initial stages it was obvious that they could not produce their own feeds locally. Not even the South itself was prepared to supply so heavy a demand. Millions of tons of grains were shipped into the region from the Midwest and Northwest, and the big national milling companies sent along branch mills to grind feed near the places of its use. Following the examples of the feed suppliers, hatcherymen developed egg-producing and hatchery centers for millions of baby chickens. In the larger centers, processing plants were developed to dress and prepare for the market the steady flow of broilers. Rapidly, towns and cities in broiler-producing areas changed their appearances. They grew into important industrial centers. Gainesville, Georgia, for instance, became a thriving poultry center, with feed mills, hatcheries, and processing plants. Beyond the Mississippi, Little Rock, Arkansas, supplied a prosperous poultry industry.

This complex new semi-agricultural industry adapted an age-old financial practice to modern business usage. Chicken raisers actually had little more than small farms and strong wills to work to make a living. They had to be financed in building brooder houses, in acquiring heating and feeding equipment, in providing proper sanitary conditions, and in the purchase of stock and feeds. There arose a new type of farm furnishing merchant who extended production credit for a crop which made a more rapid turnover than did cotton and tobacco.

Feed dealers assumed the role of the old country merchants who extended long-term credit to cotton farmers between the Civil War and the great depression. They now supply chickens and feed, maintain inspections, and locate markets for broilers. Farmers in turn supply housing, fuel, and labor to bring baby chicks to maturity. When the brood is sold, the feed dealer either pays the farmer a fixed head price or shares profits with him. The farmer enjoys a side income from the fancy-figured feed sacks, which he sells for dress goods, and from accumulations of chicken manure.

Broiler growers have become major purchasers of grains. Feed grinding has become a southern industry, in contrast to conditions earlier, when the region failed to produce its own feeds and breadstuffs. Since 1945 the South has produced increasingly greater amounts of grains to supply the livestock and broiler industries. Throughout the broiler-producing areas feed mills are important, and many of the towns have poultry processing and packing plants as well. In some places feed- and poultry-processing gentry have become economically more important than were the ante-bellum cotton planters. Georgia and Arkansas lead both the region and the country in this rising industry. By 1955 one-eighth of the South's total income of some $8.8 billion came from the sale of poultry and eggs. The South produced 69 per cent of the broilers consumed by the nation.

Modern refrigerated trucks and improved highways have placed southern poultrymen in reach of the major national markets. Chain stores, with their long refrigerated meat counters and leader sales, have emphasized the importance of chicken in the national diet. The machine age in the southern hill country has spared the squeamish housewife the tedious job of preparing chicken for cooking. Boxes of meat are delivered ready prepared, and even choice pieces are offered in special packages.

The cooler southern Appalachian climate has concentrated the broiler industry in the mountains and foothills. It was here that staple agriculture first sagged. Margins of profit, never very great, grew progressively smaller as lands were leached and eroded and the boll weevil took heavier annual tolls. So slender was the margin of income that for many years cotton farmers fought hard just to gain back the cost of production. The same thing was true in grain production. Corn fell below a twenty bushel average. The old southern story of agricultural failure was often repeated in full measure. Introduction of the broiler industry meant economic salvation for the people, and the land itself profited. Manure from brooder houses restored rich deposits of nitrogen, and humus restored soils to their virginal qualities. In many places grain production was boosted to unheard-of yields. Half the corn acres in 1954 produced more than was grown in 1920. Cherokee County in northern Georgia reflects the transition which has come to the foothills. Corn yield increased from 11.2 bushels an acre in 1939 to 22.3 in 1949. In the early 1930s Cherokee farmers harvested around 12,000 bales of cotton a year, but in 1955 the yield had dropped to 574 bales.

Farmers in the southern broiler-growing states have learned that it is far easier to let a machine pick a chicken than for them to pick "bumble bee" cotton for a living. So long as Americans eat fried chicken and the population continues to increase, a considerable part of the hill South will be assured a fairly stable income. Not only are farmers reasonably certain of gaining a satisfactory livelihood, so are thousands of people who supply broiler producers with feeds, equipment, fuels, and drugs.

The meaning of this new assembly-line farming lies deeper than mere economy. There has come a marked change in the appearance of much of the southern countryside. Fields once worn red by wasteful cotton cultivation are now being reclaimed by heavy manuring and scientific cultivation. Where scrawny flocks of weed-bred chickens once rustled for a living about shabby run-down houses, there are now houses of improved quality. Intellectually, people are far more willing to accept new ideas and changes in their way of life. Already they have made changes within a generation which exceeded modifications made in southern life in the past century. Riding through areas where the broiler industry has shown its greatest expansion one cannot help but agree with that startled hillside Georgia native who observed, "Who'd ever thought a dad-blamed chicken would scratch cotton off the land!"

The rise of livestock and poultry industries in the New South has brought radical changes in the tempo of life. Though this kind of farming requires close attention, it does not demand the back-breaking and unpromising labors of row crops. Southerners have become conscious of many factors in production which they largely ignored in the past. Production costs and profits are so important that large numbers of farmers have turned businessmen. Also, resources of the soil are now being used with considerable concern for their conservation. Use of non-row crops of grass and hay has removed one of the main causes of erosion. A glimpse at the main streams in the region reveals the extent to which soil and water conservation are now being practiced. The production of livestock and poultry, though requiring a greater initial outlay than cotton and tobacco, has tended to spread farm income evenly throughout the year. No longer are large numbers of farmers dependent upon the annual harvest season for their income; thus the possibilities of ruinous failures and agricultural panic are cut down considerably. Certainly the use of livestock as collateral has eased the problem of securing farm credit.

The revival of a traditional southern economy has brought new implications. The advice of dairying professors, country editors, and livestock men is now heeded. That the South has again become a livestock-producing area does not mean that the region has reverted to past conditions. There is a vast difference between the South at this time in the twentieth century and the sedge-choked region through which Governor Henry A. Wise chased his stump-tailed steer in the 1850s. Southern farming has been changed greatly for the better.

VII

On the Face of the Land

The country was very thinly peopled; lone houses often being several miles apart. The large majority of the dwellings were of logs, and even those of the white people were often without glass windows. In the better class of cabins, the roof is usually built with a curve, so as to project eight or ten feet beyond the log-wall; and a part of this space, exterior to the logs, is inclosed with boards, making an additional room — the remainder forms an open porch. The whole cabin is often elevated on four corner posts, two or three feet from the ground, so that the air may circulate under it. The fireplace is built at the end of the house, of sticks and clay, and the chimney is carried up outside, and often detached from the log walls; but the roof is extended at the gable, until in a line with its outer side. The porch has a railing in front, and a wide shelf at the end, on which a bucket of water, a gourd, and hand basin, are usually placed. There are chairs, or benches, in the porch, and you often see women sitting at work in it, as in Germany.

Olmsted, a journey in the seaboard slave states, pp. 384–5

The revolution on the southern farm just described is only a part of the changing pattern of southern rural life. Stereotypes and local traditions notwithstanding, a central characteristic of the South's social organization has been a lack of cohesion in its community structure. From the opening of the nineteenth century to the advent of the Tennessee Valley Authority, the regional community pattern was static. The old-fashioned double-log house symbolized the spread of civilization westward. Subsequent oblong bungalows, with their impending porches, reflected the complacency of a postwar era. Barns and outbuildings cluttered southern homesteads, and public buildings added little sense of form and order.

Physical qualities of homes and farm buildings, however, were not necessarily a proper gauge to the South's social and cultural impulses. By 1930, the region had finally outgrown its frontier background, and, later, the development of improved schools and roads and the introduction of electrical power had elevated the southern cultural perspective.

The old way of southern community life contained a germ of defeatism. Frustration was a fruit of civil war and reconstruction, of the failures of staple agriculture, and of sinful waste of the soil. A homogeneous population brought to the frontier South a complacent sense of social responsibilities which deterred progress. Thus it was that twentieth-century southerners found themselves existing largely in a rural vacuum.

Social failures in southern life prior to 1940 inspired some highly valid regional literary contributions. Before the end of the nineteenth century, Charles Otken of Hazlehurst, Mississippi, had analyzed the causes of social and agrarian discontent in *Ills of the South* (1887). Subsequent books on populism and the southern economic struggle have exhibited greater maturity of understanding. In fiction, Thomas Stribling dealt with regional battles against social and economic failures in his trilogy, *The Forge* (1931), *The Store* (1932), and *The Unfinished Cathedral* (1934). The South's most distinguished novelist, William Faulkner, emphasized the way that social and economic depression shaped the lives of his fellow Mississippians.

Homes, soils, and human character had been deeply eroded by the end of the first quarter of this century. The dreary conditions endured by numbers of southern people became the substance of critical appraisal of the South. Faulkner's novels have involved much of this social fabric. Concurrently, scholars and critics are searching for the mainsprings of this author's materials. Oftentimes they fail to see in much of the more recent economic background of his home country some of the answers. Eroded hillsides, depleted land, and wasted resources go far to document the Faulkner material.

Tobacco Road became a popular social term in describing degeneracy in the South. Jeter Lester, a sordid Jeremiah of old, spoke profanely for a veritable multitude who lived by a hard economic pattern but who spoke more meekly and viewed the future with greater concern. Whether or not Tobacco Road itself existed matters little in the over-all view of social conditions in the depression-ridden South. In *God's Little Acre*, Erskine Caldwell dramatized for the nation the beginning of the end for the old yeoman South. In an age of community failures he preached eloquently the sermon which grangers and populists had prepared for him.

Novelists were not alone in analyzing the rural South. Others attempted realistic appraisals of the region's failures. A constant stream of articles, pamphlets, and books describing the crisis came from the presses. A slight pamphlet entitled *The South, The Nation's Number One Economic Problem*, published by the Federal Government (1938), had an appreciable effect in shaping regional attitudes toward prevailing conditions. That same year the President's Committee on Farm Tenantry published a searching analysis of the condition of agrarian society in the South. It was a grim diagnosis. It left no doubt that people, land, agricultural system, human character, and credit methods had failed. In text and statistical table this report evaluated the erosion of sharecropping and tenancy. Farm Security Administration photographers caught the South in an extreme condition of social paralysis. No observant traveler had ever recorded so precise a description of many southern conditions.

Graphically, the Committee on Farm Tenantry revealed the cause of social failure. Insecure tenure had deleterious effects upon both land and living standards. Sub-marginal economy destroyed the affection and respect for buildings, lands, and institutions. Communities were caught in a catapulting downward spiral of economic opportunity. More optimistically, the Committee expressed a belief that security of land tenure promoted the building of better homes and the preservation of the lands. "Stability," it said, "increases the family's interest in community activities and makes it possible for the children to remain in school. Secure tenure does not produce large speculative profits, but greatly increases the opportunity for a steady income to owner-operator, tenant, and landlord."

Southern country life had failed in too many places. Rupert B.

Vance wrote, "On church and school, farm tenantry lays a heavy hand. Many rural schools are disorganized by wholesale changes in pupils around moving time. This mobility has created a heavy load of ignorance and retarded the progress of hundreds of thousands of farm children." This condition of land tenure laid a hand on everything in the South. Townsmen and countrymen alike were dragged to destruction. Farmstead and village were in decay and shabbiness because of economic failure.

In 1935 vast areas of the rural South were reduced to shabbiness. Farmsteads were cluttered and run-down, reflecting a deep-set state of poverty. Rusting implements and vehicles were scattered about in disarray of abandonment. Barns, outhouses, fences, and grounds sagged under the weight of sun and time. Even country churches stood on careening foundations atop ground that receded with the wash of recurring wet seasons. Agricultural backwardness, if not complete failure, was stamped upon homesteads as indelibly as the thrust of the hills and the slash of the streams. From 1865 to 1935 an objective observer could hardly have been favorably impressed with farming and small town existence in the South. There were islands, of course, where land and people helped organize community life in a pleasant manner. There were individual farmers everywhere who maintained attractive homesteads amid the general shabbiness. Armies of visitors came South to view the scene and to write books describing their experiences. From Oliver Hudson Kelly to Sir Philip Gibbs their writings tell vivid stories of the South in the hard years.

Rural southerners' lack of any aesthetic taste showed on the land. Both white and Negro were devoid of a sense of orderliness and beauty. Where the white man failed to maintain an attractive house, the Negro lived in an abode that was much shabbier. Unpainted boarded houses and the big rambling natural pine structures were more characteristic of many parts of the South than pillared mansions. Between Charleston and Natchez there were hundreds of thousands of modest dwellings which sheltered the great mass of the population. "Nigger house shabbiness" was more descriptive than "Tara," "Rosehill," "Afton Villa," and "Llangollon" splendor.

Architecture after all, however modest or impressive, was only a symbol of the quality of social life. The way of life of the people was more revealing. It cannot be overemphasized that much southern yeoman culture down to 1920 was still the culture of the American frontier. The age of a community had little to do with fundamental social and domestic advances. Old coastal and delta blackbelt regions alike were often areas of inferior homes, and there were disorganized communities without social leadership. Southern politicians were either oblivious to conditions about them or preferred not to face realities. Demagogues were able either to turn their heads to social failures or to blame someone far removed from the South for local troubles. They rationalized community failures so as to block understanding and progress.

The Tennessee Valley Authority introduced the largest program of uprooting an established pattern of indigenous society in American history. Not only were hundreds of families removed from farms and ancestral homesteads, which dated from the beginning of the famous Watauga settlements in the eighteenth century, but so were whole towns and communities. Even cemeteries were moved out of reach of flood waters. Churches and schools climbed to higher grounds. Old community lines were broken, and for some of the region social organization was begun anew.

When the TVA started, many communities in the scope of the valley were almost as primitive as they were in the opening days of the frontier. The pioneer Tennesseeans, John Sevier and James Robertson, would not have found themselves in strange surroundings at all. The first manifestation of the new era was the improved quality of homes. New houses took the place of the old ones. They were more efficiently planned, with provisions for the conveniences which cheap power would make available. No longer were country people willing to build houses without painting them. Farmers in search of land had opportunities to wander over considerable territory in locating new homes. Almost immediately they became more receptive to new ideas of farming. Agricultural test plots in the Valley made concrete and understandable arguments for change. Farmers were more willing to listen to advice about soil types, community advantages, new types of farming, and land uses. Their lives had been disrupted, and they no longer had to fight the inertia of the fixed traditions and mores of their old surroundings. They were now out to get the most for their money, and they were highly receptive to the advice of farm experts who could predict the future capabilities of the soil.

Possibly of greater importance was the fact that the rural electrification management regarded the isolated farm home as its chief customer. Under the old system of extending electrical services, this type of customer was considered more trouble than he was worth. Availability of electric power was an enormous motivating factor in the redirection of southern community life. Labor-saving devices were in reach of large numbers of people for the first time. The drudgery of farm work was lightened. Farm houses now had available to them the conveniences of houses in towns. Turning on the lights in a rural home for the first time was akin to spiritual rebirth. The first burst of bright light revealed the shabby surroundings to many rural southerners in a manner that was impossible for them to see without electricity. Dingy walls, drab furnishings, and a general lack of inspiration in their surroundings were disclosed. Lights in these shabby homes created the greatest incongruity in southern country life: it seemed sacrilegious to maintain such run-down surroundings in their presence. Almost immediately new furnishings and equipment, and even new homes, were in demand.

Availability of electricity brought more than bright lights. Farm incomes had to be increased to buy radios, washing machines, mechanical refrigerators, pressure water pumps, electric ranges, and, later, television sets and deep-freezers. Financial drains were staggering as compared with those of the past. Almost immediately the barriers of isolation which kept the farmers in ignorance of world happenings were wiped away. Too, they had made accessible to them sources of advanced agricultural information which came at strategic moments to help them make changes in the old ways of farming. If they were to meet the rising costs of the new conveniences which became all but indispensable after electricity was made available, they had to turn to a more efficient system of farming. Thousands of householders were thrust into modernity faster than their ancient homes could be readied for change. Porches were lined with washing machines and refrigerators as though these conveniences symbolized a better social status. A man with a washing machine and a refrigerator, even if they were on his front porch, was at least keeping step with the times, and was announcing to the world that he was willing to meet both the challenge of the future and the installment collector.

Along with improved roads and better communication, electricity helped change the southern rural personality. Countrymen became good customers for labor-saving machines, vast tonnages of fertilizers, annual supplies of pedigreed field seeds, more and better clothes, and mechanized farm equipment. The new way of farm life had made them customers worthy of being courted by businessmen.

The idea of community improvement is fairly old in the South, although until the coming of the Rural Electrification Agency in the 1930s it did not really have any major impetus. In the first part of this century, Seaman and Bradford Knapp, among others, sought to improve southern rural life. The Agricultural Extension Service labored at this task throughout the South. Newspaper editors everywhere made periodic appeals to farm people to improve the conditions of their lives. In Memphis, Tennessee, the rural South was fortunate in having a determined leader in C.P.J. Mooney, editor of the *Commercial Appeal*. The paper had a long history of being interested in the welfare of rural people. It had crusaded for green hills and pleasant homes in that part of the South served from Memphis. Editor Mooney struggled to break the monopoly of cotton, to put an end to paralysis of exhausted lands, tenancy, and the boredom of spiritless country life. Subsequently the *Commercial Appeal* initiated what may be considered one of the earliest community projects in its "plant to prosper" campaign, directed to the individual farmer.

In the midst of World War II the community contest idea was born in Knoxville. There is some disagreement as to its beginnings, but the originating organizations were the Tennessee Valley Authority, the University of Tennessee Agricultural Extension Service, and the Knoxville service clubs. In 1943 the public service agencies, a group of Knoxville businessmen, and the service clubs formed a community committee to conduct an improvement contest in neighboring rural communities. These localities were to be scored on the basis of 1000 points to be prorated among a series of farm and home improvement categories, with emphasis upon improved farming practices and home food supply. Three or four features of this program were ingenious. Prizes of substantial value were given to winning communities rather than to individuals; it was necessary for the people participating to work together to win, and local leadership was indispensable. One result of this common interest was the development of test plots where agricultural experts could demonstrate locally new methods of farming. Home demonstrations were handled in the same way, and, finally, in judging the success of communities, people visited back and forth to compare results. Crosby Murray of the Tennessee Extension Service and Pat Kerr of the Tennessee Valley Agricultural Fair were particularly successful in persuading rural people to accept the challenge to improve the conditions of their lives while these community improvement contests were running.

Businessmen, many of whom had rural backgrounds, gave money to finance prizes, and then served as advisers and judges. One community was pitted against another in friendly and highly communicative rivalry. Major sections of Tennessee were placed in competition. Regularly people in participating communities were brought together to hear discussions of new farming methods, better homemaking, recreation, the importance of leadership, and national and international political problems. Never in the South's history had so much friendly rural communication taken place. While businessmen and farmers in Tennessee perfected their organizations, leaders in other southern states were busy. One of the best of the community improvement programs was developed about Asheville, North Carolina. At Tupelo, Mississippi, George McClean sought an answer to the problems in Lee County. Home from the Navy, the young editor of the Tupelo *Daily Journal,* introduced the community improvement idea. He had visited Tennessee and was familiar with the Memphis *Commercial Appeal's* "plant to prosper" crusade. In Tupelo, businessmen subscribed funds to finance a community program. A decade and a half later, community organization had yielded significant results in almost every phase of rural life.

Community improvement programs have attempted to compre-

hend all the needs of the rural South. Beautifying and modernizing the home ranks as a prime objective. Homesteads were restored, houses painted, outhouses improved, lawns landscaped,
and trees and flower gardens planted. Early improvements seemed
small in the face of obvious needs. To outsiders they hardly
seemed improvements at all. It was so simple to relocate mail-
boxes, to place them on uniform posts, and to print clearly the
names of owners on the side of boxes. The naming and posting of
local roads might not seem a vital change, but to a backward
community it was a forward step. So was the improvement of
farm entry-ways. To remove the accumulation of rusting farm
implements from sight broke a long-standing southern tradition.
These were little things, but they reversed a custom for many
southern countrymen.

A bigger task was the human problem of bringing people together and planning for community betterment. Extension service workers and city promoters of community projects were
greatly tempted to push people faster than they were ready to go.
The path of rural southern improvement was a narrow one indeed. Churches represented an all but impenetrable barrier. Some
ministers objected to community programs because they brought
people together outside the churches. Often these ministers were
not qualified to assume community leadership, and their denominational attitudes sometimes destroyed general confidence in
their capacity to do so. Yet ministers struggled to make themselves central community figures. One of the first challenges in a
community improvement program was to organize it without
becoming beholden to the local church organizations.

The coming of cheap power to the South marked the beginning of a new outlook for the people of the region. As R.E.A.
extended its lines, community improvement groups increased
their demands for electric power. In scores of southern counties
more than 95 per cent of the rural people have access to power.
The land of the great unwashed is rapidly becoming as fastidious
as a woman's magazine advertisement. Annual community contests reveal tremendous changes in an ever-widening area in the
domestic patterns of southern homes.

Community leadership has been able to hasten acceptance of
new ideas by farmers. Where there has been will enough to main-

tain a well-organized community, there has been intelligence enough to accept advanced farming methods. Community demonstration plots cultivated by neighbors have proved highly instructive. Where these demonstration plots have been used, farmers have made progress. A half century before, Dr. Seaman A. Knapp introduced the idea of rudimentary test plots in his agricultural clubs for boys and girls. Grangers met and discussed the problems presented by farming as a way of life; they fussed about political failures and in a clumsy manner undertook to provide entertainment. Seldom did they approach the problems of farming scientifically. They knew little of soil types as determined by detailed testing. Soil classification was as foreign to them as an Italian phrase, and test demonstration plots were still in the future.

Wherever successful community improvement organizations have functioned, southern land has been turned into designs of whorls, triangles, scallops, and modernistic patterns of contours. Gullies have disappeared, and grass has sprung up to bind the soil in place and to produce grazing for a flourishing livestock industry. Even the scrub bull has been shoved off the land by the new community projects, with their co-operative artificial breeding stations.

Visitors in southern states where community improvement programs are active have revised their earlier judgments of the region. The quality of the new southern home is far superior to that of the past. Romance and tradition of the Old South may be symbolized by the pillared mansion with its adjoining slave cabins, but it never was as comfortable or efficient as the better modern southern farm home, which is modest in size when compared with earlier plantation homes, and is flanked by tractor equipment sheds and cattle barns instead of slave quarters.

Pressures of various sorts have brought about vast improvements in rural roads. Country voters still have strong influence in the state house; politicians have not yet discovered the wane of an agricultural voting population. As a result, rural roads have figured prominently in the scheme of legislation during the last decade and a half. Organized communities have proved powerful influences in hastening the building of farm-to-market roads. Hard-surfaced roads penetrate back country, replacing dirt roads

which even the most optimistic prophet of two decades ago would
not have predicted would ever be improved. A web-work of improved local roads into the heart of the rural South has been re-
routed and marked. No longer is a stranger left in many places to
his navigational sense to find his way. In the past quarter of a
century the South has sealed in the mud on its country roads.

As barriers of isolation have been lowered, and community
pride has been nurtured to a corresponding degree, the crime rate
has dropped in many rural places. In some Tennessee communities, for instance, this has been one of the most appreciable advances. As conditions have been improved, the pride in community welfare has reduced the tendency to misbehave. At the
same time a greater spirit of tolerance has been developed. Negro
community projects have succeeded. In some places the Negro
makes a better response to the challenge of improvement than
does his white neighbor. Eleven Negro communities have made
genuine progress in this area — in particular, communities in
Wilson and Sumner counties and Bakewell Community, all in
Tennessee, and Lee County in Mississippi. One white leader in
an eastern Tennessee community program has said, "prejudice just
naturally disappears in community betterment programs." So long
as local people were not sensitized by extremists both within and
without their ranks, the community programs were making headway toward more amicable race relations.

Like almost every phrase of modern southern life, the community improvement program has yet to experience an intensive
economic depression. But even this would hardly change many of
the gains. Through guidance and encouragement of promoters
of community improvement undertakings, local leadership has
been developed. Men have learned to accept social responsibility.
In earlier years in the South they would have been wasted in the
apathetic social system. Some of them have become articulate on
a bigger stage and have been able to exert a far-reaching influence
on the region.

Public agencies have encouraged the organization of community improvement programs, and private utility companies
have done the same thing. In many areas these companies have
changed radically their attitudes toward rural consumers of
power. In several states the companies offer guidance and en-

couragement to local improvement bodies, and in many instances they have endeavored to bring semi-rural and small urban-type industries to the South.

Some of the history of the community improvement movement in the South can now be written in positive terms. Accomplishments outweigh failures. There are failures; some communities which embarked upon improvement programs have relapsed for one reason or another to their old ways. These failures are at once visible. Paint has scaled off the once proud roadside signs announcing community borders, and the countryside has taken on a look of defeat. Not all religious sectarianism has been destroyed, and thousands of people have refused to change their political behavior. Racial tensions have grown, and in some communities which have made marked physical gains they have mounted fearfully. In fact, where extremist organizations have superseded community improvement leadership, little if any fundamental and permanent change has been wrought in these important areas of human relationships. It will take far more intensive urban-industrial development and a revolution in local and national political behavior to bring this about. Extension services and utility interests have largely kept their activities clear of politics, and so long as local leaders followed their examples community development has wrought significant change in the modern way of life in the South.

It would be fallacious to say that the South has experienced a spiritual rebirth because of the influence of scattered community improvement projects. There are, however, manifestations that conditions of southern life are improved. Painted houses, attractive farmsteads, and active co-operative farm endeavors have all drawn the rural South into a tighter social organization. More important is the fact that for the first time southerners are feeling the impact of this organization at the community level. People sense a necessity for better institutional services and are more willing to accept new ideas and social counseling. This may in turn prepare the way for the readjustment of many deep-seated southern problems.

VIII

Mr. Grady Wins

Land rent, water-power, timber fuel, and raw material for cotton manufacturing, are all much cheaper in Georgia than in New England. The only other item of importance in estimating the cost of manufacturing, must be the cost of labor, which includes, of course, the efficiency of the laborers. By the census, it appears that the average wages of the female operatives in the Georgia cotton factories was, in 1850, $7.39 a month; in Massachusetts, $14.57 a month.

OLMSTED, JOURNEY IN THE SEABOARD SLAVE STATES, p. 543

The South has already passed through the initial stages of modern industrialization. Optimistic southern prophets predicted in 1955 that at least 3000 new plants of multi-million dollar value would be built below the Potomac during the decade 1950–60. Every new plant that towered above cotton and tobacco lands disturbed the equilibrium of placid towns and communities; nevertheless it affirmed Henry W. Grady's eloquent pleas in the 1880s for industrialization to balance southern agriculture.

Since 1935 at least two southern myths have been exploded: first, that the agrarian South does not favor change, and, second, that southerners are not readily adaptable to conditions of industrialization. History of southern industry lacks continuity. From the appearance of the first factory in the region, industry has been immediately dependent upon either agriculture or local mineral resources. A lack of capital, management, transportation, and markets helped to keep the South economically agrarian. At the outbreak of the Civil War the region was woefully short of manufacturing facilities to sustain a people at war. In no instance was a mineral resource adequately exploited, and the processing of agricultural products fell short of the demand.

No southern state had a surplus labor supply before the Civil War. Much of the region was still frontier country, where people expended enormous energies in their thrust against the backwoods. After 1865 the displacement and disorganization of regional agrarian economy created an artificial labor surplus, but it was not until the appearance of the boll weevil in the first decade of this century that laborers in large numbers were released from the grind of the farm. Had it not been for the outbreak of World War I, with the resulting demand for workers in war industries and the slight boom in agriculture, the South would have become a surplus labor region much earlier.

Growth of heavy industries in the North during and after the war, particularly in the automotive and extractive fields, absorbed a large portion of surplus southern labor. Detroit, Akron, Cleveland, Chicago, St. Louis, and east-coast cities attracted southerners in droves after 1918. So did the Appalachian coal and iron fields. Surplus workers drifted away from sub-marginal farms in search for a livelihood. In the dark days of depression and unemployment this movement was reversed by returning natives.

Four basic industries have expanded in the modern South — textiles, lumbering, petroleum, and chemical manufacturing. Since the 1870s, lumber production has increased annually. After 1900 this industry reached its peak of importance. Millions of acres of virgin pine forests spread out from the top of the tidewater crescent on the eastern shore of Maryland and Virginia to the plains of Texas. Hills and swamps were buried alike under massive covers of pine and hardwoods. In six states, mountain ranges lifted their wooded crests higher with gallant poplars, chestnut, oak, hemlock, walnut, and cherry. Greedy lumbering operators tore into this priceless legacy. Roistering mountain raftsmen drifted downstream on spring floods atop piles of enormous logs to outside mills. Lowland mills ripped into the southern highlands and sawed off millions of feet of the choicest hardwood logs to be found on the North American continent.

Along the sluggish rivers of the lower piedmont and tidewater grew giant slash pines, cypress, oaks, hickories, and poplars. In time these too came crashing down to yield lumber to build a nation's houses and machines. Often a single tree contained board feet enough to construct a cluster of small houses. Gaps in the horizon recorded the prodigal butchery of the South's virgin timber resources.

Wasteful harvest of virgin timber from 1880 to 1930 did more economic harm to the South than Grant, Sherman, and all the carpetbaggers put together. Waste in the woods, at the mill, and in the finishing plants symbolized a lack of appreciation of the basic importance of forest resources to the southern way of life. So plentiful was the supply of timber that few southern mill-owners stopped to consider the sobering fact that they were plundering the storehouse of centuries of growth. Most of the lumber industry was of a "fly-by-night" nature, with no plans for long and continuous operation of mills as stabilized businesses. Millmen were as transitory in their habits as the cattle grazers who straggled through southern forests ahead of settlers a century and a half ago.

Years of depression sobered an appreciable number of lumber-men. If they were to continue in business, both they and their neighbors had to revise their ideas about forest management. Unemployment during these years was a blessing in disguise. The Civilian Conservation Corps offered employment and con-ducted a giant test demonstration that revealed both the possi-bility and value of reforestation. Lumbermen, paper company and state foresters, county agents, and farm journal editors, all began to preach the gospel of reforestation and timber care. For the first time lumbering promised to be a stable and permanent industry, with millowners giving their own timber stands expert care.

Today 40 per cent of the southern region is growing trees. In parts of the South pines grow fast enough to produce pulpwood in ten to fifteen years. In fact, loblolly pines grow so rapidly that pounding rains have not erased the ripple of cotton rows before a crop of pulpwood has matured. In thirty to forty years a heavy growth of saw logs can be harvested from a once-exhausted cotton field, and some hardwoods mature as rapidly. Even a casual ob-server driving or flying across the South can detect widespread effects of good forest management. Highway signs, advertisements in country newspapers, experiment station bulletins, and farm journals have convinced most southerners of the economic importance of timber. Organized fire protection is maintained as a guard against the profligacy of a wasteful public. Farmers and timbermen are given a clearer concept of the economic meaning of trees by forestry schools, such as those at the University of Georgia and at Duke, and by state foresters. Like cotton, tobacco, and cows, trees have become sources of continuing income. One aspect of management is that control of woods fires has made a marked advance in the modern South.

The inefficient "peckerwood" sawmill still prevails, and it is still possible to spot raped hillsides where it has gnawed its way closer to oblivion. Mounds of slabs and sawdust at the mills and wilting "laps" in the woods tell a baleful story of carnage and depleted timber stands. But both wastrel millowners and ignorant farmers are vanishing southerners. The sawmill has exacted the most arduous labor from men. In large numbers, men who have been both ignorant and hungry have operated the small mills. They have been ignorant of good forest care and too hungry to learn. Much of the southern timber harvest has been made by the rule of "get in, get as much as you can quickly, and get out." Federal and state governments have set good examples of forest management in the national and state timber and game preserves. Landowners in increasing numbers also realize the possibility of getting a steady income from scientifically managed woodlands. Today tree culture is regarded as a profitable use for poor lands.

Southern timberlands supply 39 per cent of the nation's lumber and 56 per cent of its pulpwood. Annual growth and harvest figures have almost reached a balance. Wood-using industries produce a significant part of the region's major industrial output. Lumbering and its closely allied industries still constitute a prime source of income and employment. In 1956 it was estimated that 120 acres of South Carolina timberland would yield an annual cash return equal to that from $41,000 worth of United States Government bonds.

Furniture manufacturers operated plants in all the southern states. Little fellows produce crude furniture for modest homes; regional craftsmen supply an astonishing number of cedar chests each year; and pencil manufacturers follow the rock and cedar ridges in search of suitable wood. Reproducers of antique furniture take a heavy annual toll of maple, walnut, cherry, and poplar. In Virginia, North Carolina, and Tennessee the big manufacturers supply a national market with all kinds of furniture. Furniture made in Stanleyton, Bassett, and Martinville, Virginia; High Point, Durham, and Mebane, North Carolina; and Morristown, Tennessee, and Louisville competes with that made in the East and along the Great Lakes. As television has become available to everybody, the chair manufacturing industry has thrived. Three major companies in Morristown supply a nation with seats to sit before home screens.

Thirty years ago the South produced a negligible amount of paper. Southern papermakers consumed only a million and a half cords of pulpwood, but a quarter of a century later they used more than sixteen million cords annually. In 1955 the industry produced 9,970,000 tons of pulp paper, and this represented an increase of nearly 2,000,000 tons within the year. The South now produces more than half of the nation's chemical woodpulp, and the total exceeds all Canadian production. In 1956 there were more than two billion dollars invested in the southern paper industry, and approximately 600,000 people got all or part of their income from papermaking.

Paper mills are fairly well distributed over the South, with large plants located in reach of all the important pine-growing belt. Now recent developments have turned the paper industry to hardwoods as well. The stand of so-called trash timber in the South is large, and utilization of this resource could be enormous. Two direct social and economic influences of the pulpwood and paper industry are to be found in the weaning away from agriculture of vast numbers of unskilled laborers and reversion of lands to forests. Corporate ownership of large blocks of southern land should mean that regional timber development is increased. This fact also reflects a change of political attitude toward corporate land ownership in many parts of the South. In June 1956, the Governor of South Carolina called a special session of the legislature to amend a Populist-inspired law which limited alien ownership of the land in that state to 500 acres. This was done as inducement to the Bowater Company to locate a paper mill in

York County and to enable it to purchase a large acreage of South Carolina land to ensure an adequate supply of pulpwood.

The southern paper industry has a dual nature. Craft and industrial papers account for the great bulk of regional income from the industry, but the manufacture of newsprint has expanded rapidly. The idea that southern pine might be used in the making of paper is perhaps an old one. It was not, however, until 1931 that Dr. Charles Holmes Herty, a disciple of Gifford Pinchot, perfected a process for removing rosin from southern pine pulp in order to produce sulphate-bleached papers. His work in the United States Forest Products Laboratory in Savannah reversed a rugged southern tradition of wastefulness.

Through the chemical discoveries of Dr. Herty and Francis P. Garvan the troublesome rosin and natural discoloration were conquered. Dr. Herty's promises to produce bleached paper made three years earlier to the Southern Newspaper Publishers' Association could now be fulfilled. But money to build a newsprint plant was lacking. A committee campaigned for funds, and subscribing publishers in 1938 were required to buy stock and to expend a great amount of energy to build the Southland mills in Lufkin, Texas. Before the first roll of paper came from the mill, publishers had contracted for 853,754 tons of paper and had subscribed $1,615,000 in stock to match a $3,425,000 loan from the Reconstruction Finance Corporation.

Southland Mills had not yet loaded its first roll of paper for shipment to a publisher before the shortage of newsprint became more acute. Success of the Texas mill was assured. In 1948 a second southern newsprint mill was constructed near Chilesburg on the Coosa River in Alabama. Six years later, the Bowater Paper Company of Corner Brook, Newfoundland, located its $55,000,000 newsprint plant on the Hiawassee River near Calhoun, Tennessee, and before this mill was in full operation an addition to the plant was already planned. In 1952 the South furnished 70 per cent of the sulphate-bleached pulp paper manufactured in the United States, and plant expansion was progressing rapidly.

Though the census report in 1920 did not list pulpwood and paper as a product of the South, and Howard Odum in 1935 did little more than make a prophecy for the industry, twelve southern states in 1958 received $404,660,000 from these products. Georgia led with $81,860,000, while Alabama was second with $52,480,-000. More interesting was the fact that every county in the old cotton states of South Carolina and Mississippi derived income from this young industry.

The southern textile industry shares top position with the processing of timber products. Textile manufacturing in the South goes back to the colonial fireside. As the cotton belt expanded in the early years of the nineteenth century and as gins increased the availability of raw cotton, textile mills moved southward. Jacob and William Gregg in 1843 dramatized the beginning of textile industrialization in their Georgia and Graniteville, South Carolina, factories. Across the mountains in Kentucky the Grahampton Mills made cloth for a widely dispersed southern and midwestern market, and in the heart of the rich Mississippi cotton belt, the Mississippi Mills at Wesson marked an industrial beginning in that state.

Textile manufacturing in the South grew by spurts. Closure of the British supply during the troubled years, 1811–17, encouraged domestic manufacturing, overwhelmingly in New England, in contrast to the South, and again in the late ante-bellum decades textile manufacturing grew to importance in some southern towns. It was not, however, until the 1880s that textile expansion showed the stamina which in time was to make it basic to southern economy. The story of textile milling in the South after the Civil War rested upon the same foundation as expanding industry in the present South. There was an abundance of willing labor, a cheap source of fuel and water power, friendly local communities anxious to deal gently with manufacturers at tax-paying times, cheap raw materials requiring minimum freight payments, and, in most communities, little or no competition for these advantages. There was a shortage of management and trained workers, capital, and an efficient distributive facility.

The earlier southern textile industry often gathered its people about it in isolated communities, for no southern economic development in this period brought about sufficient urbanization to attract any considerable number of immigrants. The company towns which resulted created huge problems beyond the actual manufacturing process. The present South has advanced beyond this stage. In the earlier cotton milling and mining areas, companies have disposed of their villages to their employees. The new McCormick, South Carolina, mill, for instance, has no village community but draws its workers from an area of more than sixty miles radius. So rapidly have both the social and economic pictures changed in textile manufacturing that the past is only a brief preface to the present necessity and to immediate future hopes. In fact one of the distinctive changes in industrial organization in the South is the discontinuance of industrial villages under company management.

Textile milling below the Potomac became a complex thing. Mills were moved south for several reasons. Management sought an abundance of cheaper and unorganized labor. Electrical power was cheaper, transportation was improved, and climate was more favorable. While New Englanders wailed loudly about loss of their industry, southern millmasters and farmers sought solutions to their problems. Mills which once consumed southern cotton now produced tire cord, special fabrics, and textiles from synthetics. Chemical plants in Virginia, North Carolina, and Tennessee fed new materials into the mills. The synthetic industry has chopped its fibers into staple lengths so they can be carded and spun in the orthodox way. In this manner mills can use both cotton and synthetics. DuPont, Celanese Corporation of America, Chemstrand, and others have revitalized an historic southern industry with a highly modern product. At the same time there has been a major shifting in the need for human labor for operation of the mills. In many of the processes fewer people are being employed, and in many other instances textile manufacture is becoming more specialized.

But the South no longer confines its industrial expansion to conventional regional industries. New industries are as highly diversified in nature as they are widely dispersed geographically. It is a hick town indeed which does not have at least one factory tucked away on a choice site, or is not clearing away debris from a lot to build a new one.

Smooth-talking local citizens who go dashing about the country with briefcases crammed with local statistics and descriptive matter designed to attract manufacturers are the modern southern evangelists. They represent chambers of commerce, state industrial boards, and towns and cities. These professional economic matchmakers dangle before manufacturers promising prizes of abundant labor, raw materials, balmy climate, and even southern traditions. At home, speakers describe to women's service clubs the glories of coming industries.

Statisticians in every state have spent long hours analyzing population comparisons by ages, races, and sexes, for labor is the modern South's greatest industrial asset. Generally the southern population is relatively young, and it is increasing. The revolution in agriculture has released a well-conditioned labor force sufficient to supply five or six times the present industrial needs.

In 1956 there were approximately 22,000,000 laborers in the South. It is true, of course, that much of this great force is untrained for highly specialized jobs and its educational achievements are relatively low as compared with those in the rest of the country. Deficiencies of the southern school system are revealed in the personnel records of the region's industrial laborers. On the positive side, southern labor is exceedingly willing to work, and, because of its hand-labor background, proves itself potentially capable in dexterity tests. There is a minimum of absenteeism, partly because of rugged competition for jobs, and the southerner's capacity to learn is good.

Mississippi, an intensely rural state, is becoming more industrialized. In 1954, 72.1 per cent of that state's population was rural, and it had a median age of 24.6 years. Henry V. Allen, a consulting engineer in Jackson, said that Mississippi labor, "considered in terms of the know-how and requirements of industry, is primarily unskilled." Further, "The majority of men and women available for employment in metal fabricating plants (this was doubtless true for all other industries) are persons from the rural areas who seek industrial jobs to supplement a marginal farm income. Mechanization and diversification of agriculture have greatly reduced on-the-farm job opportunities."

At the other end of the South, Virginia reflected a sharp change in its economic picture. In 1900 fully half of the state's gainfully employed people were engaged in agriculture, but in 1950 only 14.5 were so employed. Domestic food demands have increased

140 per cent, as compared with an increase in mechanical and scientific goods up to 130 per cent of the capable population. Since 1920 approximately 150,000 laborers have left the farms, and the agricultural labor supply has been reduced by half in three decades.

What is true in Mississippi and Virginia is largely true in the other southern states. The reservoir of labor is still largely unexploited. One of the reasons why labor in the region has made such favorable showing in industry is that employers have been able to use a generous range of selectivity in employing people. Generally when a new industry has selected a southern location it has been flooded with applications for jobs.

In South Carolina a firm requiring 500 to 700 laborers received applications from 5000, 7000, and 12,000 applicants in three communities. This story is repeated in the other southern states almost as frequently as there are prospects for new industry. There is no foreseeable time, under present economic conditions, when industry will have to accept the less desirable employees from the ranks of southern labor. It is doubtful that such selectivity of industrial employees is possible anywhere else in the country.

An abundance of female labor is one of the South's important economic assets. Newer types of industries and modern conditions in manufacturing plants have greatly facilitated use of female labor. Rising urbanization, changing agriculture, and lack of rural employment have brought revolutionary changes in the status of southern women. This is a significant break with southern tradition caused by industrialization.

The balance of agriculture with industry has more meaning for the small farmer as a class than for a state or region as a whole. Industrial employment boosts rather than hinders the activities of the small farmer. Under the prevailing industrial workday many farmers are able to carry on approximately the same agricultural activities as before. By converting lands to pasturage and using machinery it is possible to do a day's work, measured by earlier southern farm standards, after a man leaves an industrial plant.

In education, skills, and improved social conditions, industrialization has brought a revolution to hundreds of southern communities. Before 1930 thousands of towns and villages could deserve the reputation of being "one-horse towns," where change was imperceptible. Community improvements came only by extreme force of circumstances, or as the result of pesky crusading by ambitious citizens' groups. Small southern towns were geared to the interests and the pace of the farm. Schools, libraries, hospitals, sanitary facilities, and amusements were limited by lack of leadership, patronage, and capital resources. In the face of modern industrialization, however, social change has become a prime necessity. Communities which have continued to take an indifferent attitude toward social betterment have been ignored by industry. Specialized and technical personnel have been reluctant to move families into areas where schools, medical care, amusements, and local pride are lacking.

The modern southern educational system has been challenged as never before by a demand for quality performance. Southern labor is still largely unskilled. Many companies which come south, however, demand a large number of highly trained and skilled employees. The chemical industry is one. Its use of common laborers is limited, and its very success rests in the hands of trained and skilled employees. While it is true that southerners have been gaining industrial skills outside the region ever since the "Detroit" migration began in the 1920s, today there still are not enough skilled southerners to go around. Southern universities and colleges could devote most of their efforts to training scientists and still not flood the current regional market with specialists. This fact has already brought radical reversal of southern attitudes toward technical education. Dr. Frank J. Soday, of the Southern Association of Science and Industry, Incorporated, told the Southern Governors' Conference, meeting in Point Clear, Alabama, in October 1955, that the South had been building laboratories at a rapid rate, and that it would build a thousand more within a decade. These would require 16,000 technicians, but the region was training only 17 per cent of the nation's scientists and engineers.

It is doubtful, however, that southern industries need skilled labor as much as southern laborers need industry. All of the southern states have industrial and agricultural boards. Their common purpose is to attract new industries into the southern states. Most of the boards employ competent specialists who can analyze local opportunities for manufacturers and give them other necessary technical information. These boards have organized large bodies of materials pertaining to the South, and their influence has been significant. All of them list impressive numbers of new industries which have been attracted to the states in the last decade.

Two of the most interesting attempts of agrarian states to attract industry were those of Mississippi and Louisiana. In 1933 these states faced what was probably the most pinching economic crisis of any of the southern states. In 1930 farming and lumbering were the major industries, both unpromising in the matter of future expansion. Farming suffered from a long accumulation of ills, and lumbering from depletion of timber resources. Towns which had boomed when the big mills were going promised to become ghost towns in depression. Columbia, Laurel, Bogalusa, and scores of others were caught in the depression of lumbering. People were unemployed, and businesses were discontinued or operated on a limited scale. There was no possibility that the old system of agriculture could absorb the surplus of labor or supply capital for new economic ventures. Clearly Mississippi's traditional economic system had come to virtually a complete halt.

The general assembly enacted legislation in 1936 which proposed to broaden the industrial path to Mississippi. Reflecting the long agrarian history of the state, the new law paid its respects to the past and courted the future in its title, "Balance Agriculture with Industry." An agricultural and industrial board was created, and Mississippi went on an advertising spree to attract industry. Signs along main railroads proclaimed the glories of local communities, with the hope that they would catch the eyes of business executives as they raced by in Pullman cars. National magazines carried advertisements, and news stories described the glories of Mississippi's industrial future.

The Mississippi law anticipated that both outside management and capital would bring industry into the state. Native sons had operated many of the big sawmills, but rather generally they stayed away from most other forms of manufacturing. There were too many complex problems of adequate financing, management, and marketing for inexperienced local sons to undertake industrial organization. Much of this no doubt was timidity, but the prevailing attitude has been one of looking to outside management and capital to locate and operate the new factories.

Mississippi's new industrial law permitted communities and counties to offer inducements to industries in building and in tax concessions. Local citizens were asked to vote special bond issues to finance plant construction and even waive tax payments on capital outlay of the business for five years. Control of the plan rested with the state board, which decided whether or not a community had enough labor and other resources to sustain a factory. It then authorized a bond issue election and sent representatives to court an industry.

All of the southern states have been abused by unscrupulous manufacturers who exploited community enthusiasm to secure industry. These men have used plants for a period free of taxes, and then departed. Possibly worse were marginal industries, plagued elsewhere by labor troubles, restrictive state laws, and bankers, which accepted southern concessions and left their troubles behind. The ills, however, which caused them trouble in the first place frequently traveled south with them. Ferreting out the mountebanks and exploiters has required considerable awareness, and only time and a slackening of the present boom conditions will actually reveal the full value of the balance-agriculture-with-industry plan.

Industries which have responded to the Mississippi plan and have paid annual rent on the use of public plants have grown more numerous. For twenty years, industries pay rent which equals mortgage payments on buildings. By the end of that time they have amortized their buildings, which then become their property. From 1936 to July 1955, 138 industries have located in Mississippi under the terms of this inducement plan. Local bond issues have ranged in amounts from $10,000 to subsidize the Pasgagoula Decoy Company to $4,750,000 to construct the Greenville Mills in 1951. For the most part, interest rates were moderate and local opposition to bond issues negligible.

One of the first major companies to locate in Mississippi under the subsidized plan was the Armstrong Tire and Rubber Company, a Sears, Roebuck and Company subsidiary. This industry invaded the heart of the Old South. At Natchez, under the

shadows of plantation homes, a surplus labor force converted raw
rubber into tires. This famous old cotton and river town took on
a new appearance, and a new smell.

Many of the Mississippi industries are engaged in the manufacture of hosiery, garments, furniture, paper, glass, light bulbs,
building materials, tools, and wood and metal gadgets. Some of
them are assembly plants using parts manufactured elsewhere to
create various manufactured items. In 1952, manufactured products in Mississippi were worth $1,060,000,000, or a 509 per cent
increase over the $175,000,000 return in 1939.

Louisiana has been more successful with its industrial inducement plan as measured in terms of volume of manufacturing. The
state's constitution was amended to permit a form of industrial
subsidization. With one exception the Louisiana plan differs little
from that of Mississippi. A competing industry is not allowed to
locate in a town where there is an established plant without first
securing the older company's approval.

That the tremendous efforts to create a southern industry has
paid dividends is at once evident. Sprawling modern plants with
their tall stacks belching forth vari-colored clouds of chemical
smoke are becoming almost as symbolical of the modern South as
were the Greek revival houses of earlier days.

Railway stations, airports, hotels, and highways swarm with
businessmen who rush over the South lugging impressive briefcases. They have little interest in preserving the way of life of the
Old South. Oil men, engineers, chemists, economists, and sociologists have broken the ancient cadence of southern talk in their
ceaseless discussions of technical problems. There is a marked
difference in tempo in the way industrialists talk about building
plants and carrying on a manufacturing process, and how southern cotton planters discuss the casting of crops. It is often hard to
fit the southern drawl to such pressing business.

Literally hundreds of southern communities have made phenomenal industrial changes. Ante-bellum strongholds like
Natchez, Savannah, Charleston, Nashville, Montgomery, and
New Orleans have attracted so much industry about them that a
visitor has to search for vestiges of the past. In Natchez and
Jackson, hotel lobbies are filled with oil men who drill deep holes
in ancient cotton fields in search of black gold. Cadillacs crowd

into places that once knew ornate plantation carriages. Rings of suburban cottages have been strewn about in modernistic landscape patterns which have largely dispensed with the romantic magnolias and crape myrtle. Stanton Hall and "Nutt's Folly" in Natchez stand out against this modern backdrop somewhat like maiden aunts at a wedding.

A maze of modern highways has sliced through the region's deep loess deposits. Broad roads wind about in clover-leaf spirals — a clear indication of a rural population piling out of the piney woods to find urban employment. Above the horizon of Old Natchez and its famous steamboat landing, smokestacks crowd up among church steeples to symbolize a new era in local interests. The cotton planter of a century ago would now be as conspicuous in this modern city as an abolitionist would have been in the old planter town.

Natchez is not the only famous old cotton town which has fallen under the spell of modern industry. Near the other end of the Natchez Trace, Decatur, Alabama, has bolstered a crumbling agrarian economy with industry. From its beginning the town was dependent on the Tennessee River. Located at the head of shoal water it has been from its founding nearly a century and a half ago a depot town. In the dawn of the southern railway age, Decatur marked the eastern terminus of the Tuscumbia and Decatur by-pass railroad which hauled freight around the Muscle Shoals. In time the road delivered hundreds of thousands of bales of cotton to New Orleans-bound steamboats at Tuscumbia.

For years 2000 men kept the Louisville and Nashville Railroad equipment repaired, but when the company reorganized its operating procedures the Decatur shops were closed. A hosiery mill tried to survive, but bad management, malaria, and depression brought failure. By 1933 this north Alabama town was economically dead. Its people were drifting away, farm income dropped, and there was no industry to bolster a sagging economy.

Creation of the Tennessee Valley Authority found Decatur leaders both defeated and belligerent. They received David Lilienthal and Harcourt A. Morgan in about the same spirit their ante-bellum forefathers would have entertained William Lloyd Garrison. Lilienthal sobered the Decatur fathers when he informed them that it was they who would have to erase the gloom from Decatur's way of life. From the outset he convinced his hearers that he had no intention of saving them from their defeatism.

Development of the Tennessee Valley Authority with its power, flood control, cheap water transportation, and malaria control offered new hope. Within a decade and a half two new flour and grain milling companies, a milk-processing plant, a packing plant, a ship-building company, an ornamental iron works, a copper-tubing factory, a tire-fabric and synthetics plant, and a big Chemstrand plant were producing an annual payroll of approximately $16,000,000. Most of the town's industries came from outside, and they have already converted an old cotton town into a modern manufacturing center.

Down the Tennessee near the Kentucky Dam, Calvert City, Kentucky, has in many ways repeated the Decatur story. Seven chemical firms have spent approximately $75,000,000 in building new plants there in the last eight years. Unlike its upriver Alabama neighbor, Calvert City has no proud past. Even its tiny position on the map in the shadow of Paducah hardly guaranteed its existence. In 1945 no one could have predicted that this Kentucky crossroads would become a center of modern industry. It scarcely had enough population to hold a polite Kentucky funeral. In 1955 its optimistic promoters talked of 10,000 population in the immediate future, and some day it may even become a more important city than the state capital, Frankfort.

Calvert City's first major industry was the Pennsylvania Manufacturing Company, which located a chemical plant there in 1948. Since then, the National Carbide and Carbon Company, Pittsburgh Metallurgical Company, B. F. Goodrich Chemical Company, American Aniline and Extraction Company, and Air Reduction Company all have plants in operation or under construction.

Cheap power, an abundance of water, and a well-stocked labor reservoir brought these industries to the banks of the Tennessee. They have converted a sleepy Kentucky farming village into a thriving chemical manufacturing center. Since 1945 more than $2,000,000,000 has been spent on twelve new industrial plants;

two of these are the $1,700,000,000 gaseous diffusion installation of the Atomic Energy Commission and the $240,000,000 steam-electric plant of the Tennessee Valley Authority.

In southwest Louisiana near the banks of the sluggish Sabine and the Gulf of Mexico, the old Cajun town of Lake Charles has become an industrial anchorage in the modern South. It is a vital link in the Gulf coastal-Louisiana-Texas petroleum and industrial chain which reaches from New Orleans to Galveston. Rice, meats, oil, sulphur, natural gas, and chemicals have made the town a port of international significance. Ships are safe from the damage and destruction of the temperamental weather conditions on the Gulf coast. Located on the deep intra-coastal canal, storm-free Lake Charles has all the advantages of a gulf port plus safety.

Industrial plants which stud Lake Charles form a part of an extensive coastal expansion which extends from Pensacola to Galveston. Oil and chemical plants almost obscure the fact that the old agricultural South also has a strong anchorage in this southwestern city. Rice elevators and a slaughter house keep it wedded to the land.

The chemical industry is one of the most unusual developments in the South. Discovery of oil, the exploitation of mineral deposits, and the manufacture of large quantities of commercial fertilizer and synthetics have required enormous professional talents, much of which has come from outside the South, for chemical instruction has always lagged in the region.

Production of oil in several states accounts for the presence of much of the southern chemical industry. The South, including Oklahoma and Texas, produces about 80 per cent of the nation's petrochemicals and nearly as much of the chemical fertilizer. Financial returns from this industry are impressive and are significant in raising the regional per-capita income. Yet the chemical industry is of such a highly specialized nature that much of its manufacture is done automatically. Approximately $20,000 is spent per laborer in each plant, and in some instances the amount is even larger. As an example, the Spencer Chemical Company in Henderson, Kentucky, has invested $8,750,000 in plant, but employs only 250 men.

This industrial change in the South has brought a radical revision in the life patterns of the region's population. While in-

creasing numbers of young southerners are crowding into technological courses in schools and colleges preparatory to entering
the new industrial fields, others are being trained in economics
and management. A veritable army of specialists works at making
directories, industrial charts and maps, special brochures, analyses
of local conditions, and prospectuses for more intensive regional
industrialization.

Industrialization has been embraced by larger numbers of
southerners as a solution to their economic life. It has nevertheless brought such radical changes to the South that it has already
submerged much of the old way of life in many localities. There
is a tremendous conservative reaction to these changes which destroy old culture patterns and reorient thinking. This institutional
reorganization has involved a most intense emotional struggle.
The frontier plea to preserve the southern way of life is as un-
realistic as asking the return of slavery. If the southern way of
life means low-geared, plodding agrarianism for both rural and
urban society, then most old southern values have passed into the
limbo of history. Regional characteristics have been modified by
the uniformity of machine-made products. Rugged southern individuality is expressed more in a determination to make personal adjustments to the manufacturing process than in outspoken
opinions on politics and religion. Even the individuality of southern cooking and prepared foods has been commercialized in trade
brands which proclaim a romantic past. In this respect, all that is
left of the southern way of life is a commercial artist's conception
of the "good old days" as he displays it on a fancy label.

Few of the modern plants were moved from outside the region;
instead, most of them are either new branch plants or newly organized industries. When they are branches of older industries
they have the advantage of being equipped with more modern
machinery and of being better organized mechanically. There is
no difference between goods manufactured in the South and elsewhere. Too, a rising southern population is constantly expanding
services and consumer markets, a fact which could ensure the
South against a severe reduction in manufacturing in case of a
depression.

Each year since 1954 the South has begun to earn a greater
share of the national industrial income. In 1939 the southern states

produced manufactured goods worth $11,000,000,000, while by 1955 this amount had increased to $60,000,000,000. Equally as significant was the fact that 26 per cent of the region's business income came from manufacturing. But also important were the many problems arising from the location of this wave of new industry.

Thus far, organized labor has not followed the migration of industry into the South. The great majority of laborers in the manufacturing industries remain unorganized. Indeed this has been one of the main factors in bringing companies southward. There are bodies of organized labor throughout the region in such fields as mining, transportation, the trades, and other specialized services. Too, labor is organized in those industries which conform to industry-wide labor contracts. The common laborer, however, is still an individual bargainer. Prevailing southern opinion both within and without the ranks of labor is opposed to organization, as is documented by the fact that all the southern states, except Kentucky, have enacted right-to-work laws. Where labor is concerned, generally the southern newspaper press is highly conservative in its editorial voice. Mention of the Fair Employment Practice Committee arouses emotions. A southern governor said in protest to the civil rights plank of the 1960 Democratic platform that "FEPC" is a dirty word. By the same token some southerners regard collective bargaining with deep suspicion.

So long as industry is new in the region, and so long as there is a full reservoir of eager employees who have not produced effective organizational leadership, the labor movement in the South will make slow headway. Management is quick, however, to admit that in time this condition will change and that southern labor will be organized. Whether or not the present great body of workers speaks with an organized voice, the personnel policies of most of the new companies are in sharp contrast to those which prevailed in the earlier days of the exploitative textile and lumber industries.

The South has already gone so far in the direction of becoming both urbanized and industrialized that no longer can its reactions to larger public issues be interpreted within the narrow limits of the older historical framework. Though there have been no radical political changes because of the arrival of industries, the time is at hand when these may come to pass. Already fear is expressed by many responsible southerners that emotionalism over the 1954 Supreme Court decision may create such an unwholesome community atmosphere that outside industrialists may become reluctant to make heavy investments in the South. In Virginia and Arkansas the closing of public schools has no doubt sobered industrial leadership in planning to move south. With schools closed it would not be so easy to persuade outside management and technical employees to go south. Too, the supply of basically trained southern workers would be cut in proportion to the school-closing activities of four or five of the states. In the face of these problems, not even the abundance of labor and natural resources would outweigh the liabilities industrial management would face in many parts of the Lower South.

Thus far, industry has conformed to the prevailing social practices of the states in which plants are located. As a result the Negro is often handicapped in finding the most desirable forms of employment. On the other hand, threatened boycotts of certain manufacturers' products because of contributions to the NAACP or other organizations have given rise to considerable publicity, which in a measure handicaps the southern agricultural and industrial boards. The Federal Government also holds a whip hand in the awarding of defense contracts and in the maintenance of operational bases.

But whatever the future might bring in this area, the immediate past has already produced a far-ranging change in the South. The industrial plant, with its towering smokestacks and banks of glass windows set amidst inviting lawns, has become a more precise symbol of the modern South than some of those of the past were of the Old South. Again a modern southerner might repeat after Henry W. Grady that there is "a new South not through protest of the old, but because of new conditions, new adjustments, and, if you please, new ideas and aspirations."

IX

The Road South

The whole art of driving was directed to the discovery of a passage for the coach among the trees and through the fields, where there are fields, adjoining the road — the road itself being impassable. Occasionally, when the coachman, during the night, found it necessary, owing to the thickness of the forest on each side, to take the road, he would first leave the coach and make a survey with his lantern, sounding the ruts of the cotton wagons, and finally marking out a channel by guiding stakes which he cut from the underwood with a hatchet, usually carried in the holster. If after diligent sounding, he found no passage sufficiently shallow, he would sometimes spend half an hour preparing one, bringing rails from the nearest fence, or cutting brushwood for the purpose. We were but once or twice during the night called to leave the coach, or to assist in road-making, and my companion frequently expressed his gratitude for this — gratitude not to the driver, but to providence, who made the country, as he thought, so unusually well adapted for stage coaching. The night before, he had been on a much worse road, and was half the time, with numerous other passengers, engaged in bringing rails, and prying the coach out of sloughs.

OLMSTED, JOURNEY IN THE BACK COUNTRY, pp. 136–7

A quarter of a century after Olmsted made his notes on conditions of Virginia roads, southern country editors were pleading for improved roads. Everywhere in the region roads were poor. In winter they were mud-bound, and in summer dust-ladened. Characteristic of the difficulties encountered during the rainy season is the story told about the Ordinary of Duly County, Georgia. He had ordered an iron safe, six by ten feet, in which to preserve the county's records. This five-ton depository was shipped to Montezuma, twenty-nine miles from its final destination in Vienna. A contractor agreed to haul the big iron box for a hundred and fifty dollars, but on the way it slid off his wagon and sat mired in mud, blocking the road. The question arose about what next to do with it. A reward of a hundred dollars was offered for the best suggestion as to how to deliver the safe. Wags suggested building a railroad to it, some said it would be easier to dig a canal and float it home, others thought it might be used as a summer resort, or possibly it would be easier to move the courthouse to the safe, and one ingenious wit suggested inflating a big enough balloon to float it home by air.

This whimsical situation in the Georgia backwoods bespoke the conditions of southern roads before the organization of highway commissions and the building of all-weather highways across the South. Today, a frostbitten Yankee dashing across the Potomac River bridge hastening on to Miami is not as conscious as were his predecessors seventy-five years ago that he has crossed a sectional border. Grown prosperous from land, factory, and bonds, and jaded by persistent cold and sooty snow, northern tourists jam highways 1, 11, 25, 27, 41, and 51 in their headlong race for warm weather. Before them stretch hundreds of miles of asphalt and concrete.

Throughout the year white safety-lines guide a charging cavalcade of thundering cars, buses, and trucks through the South. From one county line to the next, and from one state border to another, the interstate roads stretch on without threat of mud or dust. Not even warning bumps denote passage from one political jurisdiction to another. This change has speeded the South onto its place of industrial hope in the twentieth century. The mud of half a century ago has been sealed under wheel, and because of this the region has taken on new economic and social promise.

Until 1920 editorial scoldings were wasted on southerners. Roads cost money and labor. The South had the labor but not the money, and there were few counties indeed which proposed raising the necessary tax money to support even the most primitive roads. This was the situation in 1894 when a small group of southern leaders realized that their region could never really overcome its economic hardships until it had breached the mud bar-

125

rier to efficient transportation. A highway convention met that year at Richmond, and a year later the crusade for good roads was further advanced in conventions at Atlanta and Houston.

Already the South was feeling the impulse of rising population and industrialization. Factories were in operation in many places below the Potomac, but they were so widely scattered as to be almost novelties in the land of staple crops. If southern optimists were to substantiate their remarks about the availability of nearby raw materials and the reservoirs of cheap labor, roads had to be built to permit easy transportation. Centuries earlier buffalo and Indian had scored the South with intra-regional trails. In the dawning of southern history, trader, cattle grazer, and plodding settler had padded trails into primitive roads, and so they left them. In 1900, these roads were little more efficient than they had been in 1860. They were disconnected and their surfaces unimproved. The southerner was still largely landbound.

By the time Woodrow Wilson became President, surfaced roads were still so much a novelty that pictures of them appeared in southern elementary textbooks as modern wonders. A few miles of worn macadam roads existed in Kentucky, while there were stretches of shell roads in the coastal South. Automobiles raised clouds of dust along many southern roads in summer, and churned them into quagmires in winter. Winter travel was almost impossible, thus making the early automobile a highly seasonal vehicle. By this time, though, the southern campaign for good roads had almost achieved the fervor of a religious revival. State legislators approved laws creating highway commissions, and by 1920 all of the southern states had created central administrative bodies.

In every southern state, highway officials struggled with public opinion on one hand and limited budgets on the other. Making surveys often involved as much diplomacy and bluff as engineering skill and management. Construction tools were comparable with those of the farm. Before passage of the new legislation roads were miserably maintained by a politics-ridden system of annually "warning out" able-bodied men and boys between the ages of sixteen and sixty-five to work a few days each year on the roads.

The rise of automobile traffic during the 1914–18 period hastened the construction of improved roads. Detroit automobile makers set off the most effective Yankee invasion that ever disturbed southern complacency. Those consecrated idealists who had preached good roads at the Richmond and Houston conventions in the 1890s little knew that these would finally be brought by benefactors roaring out of the industrial plants along the Great Lakes. Such names as Ford, Chrysler, Olds, Willis, Nash, Shakespeare, Reo, Studebaker, and Dodge had more long-range economic meaning for the South than all the Civil War generals combined. The established way of life in the South was shaken to its very foundation by this new Yankee machine.

The automobile was no reluctant invader. It ran roughshod over established social and economic institutions. Fortunately, the omnivorous invader from Detroit brought with it a partial solution to the first great problem — the cost of providing for it. Gasoline could be measured and taxed at the point of sale, and car owners could be saddled with privilege taxes, which made revenue collection for financing highways certain. There could no longer be the traditional political dodges of sparing the poor man, or of tinkering with assessments. A man who owned a car was assumed to be capable of paying taxes, and unit taxes recognized no favorites. Bad roads only limited the use of cars, so the important thing was to build roads as quickly as possible. Automobile manufacturers and agents supplied partial answers to an increased traffic volume by selling their machines on the installment-payment — and at the same time created new problems.

The automobile destroyed much of the myth of the old-style southern poor man. Afoot and on muleback his poverty was on public display. The public could see his bare feet and ragged clothes, but seated in a car, his feet were hidden from view and his rags could not be seen. New-found mobility and speed gave the southern yeoman his greatest release from the bonds of the past. In his new vehicle he found both dignity and independence. Distance no longer held him in its stifling grip, and the persistence of payments on his car blasted him loose from the ancient routine of a southern agricultural past and its uncertain year-end returns. The automobile became actually more important to the poor southerner than either medicine or dress.

By 1918 the South faced a dilemma. States debated whether or not they should issue bonds to be redeemed by direct taxes, or whether they should pay for their roads as they used them. Shortly before, Virginia rejected the idea of a general bond issue and chose to build its roads as it collected gasoline and use taxes to pay for them. North Carolinians were more venturesome and voted a staggering bond issue of $50,000,000 to survey and build a widespread system of improved public roads. The old aim of connecting every county seat in the state with an improved road was nearing a reality. This fabulous program created both a regional and national sensation. Highway promoters from everywhere came to view the results of the North Carolina plan. Some came to copy it, others to bemoan the fate of the state which would surely be bankrupted and sold to the highest bidder at the state house door. Even economists and political scientists viewed the North Carolina venture as a dubious undertaking. Changing times since 1921 have brought changing attitudes. In 1956 North Carolina assumed the heavy fiscal obligation of $76,000,000 for 1771 miles of new roads, in addition to all of the other expenditures which will be made under conditions of the Federal Highway Act of 1956.

While North Carolina was organizing its extensive highway program in the early 1920s, Tennessee assumed a burdensome indebtedness to pull itself out of the mud. It planned a system of roads which would link together the diverse sections of that elongated state, from Bristol to Memphis and from Clarksville to Chattanooga. More than any other southern state, perhaps, Tennessee wrestled with natural hazards — mountain and river alike — to cut roads through the land. Old mountain trails that had carried pioneers westward have now been graded into roads which gnaw deep wounds into the ridges; other roads now skim over river valleys. But the North Carolina and Tennessee patterns have not prevailed in many other states, to their detriment. For those that followed the more conservative course of paying as they traveled have made a poorer showing in the general quality and mileage of roads.

While southern state highway commissions were being organized and the task of developing state-connecting road systems was still in its initial stages, Congress passed the Federal Highway Act on November 9, 1921. This legislation cleared the way for the realization of one of the major objectives of the pioneering highway conferences. Interstate roads were to be constructed with the aid of the Federal Government. This resulted in the planning of an inter-southern highway system which not only brought the South into fairly rapid communication with all its sections, but also with the rest of the country. In 1926 the American Association of Highway Officials voted to bring order to interstate travel by assigning numbers to continuous main cross-country roads. At least a dozen of these interstate routes crossed the South. Highway 1 connected the far northeast with the southernmost tip of Florida at Key West, crossing the Old South en route. Highway 11 angled across the region from the tip of Maryland to New Orleans. Main roads came down from the Great Lakes to end at Gulf and ocean, while east-west roads sliced the South at intervals from the Ohio to the Gulf. Federal highway aid had an enormous influence in reshaping southern society and economy.

Since 1921 the Federal Government has made a heavy contribution to the construction and maintenance of primary interstate and secondary roads in the South. Passage of the Federal Highway Act abruptly ended a century-old political argument over federal aid to internal improvements. The central government and the states were placed in a new relationship. Not only did the Federal Government offer material assistance to the building of roads, but the Bureau of Highways set specifications for roadbeds, bridges, and road markings, and maintained overseers to enforce the rules.

With the adoption of a federal highway use tax, the greater burden of support was shifted to the more populous centers of the nation. Thus, the eastern and midwestern states paid a major portion of the levy, while the southern states, with long stretches of interstate and secondary road systems, in turn, received disproportionate benefits. This has resulted in a dramatic paradox in the current sectional political cannonading. Amidst the uproar over states' rights, no responsible southern voice has cried out against federal support of the expanding interstate highways, or against the rather strict supervision of the Federal Bureau of Highways.

Intersectional roads were opened in time to transport migratory southerners flocking to rising industrial centers in search of employment. The late 1920s saw this army rushing northward by car and bus from cotton and tobacco fields and from mountain farms to help produce the automobiles that would further crowd southern roads. Highways 25, 27, 31, 41, and 51 ran flush with this flood of immigrants. The Appalachian Highlands alone freshened this run to near flood proportions in the promising pre-depression years and during World War II. In the gloomy days of biting panic this despondent army has retraced its steps homeward. The hand of trouble, however, has not necessarily lessened the flow of this stream, but it has at times severely chastened its movement.

The roar of private traffic in the South was but a gentle purr compared with the rising crescendo of heavy commercial, multi-wheeled vehicles which came crashing down upon flimsy roadbeds and shaky bridges. Every year after 1920 saw a major increase in heavy truck traffic across the region. By 1935 southern transportation had undergone a complete revolution. Local railway lines serving scattered county-seat towns were pulled up to exist no more except in sentimental memories. For the first time towns without rail connections were relieved of the stigma and handicap of being landlocked. Trucks and buses delivered freight and passengers to remote places. In this period the South began to gain ground in its long battle with the Interstate Commerce Commission over the sore point of freight differential. Truck freight in many places effectively broke a restriction which had seriously handicapped industrial expansion of the South. Not only did good roads and the rise of truck traffic help to bring about an equalization of freight rates, it wrought changes in the nature of political pressures on the state houses. Truck owners now compete with railroad lobbyists for votes, and the truck lines are gradually winning. They can now exert near decisive influence on the course of southern politics.

Industrialization of much of the rural South was an impossibility before 1930. Many of the region's resources lay unexploited for want of transportation and markets. The whole system of regional agriculture felt the fresh surge of economic life. Vegetable growers in Alabama could now rush their produce to Chicago, and fruit growers in Florida found markets all over the eastern half of the United States. But, most important of all, livestock producers converted vast areas of southern lands to pasturage with the assurance that they could find nearby markets for their livestock. One of the main reasons livestock growing had failed in the South during the earlier years of its history was the lack of dependable markets, a condition which railroad and river had largely failed to correct.

The automobile has brought faster change to the South since 1920 than any crusader for industry and good roads in 1894 could have foreseen. The prophesies of those crusading editors who pleaded with the people to pull themselves out of the mud were more than fulfilled. It may be that modern southern roads are not as wide as they should be, and that total mileage is more impressive than the actual quality of the roads. The main thing is that the roads are passable in every season. Since 1945 public roads have been redesigned and rebuilt. Now many of the main lines of travel are even being redirected, and, in some instances, new arterial routes of travel are being located directly from aerial photographs and from drafting boards. Not only has there been a tremendous change in the character of southern highway transportation on the ground, but these new roads have produced a change in a fundamental southern creed — namely, that the central government in each state should be given as little power as possible. Louisiana, Florida, Kentucky, Virginia, and North Carolina, for instance, have established central authority over tremendous web-works of highways which range upward from narrow back-country farm roads to primary state roads. In the past half-century this process of centralization has concentrated in the hands of state highway commissions staggering sums of money and political influence. In many southern states one of the best gauges of political behavior is to be found in the attitudes and activities of the highly centralized public-roads authority.

Louisiana has assumed responsibility for approximately 47,000 miles of road of every class. In 1952 that state made a comprehensive survey of its highway needs, and two years later issued bonds worth $104,611,000 to be redeemed by 1989. This large sum of money has enabled the state to embark upon an extensive highway construction and building program which either has reshaped, or promises to, a good portion of the local economy. The financial servicing of so large an amount of money is within itself a fascinating commentary on the cost of twentieth-century progress. The interest payments on this sum between 1954 and 1989 will more than equal all money spent on roads by Louisiana from the coming of the French explorer LaSalle to the outbreak of World War I. Sitting astride the Gulf coastal passage from east to west are 600 miles of projected federal interstate roads in Louisiana, which will form a key link in the general national plan of major intersectional highways.

North Carolina and Florida equal, if not surpass, the statistical position of Louisiana. These states maintain two of the largest road systems in the South. In 1956 North Carolina had approximately 70,000 miles of roads, of which 22,074 were hard-surfaced. At the same time 1,500,000 locally licensed vehicles shared right-of-way with an almost equal number of vehicles of outside registry. Repeating its bold course of 1921, the state issued $200,000,000 in bonds to modernize and extend its roads in 1956. Again it has tempted fortune on one hand and mortgaged its future in enormous service costs on the other. From the standpoint of combined area and population, North Carolina was in first position in the nation in maintenance of hard-surfaced roads.

Among the smaller southern states, South Carolina has lined its countryside with new roads, and has improved earlier roads, some of which have been in existence since colonial days. Not only has that state made vast improvements in its primary roads, but in recent years its legislature has provided for an extensive network of farm-to-market roads. The centralized highway authority had in 1956 responsibility for 25,358 miles of rural and urban roads. In 1917 South Carolina was hopelessly bogged in the mud, and its 39,400 motor vehicles were restricted in travel by seasonal conditions. Forty years later there was a motor-vehicle registration of 649,742 vehicles, and the interstate highways carry an even greater number of vehicles of outside registration each year. If the number of vehicles has increased in such large proportions, so has the expenditure of funds for highways. The Federal Government has spent $98,000,000 on South Carolina roads from 1917 to 1956, and the state has spent $395,000,000.

In 1930 Mississippi was behind the other southern states in highway construction. Motorists who crossed the state faced a constant struggle with mud and dust. Automobiles driven for any length of time on Mississippi roads acquired unmistakable evidence of a lack of roads. By 1956, however, no traveler, however critical, could find much fault with that state's roads. In sixteen years since 1940, automotive traffic has increased in this state by 104.6 per cent. In 1955, 636,544 motor vehicles were registered. More significant was the lifting of gross-weight limitations on commercial vehicles, thus bringing about a great increase in the volume of freight carried on the highways. Revenue still remains a problem. In 1952–53 Mississippi collected the smallest income from all its road financing sources of any southern state.

Expenditure of vast sums of state and federal money for highways has always involved politics. Governors, highway commissioners, and local county officials have found highway funds bottomless tills from which to dispense political favors. Long ago some machinery manufacturers and dealers learned lessons in the practicalities of southern politics. Campaign chests have profited from the benevolences of friendly dealers in search of congenial customers. For the citizen the building and maintenance of highways has become one of the surest sources of public employment. In some states, cutting weeds along the roads, whether done by hand or machine, often has more political significance than a genuine promise of reform. As a matter of fact, a good crop of carefully chosen weed-cutters in some southern states might well hold a balance of political power in a hotly contested election. On the other hand, the tremendous effort necessary to build and maintain roads across vast distances of the South has created a demand for trained engineering talent which oftentimes taxes the region's educational capacity to supply. In the field of engineering more and more trained southerners are being kept at home, and, because of the scarcity of engineers, politicians are reluctant to involve them in politics.

Whether travelers go south on Highway 1 or 41, the story is the same. Unlike Olmsted and his colleagues who lumbered across the South a century ago, there is little time for the modern traveler to contemplate regional conditions along the way. He may pick up a grunted half-notion of what is happening locally from a poorly informed filling-station attendant, or pass a few words with a motel-keeper while he is in the process of registering for the night, but he gets no really mature idea about the South on his travels. He may contemplate how the people make a living on such red land as he drives along, but a constant stream of speeding cars and roaring trucks is distracting. A continuous line of commercial advertising signs telling of the wonders of everything from beer to pecans, from gasoline to antiques, all but obscure much of the countryside. In many instances even the historical spots of the South are located in the mad swirls of traffic. Today it might be more hazardous to pull off a main road to take a leisurely look at the scene of a Civil War battlefield than it was to have engaged in the battle itself.

The South is no longer a land of muddy roads, and it is no longer a land of leisurely travel. The new roads reflect a haste not hitherto associated with the southern temperament. Even Mississippi has gradually lost its reputation for being the only place in the land where an obliging motorist would stop and help another change a tire. It would be difficult to find a public road anywhere in the South today that would be as poor as was the highway between Washington and Richmond in the 1850s, or in 1918. Rivers and creeks have lost their identity in flatbed bridges which hasten travelers over them in distressing ignorance of their existence. The ferry is all but a museum piece, and the modern southerner has come to think of a ford as something that comes out of Detroit. Hazards of modern travel are in keeping with the expansion of the roads themselves. The automobile and truck are fierce killers in the South. They take an annual toll of life that approaches that of the old regional diseases. Riding across the modern South in an automobile offers a more serious threat to human safety than did a lifetime spent in a hookworm-infested region fifty years ago. In many places straight roads are conducive to excessive speeds and highway hypnosis, and low percapita income has contributed further hazards in weak tires and defective machines.

High-speed expressways and interchanges which facilitate traffic movement around some of the southern cities are major examples of skilled engineering. Expressways in Miami, Atlanta, New Orleans, and Washington are parts of a regional highway system which serves the fast long-distance traffic which has developed in the industrial South. It is hard to recall that once stagecoach drivers hunted for the road or fetched rails to enable them to cross stretches of ungraded swamplands where now four and six lanes of high-speed expressways with their complicated system of clover leaves and spiraling turn-outs are located.

Urban centers are being forced to free their streets of heavy traffic. Sleepy southern towns, which never experienced traffic rushes greater than those of court and circus days, now find themselves caught in vortexes of churning vehicles struggling to break the restrictive clutches of narrow street bottlenecks. Horse-and-buggy southern town budgets long ago proved inadequate to finance the building of continuous roads through urban areas. State and federal funds have been drawn upon to maintain efficient continuity in the southern interstate road systems. An increasing number of four-lane bypasses drift traffic around towns in constantly flowing streams. A lack of planning and restriction, however, has allowed jungles of cluttering service businesses to entrap these passways in death grips. Driving through a modern southern bypass jungle on a free-access road is a more hazardous undertaking on the face of the record than was riding across the Choctaw Indian country along the Natchez Trace in the early 1800s. Many southern towns are being sucked away from their historic cores by this feverish rush to grab at easy dollars in roadside merchandising and inn-keeping. Even southern cities are suffering enough decentralization pains to stimulate crusades to preserve main streets.

The South is perhaps only beginning its highway revolution. Already the outline of super-interstate defense roads form a fairly intricate pattern of cross-hatching in the region. By 1959 the United States Bureau of Public Roads said the South would have spent $1,846,559,276 on highways and maintenance. Thus in three years the region would have built more roads of far superior quality and at a greater mileage cost, than it built from 1789 to 1930.

Impressive though comparative statistics of southern highway construction are, the real significance of the new roads lies in the fields of social and economic change. Today the southern population is highly mobile. It is difficult under these conditions for a social situation to become a provincially static one. There is little possibility that such a population can be kept in a state of social self-satisfaction under these conditions. The modern highway has not only hastened the draining away from the South of hundreds of thousands of people, but it has brought about greater meaning to firsthand comparisons of local conditions with those in the rest of the country. Provincialism is less a factor in the modern South than ever before in the region's history. Conversely, the rest of the country has gained a closer look at the South.

In a more fundamental way improved roads and means of transportation have given southern labor the same mobility as industrial goods. Industrial management is safe in locating plants in isolated communities near sources of rural labor supplies because cheap trucking facilities are available. The employment radii of industrial plants have been enlarged fiftyfold by good roads and the automobile. In the same manner an intensive move in the future to organize southern labor might be greatly facilitated by this mobility. In cases of labor strife, larger industrial areas might be drawn into disputes than was possible prior to 1930. In the strike around Gastonia, North Carolina, in 1929 textile employees were able to communicate their grievances to their fellows over a considerable area.

The transformation of highways in the South is, of course, a reflection of a change which is happening throughout the country. But nowhere else have improved roads done more to shape the economic and social structure of the region. Automobiles and trucks have become as fundamental to the southern way of life (financially at least) as food, if not more so. In 1958 the Charleston field office of the Department of Commerce reported that southerners spent $16,000,000 more on automobiles and supplies in 1957–58 than for food.

The automobile and transport truck have greatly facilitated the urban growth of the South. The transition from a purely agrarian system to one balanced by industry would have been utterly impossible in 1920. Too, the conveniences which are now fundamental parts of the new southern way of life can only be maintained over passable roads. Even the race problem has felt the impact of the modern highway, and the Negro is able to live in towns and villages because he has ready access to the roads. The South's historical provincialism will be further broken down as the highway system expands. Already this is to be seen in the fact that many defenses being made by extremists are against specific groups rather than against the North of years ago. The South is now able to see tourists to its region as individuals with their own views and emotions rather than as the conventional "Yankees" with supposed ill-will toward the South.

X

Picking Yankees

Presenting myself and known only in character of a chance traveler, most likely to be in search of health, entertainment and information, usually taken for and treated as a southerner, until I stated that I was not one, I journeyed nearly six months at one time (my second journey) through the South. During all this journey, I came oftener than once a week, on an average, to public houses, and was thus generally forced to seek lodging and sustenance at private homes. Often it was refused to me; not infrequently rudely refused. . . . Not once with the slightest appearance of what Noah Webster defines hospitality, the "practice of receiving or entertaining strangers without reward."
OLMSTED, A JOURNEY IN THE BACK COUNTRY, p. 407

To call a southerner inhospitable is comparable to calling him un-Christian. From the beginning of English settlement on the banks of the James, southern people have laid great store by the word hospitality. Hundreds of travelers, both foreign and domestic, have visited the South during the last three and a half centuries. The southern states were major links in the "grand tour." Visitors came first to see the wide expanses of the physical region, to visit Indian tribes, to view and denounce slavery, to criticize the southern yeomanry, to assess plantation economy, and, later, to see what had happened to the South and its people during the Civil War.

Travelers came south to "stay awhile," to spend a night with a family, or to eat a meal and be gone. Many of them went away to publish travelogues describing what they had seen and thought on their journeys. They commented on food, beds, company, traveling facilities, the personal eccentricities of householders trapped into being reluctant landlords, and the graces or lack of graces of the people in general. Slavery was a whipping-boy, and seldom did the institution escape severe arraignment both as to its moral and economic failures. The ignorance of southerners, their habit of spitting, their insatiable idle curiosity, their sloven speech, and lack of industry filled many pages of the travelogues. Frederick Law Olmsted dealt southern pride a heavy blow when he spoke harshly of the region's hospitality, a thing which landed him in a hot controversy with James D. B. DeBow. Olmsted, like all the other travelers, frequently rode up to farmhouse doors seeking food and lodging without any forewarning to a family that he was on his way. Then he complained about the accommodations.

If Olmsted should ride across the South today, though, he would find the landlords ready to receive him, no matter how brief the notice of his arrival. If they were not they would tell him positively by flashing a "no vacancy" sign in his face. There is some difference in the cost of lodging and the attitude of landlords in stating their charges over those of a century ago. As a matter of fact the modern landlords state their charges and collect them before a guest settles down for the night. In the early South the average householder was naïve indeed in the art of exploiting the traveler; today he has either mastered the art or he does not keep travelers at all.

Again the South is on the "grand tour" during all four seasons of the year. Corn, fodder, and oats may be in short supply, but there are plenty of high-octane gasoline, motor oils, and water for cars. The only real difference, if any, between southern gasoline and oils and those sold elsewhere is in the service. There might have been a period, for instance, when a Yankee was not enthusiastically welcomed in the South by some people, but, if this were ever true, it was in a day before statisticians, high-pressure promoters, park directors, and politicians began writing dulcet perorations in their annual reports to governors and tourist commissions.

Actually, in courting tourists the South has come to make a momentous distinction between "good" and "bad" Yankees. Good Yankees come in automobile loads. Hungry as wolves, they are in search of a fleeting glimpse of the past, and are firmly wedded to the idea that a night's sound sleep in a motel is necessary to the good life. They usually have well-developed appetites for candied pecans, apple cider, Coca-Cola, ice cream, milk shakes, "art objects," french fried shrimp, and southern fried chicken. Of course a good Yankee can turn bad quickly in the eyes of tourist promoters. All he has to do is to bring his food with him and prepare it on the roadside, sleep in his car, and shout critical opinions around freely. The worst thing he can do, however, is to stay at home. Good or bad as he may be, the tourist is about as necessary to the welfare of the southern economy as cotton, cattle, burley tobacco, and pine trees. A well-loaded station wagon coming down the road from Pennsylvania headed for a ten-day Mardi-Gras-garden tour in New Orleans and Natchez can quickly be translated into economic terms comparable to those of a small crop of cotton, or a good thinning cut of pulpwood. When tourists are converted to terms of their expenditures they come to represent a good cash income.

Almost every issue of the Sunday *New York Times* carries a section proclaiming southern love of Yankees. In seductive terms and pictures, promoters use warm weather, beautiful gardens, ladies in bathing suits, and food-a-plenty to lure people southward. Come South is the solid refrain, whether it be winter or summer; properties are shifted with the changing seasons, and the summer offerings are made to sound as inviting as those of winter.

Since 1945 the roads southward have been swarming with visitors. They come in search of all sorts of things. Some come to find out the region which receives so much publicity, favorable and adverse. Some come to fish and hunt, others to thrust themselves back into an imaginary world in which they can dream for a fleeting moment that they own slaves and run plantations. The gardens are beautiful — so beautiful in fact that the original owners would be uncomfortable in them in their present well-kept condition.

Southerners now have for sale an almost inexhaustible resource of ante-bellum romance and atmosphere. Where once a fine old home and its furnishings were a virtual millstone about an owner's neck, and often drove him to drink trying to keep up interest payments on a mortgage, they now produce revenue. The house has been placed on "the tour," and the land is in the Soil Bank. Parlor doors have been flung open to tourists, and for the first time the roses and magnolias bloom sweetly, and the moonlight falls softly, on an old homestead which is at peace with itself. The owner

stands in a new relationship with both his property and the mortgage companies. Indeed, he now most likely owns stock in the
latter.

Less aesthetic visitors than those who come to see homes and
gardens are those check-shirted gentry who drag millions of dollars worth of boats and fishing and hunting equipment from one
man-made lake and hunting preserve to another. Every hydro-
electric development from Norris Dam to a private utility-owned
impoundment has created a fishing resource. Almost before the
sediments settle in a new lake, economists are figuring its side-
income in terms of the tourist trade it will draw. The announce-
ment of a new hydro-electric facility in a community touches off
a rush among real-estate dealers, motel-keepers, and concession
operators to be first on the grounds to purchase choice lots.

The tourist trade has presented some major problems in road
location for the South. Once almost all state highway departments
had to worry about were rows with landowners, but now they
have the motel and roadside stand people to think about. The relocation of a road can often mean a staggering displacement of
income-producing property.

Motel- and tavern-keeping has become a modern southern profession. Actually the modern South is well on its way to placing
this calling alongside those of a long and dignified heritage. By
1954 there were 3857 motels and tourist courts in eleven southern
states which had payrolls, and many others which were not reported by the Bureau of the Census. Naming motels is as big a
challenge to many southerners as was selecting plug tobacco
brands in the 1880s. One can take his choice on almost any highway. He can sleep in the Alamo, in a ranch, he can dream about
the mountain view, the river view, the old homestead, and hundreds of other places where owners have been able to think up
romantic names. The *Tourbook* of the American Automobile Association is almost a lyric poem in names of motels. Names from
the Old South, the Old West, the natural surroundings, and even
weird combinations of man-and-wife names now are flashed in the
eyes of travelers from neon signs.

Kentuckians estimate that in 1958 they collected the staggering
amount of $500,000,000 from tourists and travelers who crossed that
state. If this be even partially true, then the farmers who are ready

at the drop af a gavel to exert enormous pressure on the state's general assembly should give up in defeat. The entire agricultural income of the state was only $399,573,000, of which $207,337,000 was from the sale of tobacco. In 1953 Tennessee business firms estimated that receipts from tourists and travelers amounted to $460,000,000 a year, or 15 per cent of the state's three-billion-dollar retail and service income. The value of all farm products sold in Tennessee was only $333,215,000. Actually, recreational travelers alone are estimated to have left almost half again as much money in Tennessee as the entire farm income. Cattle brought Texans an income of $386,000,000 in 1955, while the tourist business yielded $412,000,000, or more than half the value of a $700,000,000 cotton crop. Florida's state advertising budget in 1955 was $450,000, and the tourist business estimated that the various resort cities spend $1,800,000 more. If the state yield was $125.00 for every dollar spent in advertising the return was $282,250,000. Actually, the state estimates its tourist income at a staggering billion dollars a year. The year before, income from all farm products sold in Florida was $466,116,000. It may be true that in the long-run southern history and atmosphere in the raw will be a more profitable and dependable source of income to the region than cotton ever was, even in its golden era.

During 1958 southerners estimated conservatively that they collected more than two billion dollars from tourists and visitors to their region. This, however, is one of the hardest figures in all kingdom come to substantiate. If the estimate is taken state by state, the total is far higher than when estimated on a collective regional basis. Because of the pressure by tourist commissions to secure increased state advertising appropriations, one can never be certain just what the actual tourist income might be. But to those who advertise the South it appears to be good business to brag high.

A vast pilgrimage comes south in increasing volume to view the scenes of the Civil War. As the centennial celebrations of that struggle arrive, the South anticipates an enormous cash harvest. A good motel site by a popular battlefield can be worth more in cash income to an energetic landlord than was any cotton plantation in the old blackbelt. The South fortunately has its share of historic spots and shrines. Through the colonial period, the Revolutionary War, and the Civil War, the region has been well endowed with places of more than local regional interests. Virginia led the southern states in the raising of historical markers. An imaginative markers program has made at least a bare incidental outline of Virginia history available on the roadside. Markers, monuments, and roadside signs review the state's past in terse paragraphs at almost every bend of the road. Following Virginia's lead, other southern states have erected historic markers by the thousands. In some cases, markers commissions have all but exhausted places of major importance, and many of them have now been brought to the cemetery gates with mandates to call upon the heroic dead to strike a public blow for history and tourism.

Still, the Civil War represents the major historical tourist attraction, and indeed promises to be one of the most profitable, and continued revenue-producing business adventures in southern history. Almost a century after, a southerner may whimper a bit that his family and state were bankrupted by war. Occasionally a nostalgic son or daughter will detain a tourist long enough to go through the ancient ritual of describing how heartless Yankee brigands during the war beat down private doors, chopped open trunks, dumped the contents out of sideboards, stole the family silverware, and rushed northward with family treasures.

Those notorious silver thieves who marched with Sherman to the sea, and that masterful "spoon snatcher" General Ben Butler who plundered New Orleans so methodically, are now almost warmly remembered in the South. Such a remarkable change has come with the passage of time that these once-hated freebooters have all but become sentimental characters in this day when every place a hundred years old is a potential tourist attraction. Every scorched place on the woodwork of an old house and every bullet mark is now a profitable scar. The aura of time and a certain amount of romance surround this extra-military aspect of the war.

Where there are no landmarks of war, there are natural attractions. There is a certain amount of prestige for travelers when their automobiles come home bearing placards, and placard men are anxious to add prestige to tourist cars to document the fact that travelers stopped at Rock City, Silver Springs, Natural Bridge, or Dog Patch, Kentucky. In fact advertising signs from Salt Lake City to Philadelphia, and from Detroit to Mobile, proclaim the natural beauty of Rock City and suggest that if a tourist has not strained his eyes to see seven states from its pinnacle, or admired nature's handiwork, and filled his lungs with mountain ozone, he might well consider himself untraveled. The income from paint and printing alone for all the signs and placards, goofy letters, colored postcards, and literature describing tourist attractions in the South may be twenty times greater than that from books for general readers and literary magazines. The southern landscape has been sacrificed in many places to this mad campaign to snatch the tourist dollar. Scarcely a roadside post, tree, fence, or barn has escaped the signmaker. On some of the main highways there is hardly a quarter of a mile left undefiled.

If local sons run out of ideas about historical places to exploit, or curious things to put on display, the United States Department of Commerce stands ready to give expert suggestions. Under the title, *Your Community Can Profit from the Tourist Business,* the Commerce Department shows that all that is needed to attract the tourists is a road and plenty of roadside attractions, with enough signs, mile by mile, to convince the tourists that they are approaching one of the great southern wonders. In a coy piece of advice the federal agency assures the local promoter that, "Tourists perk up when geological formations are called 'faces,' when a narrow valley becomes 'a pass,' when rocks become 'painted,' or when a cliff is called 'Devil's leap.'" The agency lists a number of man-made attractions which range from battle sites and burial grounds to fish hatcheries. Not only can man make his own attraction, he can organize a series of special tourist-attracting events. The southern list today ranges from Hillbilly Day in Highlands, North Carolina, to the wild pony roundup on Chincoteague Island in Virginia.

When Department of Commerce authors urged imaginative citizens to create man-made attractions, they must have had in mind the horse farms of Kentucky. Stud barns on Bluegrass estates swarm most of the year with tourists who have come to gawk at single stallions valued at figures greater than the cost of a modern science building on a southern university campus. A groom, and showman, in anticipation of a generous lecture fee, extols the virtues of his charge. He gives a statistical recitation on such matters as number of races the horse has run, his track time, dollars won, the success of his get, and the size of his service fees.

Thousands of visitors to the South learn more realistically about the facts of horse racing at the tracks. They pay high tuition fees for this schooling through pari-mutuel windows at Keeneland, Churchill Downs, Hialeah, Gulfstream, and Tropical Park. A good day's gross take at these tracks would make a solid down payment on Civil War losses. But this is not all, for the tourist also swallows a generous amount of locally distilled bourbon, eats ravenously of fried chicken and other specialities, and feels very little pain in paying over millions of dollars in doing so. Long ago Louisville, Kentucky, businessmen learned that selling goods and good old southern atmosphere to throngs of people ready and willing to pay homage to a race horse is a painless way of doing business.

One of the major complaints lodged against southern labor in by-gone years was its ruinous absenteeism. It was generally assumed that the average southerner, black or white, was compelled to do a certain amount of fishing every year — come high grass or bankruptcy. In fact the South gained the reputation of being such a leisurely place that no one ever got anything done. The cards are now reversed. Southerners have to work their heads off to serve other Americans in search of leisure. It is ironical that in these years when the South is exerting its greatest efforts to become industrialized it is proclaiming its recreational facilities to outsiders. Recreation is offered as one of the attractions to industries to convince management that it should locate factories in the South. The shorter work day and shorter work week give greater validity to this argument than was true half a century ago.

John Smith in his *History of Virginia* described primitive efforts to catch fish in the James River and Chesapeake Bay. As a matter of fact fishing at Jamestown had helped ease settlers through the starving time. Great natural bodies of water have attracted visitors ever since the first Spanish explorers pushed inland. But the creation of many artificial lakes since 1920 has added extensively to the water surface of the region. The Tennessee Valley Authority has made possible a major side-income for the people in that area. A good part of the estimated two billion dollars which tourists leave in the South annually is spent on fishing, boating, and other recreation activities centered about the lakes. A warm week-end in April will fill most of the main roads with mobile fishermen. Like migrating geese and ducks, they flock to the Cumberland Lake, to the Catawba, Norris, Kentucky, Saluda, Savannah, and hundreds of other lakes and streams to fish and race their boats. In the Tennessee Valley alone the income from boat building and the manufacture of fishing equipment is big business. Sale of fish bait in the modern South must almost equal the annual income from cattle in 1900.

Every southern state makes considerable effort to attract tourists. Publicity bureaus, hotel and motel associations, departments of public parks, organized gasoline dealers, and chambers of commerce, all conduct active campaigns to create and advertise attractions. As Arthur Gordon said of the people of Savannah, southerners generally will dig up anything if it will interest a tourist. They will forget crass materialism long enough to offer a bit of seductive relaxation in the form of scantily clad maidens paddling lazily through quiet lagoons. The pleasant way of life is further revealed by a picture of the Atlantic surf as viewed through a picketline of shapely girls.

The influence of the tourist business upon the South is to be measured in many ways. To indicate how profitable it is, the Eastern Airlines strike in December 1958 threatened such heavy losses to Florida that it put business in that state into momentary panic. Losses were felt not only by those businesses catering to the tourist but by the state's educational system, which was threatened with a curtailment of funds because of a disastrous drop in state revenue.

Few other interests could have made enough impact on governors and legislators to force them to supply funds for the purchase and maintenance of state parks and recreational facilities. All the state parks have been planned with recreation in mind. Where history and recreation could be served in a single area, the historic places have been exploited. Many of the Civil War battlefields have lent themselves to a combination of purposes. The scenes of great battles such as Vicksburg, Shiloh, Chickamauga, Lookout Mountain, Missionary Ridge, and the numerous battlegrounds in Virginia are attractive places.

Virginia has the added attraction of its colonial landmarks. At Jamestown several of these are brought into focus with its historical pavilion and restored village. The surrounding country was battleground in both the Revolution and the Civil War. In addition, the Federal Government has converted several major natural areas of the South into national parks. Possibly the five most important of these are the Mammoth Cave Park, the Lincoln Farm, the Great Smokies National Park, the newly opened Cumberland Gap National Park, and the Everglades National Park.

For the South, aside from the tourist business, the opening of state parks is almost a reversal of attitude toward its natural resources. For the first time in its history the region is making a public effort to develop a sense of conservation for both private and public property. Resources which once were wasted with open-handed profligacy are now being husbanded with care. Land which was allowed to wash away, and timber which was slashed to pieces, and historical spots which were either obliterated or badly abused are now looked upon as wasted capital assets. State management of large areas of woodlands has set a highly instructive example of how southern resources respond to management, and the income from tourists adds further incentive for careful management.

Conservation is carried into other fields. State legislatures and local governments have come to appreciate the importance of game laws. Again it is possible that southern woods and fields will once more be full of game. It is not impossible to find a place where deer, bear, wild boar, and turkeys range as they did in the pioneer period. A wild-boar hunt in the Great Smokies is already an annual event, and in many areas deer seasons are looked upon as significant sources of income.

State and federal statisticians have learned much about the spending habits of the tourist. They have divided his dollar into minute parts, and they can tell before he leaves home how much money he will spend and what he will buy. If, for instance, he goes to the Tennessee Valley and the Great Smokies in the Knoxville area, he and his fellow visitors will leave approximately $35,000,000 or more with the local purveyors of goods and services. In 1955 tourists to this region left behind them a tax tribute of $1,262,000 — enough to relieve the natives of 50 per cent per capita of their tax burden.

In the sales-tax states the tourist business has enormous meaning in boosting tax income. Educational programs are financed heavily from sales-tax sources. Whether he knows it or not, the tourist has helped several of the southern states make the supreme effort to equalize Negro educational opportunities when it became evident that an adverse decision of the Supreme Court would be forthcoming. Had it not been for extra income from outside sources, this effort would have brought the states to a point of bankruptcy.

One of the most unpopular things a candidate for public office could do in the present South would be to oppose further friendship with the tourist. More than one state has been rocked by arguments among gubernatorial candidates over the abuse of tourist attractions, or the failure to provide funds for further expansion of state attractions. Taxes from the tourist trade are the most politically acceptable taxes extant. The taxpayer is here today and gone tomorrow, and he is without voting influence. Too, he is nearly always in a holiday mood and thus not likely to be too fussy about paying a little dribble of sales tax as he goes. The tourist never stops to consider what a heavy tribute he and his fellows pay in the gross figure.

Whether or not a thriving tourist business and vastly improved recreational and conservation facilities have any bearing upon the ways of the South may still be a somewhat open question. Certainly the availability of vast quantities of fresh water and a comparable amount of timber and other resources may be considered well beyond exaggerative error of state publicists. The recreation business may be considered a sufficiently profitable one to mean the difference between a rich profit and loss.

It would be difficult to estimate the meaning of the tourist business to the South in the broader terms of human understanding and the conservation of regional resources. At the time Olmsted traveled through the South in the 1850s, no one was much concerned about visitors, especially American visitors. Certainly no one had so far lost his reason that he regarded the casual traveler as a significant source of income. The lush annual harvest of tourist dollars today can be gathered with relative ease, and this source of income seems inexhaustible.

XI

The Great Crusade

Leisure, and bountiful provision for the future being secured, it is almost a matter of course, that men will amuse themselves with literature, arts and science. South Carolina has, therefore, always boasted several men of learning (men learned in the classics, and abstract science), and many belle-lettre scholars. Yet scarce anything has been accomplished by them for the advancement of learning and science, and there have been fewer valuable inventions and discoveries, or designs in art, or literary composition of a high rank, or anything else, contrived or executed for the good of the whole community, or the world at large (cotton and rice growing excepted), in South Carolina, than in any community of equal numbers and wealth, probably in the world.

OLMSTED, A JOURNEY IN THE SEABOARD SLAVE STATES, pp. 501–2

Education has been the South's greatest challenge. The region has struggled mightily against illiteracy and to meet the competitive standards of other parts of the nation. Illiteracy in its most elementary form has been largely erased, but the region still battles functional illiteracy. No other area of the United States has established and maintained schools at greater sacrifice than the South. Not only have public attitudes, distance, sparsity of population in places, and two races burdened the region, so have slender tax returns and a high birth rate. Lack of imaginative educational leadership in instances has further limited progress. Added to these problems is that of race relationships within the public-school system. The South not only struggles with the normal problems of education which confront the rest of the country, it is beset with the highly emotional and explosive issue of desegregating its schools. This topic will be discussed fully in succeeding chapters.

A century ago public education was in its initial stages of organization. North Carolina, Louisiana, Alabama, and Kentucky were first to provide superintendents of public instruction. All the states appropriated some public funds for school support. An outsider, however, could scarcely have detected any great social pressure to convince legislators of the educational needs of the people.

Democratic impulses which stirred the country in the 1840s brought, among other things, revision of some of the state constitutions. Virginia led by revising her eighteenth-century constitution in 1832. Across the mountains Kentuckians battled to an emotional draw on the issue of modernizing their short-sighted constitution drafted at the turn of the century. In the storm of this campaign, the voice of the fiery Presbyterian preacher Robert J. Breckinridge blasted slavery in one breath and pleaded for constitutional provision for public education in the next. Opposition to slavery kept the preacher out of the convention, but it failed to silence his plea for public acceptance of educational responsibility. Though absent from the convention, Dr. Breckinridge got an educational clause written into the new constitution, and he subsequently forced a reluctant legislature to appropriate school funds. He did not, however, succeed in getting that body to provide a specific school tax. The South was belatedly taking steps to break with the private academy tradition.

Historically wealthier southerners, for economic and social reasons, favored reduced taxation and private schools. Poorer southerners, for religious and prejudiced reasons, likewise favored private education. Some southerners have felt there was little danger of compulsion from schools in non-public hands, and that private institutions afforded freedom of personal conduct not possible in public schools. It was easier to control teaching, which might vary from certain narrow and orthodox views. Too, private schools were free from the compulsory-attendance feature of the modern public schools. Thus it is that many southerners are quick to take refuge in the private-school idea when faced with major educational problems.

Although it did not originate in the reconstruction period, the public school was given impetus in this era. Revised state constitutions and new legislation after 1876 provided for maintenance of schools, and there was even some attempt to lower racial barriers. The development of schools in the South required a longer and more stable period than that of reconstruction. Thus, southern educational history has to be considered in a much broader scope, with reconstruction one phase. Through numerous readjustments and the expenditure of enormous energy, public education became a reality for the South. Basically it was largely an accomplishment of the twentieth century. By far the most significant cultural and social advancement made by the post-Civil War South was organization of public schools.

Before modern schools could be brought into existence, an extraordinarily vigorous campaign was necessary. Most states cherish memories of heroic leaders such as Charles D. McIver, Charles Brantley Aycock, and Edward Alderman of North Carolina; H. A. M. Henderson and T. U. Dudley of Kentucky; C. W. Dabney and P. P. Caxton of Tennessee; James H. Dillard and R. L. Himes of Louisiana; Albert A. Murphree and W. N. Sheats of Florida; Robert L. Dabney and Oscar H. Cooper of Texas; J. J. Doyne of Arkansas; John William Abercrombie, Henry Jones Willingham, and B. B. Comer of Alabama; Walter B. Hill and Joseph S. Stewart of Georgia; and William H. Hand of South Carolina. These men, with scores of others, attacked illiteracy with evangelistic fervor. They conducted a holy crusade to lift the South out of ignorance. Though support for education was an individual state responsibility, the whole South was involved in general efforts at improvement. The George Peabody Fund and grants from the General Education Board offered aid to the South in this battle against illiteracy. The experience of one southern state was important to the common growth of the region. The problem of educational deficiency was attacked all the way from the beginning elementary-school level to college and post-graduate studies. George Peabody College for Teachers was established in Nashville in 1875 to train teachers for the South.

An early southern concept of education was of an elementary school extending through the fourth grade and taught by an impoverished teacher who had scarcely more training than his pupils. College preparation was left largely to private academies and preparatory departments of the colleges themselves. Thus, the southern high school is of relatively recent origin. Marked expansion of this institution has occurred since 1900, and the more important developments have come since 1918. Next to a lack of established financial support, the most serious drawback to educational advancement was the widely dispersed one-room school and its poorly trained teacher. But this condition only reflected another southern problem. Prior to World War I, southern highways were so poor that school consolidation was too often impossible. There are no definite dates to mark when consolidation was begun in the South and when it was accomplished. It has been a continuous process during this century. Alabama, for instance, had 3015 one-teacher schools in 1928 and 1417 in 1945, 1157 of which were for Negroes. Five years later, the total number was reduced to 806, of which 691 were Negro. The story was the same everywhere in the South. The one-room school faced oblivion; even the large number of small Negro schools was being abandoned. Shifting of population brought dissolution of many school districts and the enlargement of others. Some high schools, for instance, are now crowded, while others are being discontinued for lack of students.

Not until the southern highway system was improved was it possible to develop efficient means of educational transportation. Once this occurred, the South generally was able to improve educational facilities. Beginning with Tennessee in 1905 and finishing with Mississippi in 1918, the southern states passed compulsory school laws. Though imperfectly enforced, these laws did express an implicit regional faith in public education. This legislation was and still is necessary to break the educational resistance of much of the population. Presently these laws are creating a state of mixed emotions. Because compulsory attendance laws apply to white and black alike, the Supreme Court decision of May 17, 1954, gave a deeper meaning to compulsion.

The years from 1890 to 1916 were used up in planning and campaigning for better schools. Since 1930, southern youth in significant numbers has come to regard education as an economic and social necessity. Changing conditions of social and industrial America have impressive bearing upon the southern high school. In the 1960s a high school diploma in the expanding South may mean the difference between securing a job with future promise or being bound for life to common labor. Sometimes having a high school education is the key to getting a job in the first place.

Intelligent southerners dedicated to the belief that this region must progress know that the South cannot now reverse educational history. No matter how much extremist legislation and administrative action threaten to abolish the public-school system, the weight of both history and present needs will defeat such action. A good public-school system is a necessary pawn in wooing industry to locate in a community. An ambitious southern community could offer no greater discouragement to outside industrial management than an inferior school system, since large numbers of persons are imported with most new industries and one of the first concerns of families is for the quality of local education. Too, industries depend upon schools to train a sufficient number of people with whom to operate. Because of this fundamentally new emphasis, the region cannot mis-serve its youth in greater measure than to disrupt the schools.

Appraising institutional qualities in a region as large and diverse as the South is hazardous. Some southern urban high schools in cities like Atlanta, Richmond, Nashville, Memphis, and Louisville are as mature and effective as any in the country. On the other hand, large numbers of schools, urban and rural alike, are exceedingly poor when judged by any standard. This is especially true in small high schools barely able to maintain minimum standards of quality. The South, along with the entire country, faces a constant teacher shortage. Since the beginning of its modern educational history, lack of adequately trained teachers has been a heavy cross for southern schools. In earlier years the South lacked facilities for preparing teachers; today there are enough training facilities, but the South has to compete with other sections of the country which pay higher salaries. Likewise, a rising industry in the region offers serious economic competition to the classroom. Industry, in fact, has stood at the classroom door to ensnare promising young college graduates, offering salaries and fringe benefits which far exceed the rewards of teaching.

Large numbers of southern schools have failed to employ teachers in special fields such as chemistry, physics, and engineering and thus have not trained southern youth to live in this modern technical age. Only by maintaining the most favorable conditions can southerners hope to maintain standards in some areas of training. If the conscientious teacher is beset by emotionalism and the shackling of freedom and is constantly threatened with disruption of tenure then there is little hope for much of southern education. This is the challenge of the 1960s even in the face of all the headline sensationalism over integration. The present South can scarcely afford to face educational problems which beset the national school system and also shoulder an extra burden of peculiar regional problems. At the moment, some industrial personnel managers say that southern dexterity and willingness to work are high, but that educational preparation is poor.

At the start of the 1960s the rising tide of urban students in the South is overwhelming. In Alabama the number of students rose from 665,495 in 1935 to 684,908 in 1950, although there were over 791,340 school-age children. A special study in 1941–42 indicated that there were 718,089 children ready for school, and that there was one teacher for every 42 white students enrolled in high school, and one for every 101 Negroes. If the high schools had been adequately staffed, it would have been necessary to hire 1881 additional teachers. This statistical picture can be duplicated almost everywhere in the South.

For the first time since the Civil War, the charge that the South is exhausting itself financially to maintain bi-racial schools appears to be more myth than fact, at least in urban communities. Only in the old and undisturbed agrarian communities, which yearly lose population, is the charge valid, because of the loss of pupils enrolled. The South feels the educational pinch in maintaining good educational standards at all levels. One of the more serious immediate problems is that of closing the gap between white and Negro educational accomplishments. In 1952 the average per student discrepancy between the two races was $50, or the difference between $165.71 and $115.56. The teacher salary ratio was $1460 for whites and $1273 for Negroes, or a differential of $187. Nine per cent of the Negroes had less than two years of college training, while 3.3 per cent of the whites were in this category. Seventy-eight per cent of the whites had four years of training as compared with 73 per cent of the Negroes. Oklahoma has equalized educational expenditures between whites and Negroes, and in many instances the schools have been integrated.

Texas and Florida are rapidly approaching equalization, and several of the other states make no distinction in salaries of white and Negro teachers of equal qualifications.

An analysis of the gaps between rural and urban schools in the same year — 1952 — revealed a deficiency of $44 in capital outlay for rural schools. In total amounts eleven southern states spent approximately a billion dollars on rural schools, some $380 million of which came from local taxes and the rest from state and federal sources. Both average daily attendance and school enrollments have increased rapidly since 1945. The per capita increase has been even greater, thus putting ever greater demands on the tax systems. In precise per-capita figures the cost of urban white schools was $178.23 as compared with $133.40 for rural schools. Negro schools widened the gap further. Urban per-capita costs for Negroes were $125.45 and for rural schools, $85.10 — a percentage gap of 24 per cent; while rural Negro schools were behind those for white 38 per cent.

Ernest W. Swanson and John A. Griffin have presented a graphic picture of the comparative development of education for Negro and whites in their extensive statistical analysis, *Public Education in the South Today and Tomorrow*. They have used the key years, 1930–31, 1949–50, and 1951–52. Selection of these representative years reflect four facts: a low point in support of Negro education; the inroads of depression; the results of World War II; and the effects of pending litigation in the federal courts.

In 1940, the South had a Negro population of 9,261,792; a decade later this number had been increased by only 1.5 per cent. At the same time the white population numbered 27,651,141, which a decade later had increased 16.5 per cent. School population numbered 5,580,450 whites and 1,902,001 Negroes. In the ensuing decade white pupils showed an increase of 25.4 per cent, while the Negro gain was 5.7 per cent. In 1950 Negro percentages ranged from 6.4 in Kentucky to 48.1 in Mississippi. During 1955–56, South Carolina had 313,902 white students registered for a period of at least 35 days, as compared with 238,754 Negroes, with increased Negro enrollment only 76 per cent of the white increase.

Considering South Carolina as representative of the old cotton South states, an interesting human factor is reflected in its educational statistics for 1955–56. White teachers holding a bachelor's degree had increased by 1296 and Negroes by 918, while emergency certificates had been reduced from 207 a year before to 60 for 1955–56. Negro teachers showed a slightly greater tendency to drop out after a brief period of teaching, and they averaged 36 years and 6 months of age as compared with 44 years and 7 months for whites. Teaching has appealed to younger people of both races but it has failed to hold them, with the possible result that young Negroes have tended to leave the profession more readily than white teachers.

Gaps in southern education are not necessarily wilful discriminations. All sorts of factors create this troublesome condition. Historically the South has been wedded to property and special levy taxes as sources for school support. Rural landholders have ever been conservative and have held tax rates and assessments to a minimum. Politicians are careful to stay off these sensitive toes no matter how much educational costs increase. Educational demands have outrun the capacity of an antiquated and badly administered tax system to support modern schools. Assessment officials have been reluctant to come within gunshot of reasonable evaluations of real property. For instance, land has appreciated greatly in value during the inflationary years since 1940, but assessments remain virtually the same as they were for deflated cotton and tobacco land values of 1910. Another regional assessment weakness is the contention that lands removed from cultivation and returned to forest production have suffered devaluation. The contrary is more likely true, but this has not always been recorded on assessors' lists.

There is often lacking an aggressive leadership in rural communities which might campaign for improved schools as conditions change in the South. The discrepancy between urban and rural schools has been almost as discriminatory as that which has differentiated schools racially.

If the Negro is to compete socially and economically in the South or elsewhere in the nation, he has to raise his cultural and educational levels. There is no other choice; only through the schoolroom door can he hope to enter new fields of opportunity. Even the old avenue of the farm has been narrowed for the uneducated. Mechanization of farms makes some basic education a necessity. In the rising field of industrial employment the Negro's only hope for economic salvation lies in better education. At the same time complexities of non-farm or urban life force him into social commitments which were virtually unknown to his race a half-century ago.

Southern politicians have historically exerted an unwholesome influence upon school development in many places. Where local boards of trustees have controlled educational affairs, there have been political barriers. In some areas teachers have been victimized by unscrupulous board members and politicians. Conditions of tenure have been unstable, and emotionalism and the suspicion of the rural mind have often disrupted the teaching process. On top of these handicaps, costs of bi-racial education have fallen more heavily on rural than urban school districts.

A fundamental change has come in the South in the area of support for public schools. Within the last fifty years educational costs have gradually competed with highways for a major share of the southern tax dollar. Almost everywhere in the South education has become a principal public business. For this reason southern legislatures have been forced to find new sources of revenue to supplement traditional levies on real property. It was this fact, as has been said, that brought legislatures to levy sales taxes. The Federal Government has pre-empted several productive tax sources, thus narrowing drastically the regional revenue base. States such as Virginia, North Carolina, Kentucky, and Tennessee can demonstrate the fact that the Federal Government is extracting vast sums annually from them in excise taxes. It is true that this tax is on tobacco and liquor which are consumed throughout the nation, yet there is only a slender margin left on which to place a state levy. High income taxes collected by the Federal Government no doubt hurt the states more than any of the other national levies.

Over the years the South has received a disproportionate share of federal funds. Eighty per cent of the $21,000,000 spent by the New Deal between 1933 and 1935 to improve public-school facilities was spent in the South. The same thing was true in distributing the $200,000,000 provided for rural-school construction. This money was distributed on the basis of need, and need in the South was great, in terms of lack of physical facilities and of high quality teaching personnel. The southern school population was not increasing so rapidly as was patronage of the schools. School terms were lengthened and average daily attendance showed a sharp increase. Since 1930, vocational education has thrived in the region. The depression made clear the need for vocational training. Unemployed southern youth realized that only through vocational training could it hope for steady work.

The shape and proportion of southern educational need is purely a local responsibility, but the quality of the end product is of national concern. For fifty years of public educational history the South has trained large numbers of its youth to have them spend their productive years outside the region. A mere recitation of population statistics does not fully reveal the qualifications of large numbers of these displaced southerners. It is true, of course, that a shameful portion of this horde was untrained and inexperienced.

Southern migrants in large numbers could not be depended upon to assume any responsibilities where mature educational training was required. Many of them were Negroes who had attended defective rural schools that offered only the most meager opportunity for elementary training. This particular migrant group had little meaning to the South beyond the loss of its physical capacity to labor, and a rapidly changing system of traditional agriculture caused them to go without serious economic loss. Wherever uneducated southern migrants have gone, they have created social problems growing largely out of defective education and inability to make adjustments in crowded urban communities. Surveys of welfare conditions in the large industrial centers along the Great Lakes reveal severe social conditions created by this influx of migrants. In June 1957, the *Chicago Tribune* published six articles on the social background of the flood of Appalachian highlanders into that city. These articles revealed a degree of social frustration and hopelessness that is hard to believe exists. A principal of a South Side Chicago school told me that the average intelligence quotient of his 1400 children, most of whom come from the South, is only 87, and only 16 of the number have a rating of 120 or more. Philadelphia and New York, among other cities, have felt the impact of this situation in problems of teaching and discipline.

Loss of this great labor force from the South no doubt could have a long-range deleterious effect upon the region, but it is the loss of trained young southerners that is costly beyond estimate. The loss to the South of a single well-trained native son is potentially more disastrous than that of a whole trainload of illiterates. The education of expatriate southerners may cost the South a greater proportionate price than if they had left the East or Middle West, because the southern states have fewer trained people in proportion to their population, and because of the demands of new industries. In the migrating army leaving the South since 1865 have gone scientists, teachers, engineers, lawyers, doctors, industrialists, bankers, merchants, ministers, and professional people of all sorts. Many of them have gone elsewhere to make tremendously important contributions to the nation. Because the rest of the country has absorbed such a large proportion of educated southerners, many reason that to expect the South to receive some federal assistance with its educational problems is justified. In the 1930s, when racial tensions did not blur the prevailing point of view, southerners sought federal aid, and possibly they would do so again if there were no issue of integration. About the only aid the Federal Government could give the region under prevailing conditions would be an abandonment of certain tax sources to enable state governments to tap more productive veins of revenue. This might serve the same purpose as federal aid, and certainly it would avoid the troublous issue of federal control raised by political and religious groups. In 1960, conservative southerners in Congress blocked once again efforts to make federal aid available.

Despite its financial handicaps and relentless demands for new schoolrooms, the South has made phenomenal educational progress. Physical educational needs of the region stem from three sources. To begin with, much of the southern public school plant was antiquated almost the day it was built. The shabby one-room frame schoolhouses often mirrored the poverty of large numbers of rural homes. Little care was given to their upkeep; their grounds were barren and eroded; sanitary facilities were as primitive as nature itself; water and fuel supplies were collected from the countryside; and schoolroom equipment often reflected the salary and generosity of the teachers. Sentimentalists of the South have frequently paid homage to this institution, but they have done so in warm remembrance of the personality of a challenging teacher, or safely isolated from the damaging comparison of regional statistical tables and the stark realities of the schools themselves.

Architectually, many early southern urban school buildings were patterned after county courthouses. Though the schoolhouse was a community symbol of faith in learning, almost never was it an efficient structure or a source of great aesthetic inspiration. Some state departments of education early sensed the importance of pleasing physical surroundings and encouraged construction of better buildings. Since 1945 the South has been engaged in relocating and rebuilding much of its school plant. Many new buildings reflect a spirit of hopefulness for the region. Handsome new Negro schools, constructed before 1954, reflect southern anxieties over the impending Supreme Court decision.

Modern school buildings and the new industrial plants have done much to destroy the southern architectual traditions of Georgian and Greek Revival public structures. In many areas the new southern schools have advanced regional taste for modern architectual lines by at least a full generation. Some new buildings are good examples of functional architecture, taking advantage of natural conditions to achieve aesthetic harmony inside and out of the classroom. In building much of its modern school plant later than most other areas of the United States, the South has been able to profit by experience elsewhere.

Mississippi has made remarkable advances in its new school buildings. Its structures reflect a keener local awareness of the importance of schools as centers not only of educational advancement but also of aesthetic improvement for an agrarian state where many communities are still wedded to frontier tastes. Both white and Negro school buildings reflect a change in the cultural pattern of the state, a change which exceeds progress in other areas of human activities.

Inside southern school buildings some fundamental educational changes have occurred. Because of a rising industrialism, and a world-wide reverence for science, old-line fundamentalism is losing ground. In most parts of the modern South it would be difficult to create much resistance to the teaching of science. Biologists are far more secure in free discussions in the classroom at the moment than are either sociologists or political scientists. In many areas of human relations both parents and students demonstrate more liberal attitudes than did their immediate forebears. However poorly the sciences may be taught in the schools, the subject itself is no longer an unwanted stranger in the classroom.

Generally there has been a shifting of emphasis from the traditional arts and sciences to vocational training. Booker T. Washington was an apostle of vocationalism in the South. He preached this type of training at a time when many white leaders of the public-school movement were emphasizing the importance of the classics. Classicism found warm support among many educational leaders in this century, who measured educational attainment largely in terms of capacity to read the ancient languages and to exhibit skill in mathematics, astronomy, and rhetoric. Chancellor J. H. Kirkland of Vanderbilt University and his colleagues in the early years of the Southern Association of Colleges and Secondary Schools spent long hours discussing Latin and Greek as basic requirements for admission to colleges.

This philosophy of education has all but vanished from the thinking of southern educators. It might be difficult to start even a gentlemanly argument over this subject in present-day Southern Association meetings. On the other hand southerners have made tremendous headway in the field of vocationalism. Seaman and Bradford Knapp were influential pioneers in this field. They worked with boys and girls in the 4-H Club movement, which served as an entering wedge for convincing rural parents that vocational training was a highly valid educational activity. Passage of the federally administered Smith-Hughes and Smith-Lever acts brought revision of the curriculum of the public schools. By their basic requirements these acts facilitated the idea of vocationalism on the high school level, as had the Morrill Act at the college level. In the same years Mississippi developed a system of agricultural high schools which made education available to rural pupils on a reasonable financial basis.

In the present South some educational leaders have placed greater stress upon vocationalism than upon basic liberal arts. They are faced with the tormenting knowledge that large numbers of students will leave school before they have finished the twelfth grade and that they will enter industrial employment as common laborers. On the other hand, an increasing number of students are going to college each year, and high schools are being taxed to prepare them for future training.

Closely akin to the widespread philosophy of vocationalism is that of the professional educationist. Few areas of the country have struggled so desperately to train teachers as have southerners. After the Peabody Fund brought about the establishment of George Peabody College for Teachers, all the southern states organized teachers' colleges, and the older universities created departments of education to meet the need for trained teachers. In time, advanced educational ideas were imported into the region. Whether from Teachers College of Columbia University, the University of Chicago, or some other source, they constituted a major influence upon the quality of southern education. More than one observer has remarked that the South received and tried to apply many extremist educational ideas after they had been abandoned even by their authors. Whether or not this is true is open to question. It is not a matter of serious question, however, that the professional educationally trained teacher has come to predominate in the southern schoolroom, and that the old classical concepts of three decades ago have been discarded.

A relatively new and powerful influence has brought changes in southern attitudes toward education. Runaway passions for athletics have placed schools in a curious kind of public domain. In a way the South has always been a sports-loving region, but in those earlier days individualistic displays of personal prowess or personal excellence in the hunt and the chase were required. On a higher social plane was horseracing, and occasionally there were romantically inspired ring tournaments. Organized sports in the modern sense were unknown in the Old South. Post-Civil War years saw the introduction of baseball, basketball, and football into colleges. Since 1915 football and basketball have become popular in the secondary schools. Today most southern communities have developed a local mania over their athletic teams. Even hardened old rednecks who have wandered in from the cotton fields have caught the fever. Fifty years ago they would have regarded these sports as either effeminate or juvenile. Not so the modern southerner. Governor Orval Faubus of Arkansas claimed to be shocked when he heard that during the Little Rock incident the football schedule of Central High School was cancelled and the team had stopped practice. He blurted into a Columbia Broadcasting System microphone that this interfered with education.

There is no trustworthy criteria by which the present athletic mania can be adjudged either as an asset or a liability. It is disruptive of educational routine, and educational standards are frequently in inverse ratio to the successes of athletic teams. In 1957 the editor of the Brantley, Georgia, *Enterprise,* said that "One big problem is the overemphasis on school athletics. From the opening of the fall term until far into the spring our schools are in a frenzy of football activity."

This new emphasis on exhibitionist activities in southern schools has brought the public into closer association with the forms if not the substance of education. In few areas of the United States does education reflect so vividly the influence of local and state opinion as it does in the present South. The authoritarian hands of state departments of education and special commissions lie heavily on the schools. Application of administrative policies varies from state to state, with some permitting more local autonomy than others. Generally, central administrative powers exert tremendous influence on educational procedures. They set standards for teaching qualifications and tenure, stimulate educational legislation, provide economic rewards for teachers as they advance in their teaching (usually granting raises on the basis of accumulated academic hours), set terms of retirement and pensions, exercise an inspection function, and, in many cases, oversee plant construction.

Every southern state is faced with the enormous burden of equalization of educational opportunities. If there were not a Negro in the South seeking admission to a white school, equalization would still be a burdensome responsibility. Economic wealth is unevenly spread over the southern counties. States having hilly and mountainous sections are faced with need for distributing large sums of state funds to maintain schools. Without a central authority in the state there would be educational discrimination in many areas. Parts of the South would be unable to sustain teaching staffs of any quality at all. During the hard years of World War II it was necessary to certify hundreds of inadequately trained teachers. Some were highly satisfactory instructors, but the major-

ity was ineffective, and the cost to southern educational standards
was tragically high.

Legislation within the last decade has tended to place educational control in remarkably few hands. For this reason it would
not be at all impossible for selfish state political cliques to exercise
life and death control over southern schools. The regional school
system could easily be thrown into chaos, if not destroyed, by a
remarkably few wilful persons. Already Arkansas has interrupted
the operation of Little Rock's schools, and the same danger exists
in at least five other states. Few local communities receiving any
appreciable amount of state funds actually exercise decisive control over their schools. Since 1954 the tendency has been to
strengthen centralized authority by reducing the number of school
districts in the states, and to wield the club of withdrawal of state
funds. If the present state of emotionalism over segregation prevails there is grave danger that local control of schools will slip
away entirely in several states. Present southern political leadership is hardly consistent in stoutly opposing federal aid on the
ground of federal control when the states make annual statutory
raids upon local educational management.

Historically, one organization thus far has transcended both
state and politician in maintaining worthy educational standards.
The Southern Association of Colleges and Secondary Schools is
the outgrowth of years of crusading for improved southern schools.
It came into existence in Atlanta in 1895. Back of it was a South-
wide desire to elevate educational standards. Colleges wished to
free themselves of the task of preparing students for admission to
their classrooms, and to encourage development of high schools.
It was necessary for the Association to assume an accrediting function, and to make inspections to ensure that standards were maintained.

Standards were only part of the Association's responsibility.
Self-seeking politicians raided schools without fear of retribution,
but the central accrediting body was able to stop this practice. By
representing the whole South it was able to exercise stern discipline against an offending member. Three governors in the 1930s
felt the stinging lash of the Southern Association. Theodore G.
Bilbo, riding high on the wave of political restitution, invaded the
University of Mississippi and the state colleges. He discharged

Chancellor Alfred H. Hume of the University and sent several professors into political exile. The Southern Association suspended the Mississippi schools from accreditation, and powerful accrediting bodies for professional schools withdrew their accreditation from the law and medical schools. Bilbo learned that, while he ruled the political empire in Mississippi, he had no influence with the stubborn educational accrediting bodies. Across the line in Louisiana, Huey P. Long learned the same lesson.

Governor Eugene Talmadge of Georgia broke his lance on the Association when he initiated the dismissal of Professor Walter D. Cocking of the University of Georgia in 1941 because he was reported to have predicted to a class that in time Negroes and whites would sit together in the University's classrooms. The Governor had eight other staff members of state colleges dismissed. His loud shouts of defiance availed nothing in the face of suspension of Georgia schools from accreditation. For good measure Phi Beta Kappa withdrew its charter. Like Bilbo and Huey Long, the Georgia demagogue was brought to bay, and a reversal of public opinion helped elect Ellis Arnall governor.

In the 1960s, however, the Southern Association of Colleges and Secondary Schools faces its most serious test. For the first time issues which threaten the integrity of free education in the South cut across state borders, and offenders cannot be easily isolated for disciplinary action as they were in the earlier cases. Adjudication of issues concerned with the violation of academic freedom and standards which might follow on the heels of the Supreme Court decisions of 1954 and 1955 could involve not only non-academic political and administrative offenders but many influential members of the Association. The Association itself has different views on the procedures which should be followed in moments of a showdown between the southern states and the Federal Government. Again, special groups fighting integration in several of the southern states are powerful enough to render the Southern Association virtually helpless. A fear of the withdrawal of several states handicaps the Association in its actions, and might even face it with destruction. If the Association winks at violations of tenure and standards, it destroys its effectiveness, while if it is too aggressive, it endangers its existence. Some of the leadership of this body finds itself caught in a maddening dilemma. To act would not only involve persuasiveness, but would require courage in the face of possible destruction.

At its meeting in Louisville in December 1958 the Association admitted Negro school members. Some of the Association's officials warned that too many Negro members or too much aggressiveness on the part of those admitted might cause disaster. An interesting side light on this decision is the fact that Louisville might easily become the only southern city in which the accrediting body can meet where its full membership would be welcome.

No one knows the answer as to what might happen to accreditation and standards if the public schools were abandoned in favor of some type of hastily conceived private schools. This issue is more complex than the highly vocal spokesmen for private schools in some states give evidence of realizing. Under the most favorable circumstances southern public schools have enormous problems of maintaining standards in the face of sharply rising educational demands. To date this has been a main objective of the Southern Association of Colleges and Secondary Schools. What some of the private school advocates seem to ignore is the further reduction of southern educational standards which would result from closing the schools and also the enormous pressure which other regional and professional accrediting bodies could bring upon southern educational standards if it happened.

Opposition to the Supreme Court decisions has blinded much of the public, if not an appreciable segment of southern educational leadership, to the enormous educational needs of the South. Conditions in every state reveal this fact. In February 1955, Alabama's Superintendent of Education, Austin P. Meadow, and 112 county and city superintendents met with Governor James Folsom. They endorsed a $150 million bond issue for school construction and asked for an additional $25 million with which to raise teachers' salaries. At that time Alabama teachers were receiving $900 less than the national average. Further indication of the teacher problem was the fact that 3394 teachers still held emergency certificates. Dr. Meadow said that despite the support given Alabama's minimum foundation program to "bring school construction up to minimum requirements, [Alabama] is still no higher than the average annual outlay during the four worst years of the depression in the 1930's."

Across the line Georgia was no better off. In midsummer 1957, the Department of Education reported that the state was short 3342 classrooms. Allen C. Smith, head of staff services, estimated that it would take $88,641,000 to relieve physical shortages alone. In comparative statistics the southern states are still at the foot of the national educational scale.

One of the most serious tragedies of the current conflict over integration is the blinding effect it has upon a general understanding of the South's basic educational problems. It is extremely difficult for educational leadership to focus attention upon a long-range program when it does not know whether the whole public-school plan of the state might not be changed overnight by official action in a number of states. If these states should carry out threats to close their public schools, they would at the very least invoke a long legal battle before the courts; at most, the southern schools would suffer loss of momentum at a moment when progress is more essential than ever before in American history.

The South's educational system is also being challenged indirectly by businessmen pleading for better trained people. What they mean by training would involve the abandonment of the arts and sciences tradition. This comes unhappily at a time when the South might cultivate some of its traditionally liberal attitudes toward teaching and learning.

The South cannot pursue its present economic course without producing better-educated people. If they are not obtainable in the region, they will be brought in from elsewhere. No significant emotional resistance will or can be offered to this kind of an invasion. The realistic demands of business and industry, with their supporting payrolls, have a way of ignoring emotions.

Aside from having to run fast to maintain ever rising standards, southern educational leadership and the southern people need to pause a moment to ask themselves what purpose their education is designed for. If some public schools are disrupted by extremist action there is grave danger that this generation of southern youth will become the most disillusioned in American history. A price the modern South cannot afford is a lowering of educational standards or desertion of its long established tradition of Jeffersonian liberalism, no matter what the provocation is. Again it needs to repeat after Jefferson the pledge that "I have sworn on the altar of God eternal hostility to any form of tyranny over the mind of man." To block freedom of textbooks and classroom instruction or to deter the search for sustainable truth would be the most devastating blow that could be dealt the cherished southern way of life.

Wounds to a struggling school system like that in the South go deep and are slow to heal. Closing the southern public schools would be little short of preparing the way for enslavement of great masses of southern youth. The clear voice of a teen-ager in Little Rock put the issue in focus when he said, "It is I who is being injured." In Atlanta, 419 physicians endorsed a statement in December 1958, saying that the closing of public schools in that state would "constitute a major catastrophe that would result in irreparable damage to the children of our city and state. We believe that closing the public schools would materially interfere with the supply of essential scientific personnel and would ultimately damage the health services of this region. We also recognize the far-reaching consequences to the spiritual, moral, and economic welfare for our community."

These statements provide the most effective answer one could give to those who would throw the South back to a system of private education it has taken nearly a century to outgrow.

XII

In the Toils of Inequity

If the security of life and property at the South must forever be de-
pendent on the thoroughness with which the negro population is pre-
vented from acquiring knowledge, from thinking of themselves and
for themselves, it will never be felt to be greater than it is today. Ef-
forts made to increase this security will of themselves occasion agita-
tion, and agitation must counteract those efforts. Knowledge, knowl-
edge of what is going on elsewhere, of the condition of men elsewhere,
of what is thought elsewhere, must have increased currency with every
class of mankind in all parts of this continent, as it increases in popula-
tion, and the movements of its population increase in activity and im-
portance. No human laws, embargoes, or armies and navies can pre-
vent it.

OLMSTED, A JOURNEY IN THE BACK COUNTRY, pp. 454-5

Frederick Law Olmsted in a sense wrote a preface to the South
in the twentieth century. Since 1900 the southern conscience has
been deeply troubled over the low estate of education in the region,
and of Negro education in particular. Following 1930 this problem became increasingly acute. In the field of illiteracy the South
made an exceedingly poor showing, largely because of its heavy
Negro population. Wherever Negroes were enrolled in schools,
they were nearly always subjected to inferior teaching. Before
1940 teachers' salaries were so low that few hoped that the schools
would ever be any better.

The depression and World War II brought quick changes in
attitudes toward education in the nation, changes which the South
was to feel especially. The technical nature of the new army revealed gaping deficiencies in the training of southern youth. This

was more especially true of the Negro, who found it difficult to be an effective soldier. For the same reasons he found himself handicapped in the rising industrial South of the postwar years. He was now called upon to compete for jobs as never before in his history. In the political field he found his way to the polls barred on the grounds that he was too ignorant to vote.

Added to the pressures of army training and the necessity for employment in industry was the tremendous emphasis placed on the American democratic way of life. Before the nation could give validity to the democratic image it presented to the world, it had to look to its own shortcomings in this area. In condemning the practices of Nazi Germany it had to promise a revision of its own practices of discrimination on racial grounds. After the war the nation had to face the problem of providing better educational and economic opportunities for its minorities — especially for the southern Negro.

No longer could the Negro accept token education and hope to survive economically in the South. He was now raising the major legal issue that he did not actually enjoy equal opportunity under a bi-racial system of education. This has been his basic plea before the courts, and it has been where southern defense has faltered most.

Historically, the South has struggled with the challenge of educating the Negro. The development of a bi-racial system of education when reconstruction was ended only compounded regional problems. Though provisions were made for Negro schools, the vast majority of southerners were not conditioned to regard them with favor. Prior to 1865 the slave states forbade by law the education of Negroes. Even today this is a latent factor in some of the thinking about education of Negroes. There has prevailed the attitude that the field of activity for the Negro was largely physical, and to give him a classical education bordered on the ridiculous to many white southerners.

Further, to white southerners who bore the rigors of reconstruction, all public education was tainted with abolitionism and carpetbagging. The time was far off in the future when Negroes would be ready for education in the proper sense. Until then, they should only serve their basic physical needs. They had to learn to adapt themselves to the complexities and subleties of modern civilization — so ran the white-southern argument.

When reconstruction came, both state constitutions and statutory legislation provided public-school systems for the South, and in many instances missionary and Freedmen's Bureau teachers entered the region to establish schools. In some places schools were integrated, but generally the limited public-school system, like every other phase of southern public life, was blighted by the excesses of reconstruction. Public schools contributed materially to the breaking of the old private-academy tradition, and they encouraged a leveling of southern society. Above all, the new public-school system would educate Negroes largely at the white man's expense. Schools generally depended on taxes collected from real property levies, and the Negro owned little property. Thus, some southerners contended, as they did about many poor white students, that Negroes were entitled only to their share of returns from taxes paid by them.

Negro education in the last three-quarters of a century has progressed largely to the extent that white and Negro leadership have received public support and outside interests have given supplementary support. In 1882, John F. Slater established the Slater Fund of $100,000 to support Negro education in the South. Twenty-three years later, Anna T. Jeannes of Philadelphia gave the General Education Fund $200,000 for the same purpose. Caroline Phelps-Stokes willed the residue of her fortune in 1911 for Negro education. The next year Julius Rosenwald, head of the great Sears, Roebuck mail-order house, contributed $25,000 to be divided between Tuskeegee Institute and neighboring Negro schools in Macon County, Alabama. In time this fund was enlarged greatly, and in 1930, the five-hundredth Negro school, built in part with Rosenwald money, was dedicated.

Today it is an open question what effect these vital private funds have had upon Negro education. In the early 1940s, for instance, Governor Eugene Talmadge of Georgia criticized the foundations in terms which were reminiscent of the attitude of earlier Georgians toward abolition. In many instances public management of southern education left responsibility for training the Negro largely to outside interests.

In 1896, southern leadership was lulled socially to sleep when the United States Supreme Court ruled for separate-but-equal facilities for the two races in the famous Plessy *v*. Ferguson decision. Homer Plessy, a Louisiana octoroon, brought suit contesting the constitutionality of Louisiana's Jim Crow law which required separate travel accommodations for whites and Negroes. He contended that his constitutional rights under the Fourteenth Amendment were being violated. When this case reached the Supreme Court, it was ruled that separate-but-equal provisions in transportation, and in education as well, did not imply inferiority for either race. It was held that in maintaining separate travel accommodations for Negroes and whites the states were acting within their police powers. In substantiation of its position, the Court cited the separation of the races in schools, a principle "which has been held a valid exercise of the legislative power even by the courts of the states where political rights of the colored race have been longest and most earnestly enforced." Recent decisions have not reversed the Court's stand on segregation, for segregation was not at issue in Plessy *v*. Ferguson. So far as the Court was concerned, segregation was never in conformity with the Fourteenth Amendment; before 1940, it had never considered it as a constitutional issue. The Court in this case, however, was not ruling specifically on the issue of segregation, a fact which present-day southerners forget. The point at issue in this case was the quality of service rendered rather than the issue of purely racial discrimination as such.

The year before the Supreme Court rendered its historic decision, Booker T. Washington represented the Negro race at the opening of the Cotton States International Exposition in Atlanta. In his impressive oration he urged his race to concentrate its efforts to better its condition in the fields of agriculture and commerce where it toiled. To his white hearers he said that in all things "that are purely social we can be as separate as the fingers, yet one as the hand in all things essential to mutual progress."

Washington's speech received enormous publicity. Clark Howell of the *Atlanta Constitution* proclaimed it, "One of the most notable speeches, both as to character and as to warmth of reception, ever delivered to a white audience. The address was a revolution. The whole speech is a platform upon which blacks and whites can stand with full justice to each other." In retrospect, it almost seems that Booker T. Washington was uttering a dictum for his time as fundamental as that propounded by the Supreme Court in Plessy *v.* Ferguson. Further, the white South accepted both the Atlanta speech and the Court decision as declarations of enduring principles. Unhappily for southerners of today, their fathers did not understand that both of these statements presupposed a dynamic social program which would place as much emphasis on "equal" as on "separate," if the separate aspects were to prevail unchallenged in the future. Few present-day southerners realize that the separate-but-equal doctrine rests on the Plessy decision or realize the implications of the "equal" part of its doctrine.

A decade ago, just before southerners were faced with an ominous review of the separate-but-equal doctrine by the Supreme Court, former Associate Supreme Court Justice James Byrnes, as Governor of South Carolina, expressed an important segment of regional thinking when he urged the necessity for improving conditions of Negro education. "To meet this situation," he said, "we are forced to do now what we should have been doing for the past fifty years." In his inaugural address on January 16, 1951, he said, "It is our duty to provide for the races substantial equality in school facilities. We should do it because it is right. For me that is sufficient reason." Governor Byrnes may never have analyzed the tell-tale objective statistics of educational development in the South for the first half of the twentieth century. He might have observed only the physical manifestations of the failure of the Plessy *v.* Ferguson doctrine. Driving from his home city, Spartanburg, to Columbia on Highway 215 in 1948, he could have spotted surface evidence of the failures of a part of the South to close the gaps in educational opportunities between the two races. Later, in a speech at Spartanburg, he said that as Governor he had seen the number of school districts reduced from approximately 1200 to 103. One-teacher schools had become largely relics of the past. Consolidation had destroyed 824 independent schools in South Carolina, 357 of them Negro. In 1950–51, 142,000 children were being transported. The following year this number increased to 241,000, a large portion of the increase was Negro. Two-thirds of the state's school-building fund was spent for Negro buildings; of the entire fund $124 per capita was used to finance white structures, while $314 was spent on Negro schools.

Everywhere in the South there is still a yawning gap in educational facilities between the races, however badly the whites themselves have suffered from insufficient support. Judge Tom P. Brady of Brookhaven, Mississippi, wrote in *Black Monday,* "Men of the 'Bible Belt' realize fully that the Negro has not received the treatment which he should have received at our hands. We know, too, that no human being can mistreat another and escape paying a terrific price — that God's law of retribution is as fixed and immutable as God's law of gravity."

There was lack of vigorous Negro leadership in the field of public education. The intangible gaps in teacher qualifications and lack of funds caused serious injury. Also, the economic and social environment in which the average Negro lived handicapped him when he entered any school area where educational maturity was a prerequisite.

Dr. C. W. Dabney wrote in his *Universal Education in the South:* "On the whole the improvement in the education of the Negro children in the southern town and city public schools in the last twenty years is encouraging. In the country districts the schools remain very poor and inadequate. In the densely settled Negro districts, such as those in Mississippi and Alabama, where there are no compulsory laws, the enrollment will average fifty and the attendance twenty-three; 30 per cent of the school population never enter school; 65 per cent of the children in the rural elementary schools will usually be in the first three grades, and 85 per cent leave the school before the seventh grade." Failure to maintain school attendance puts Negro children at serious disadvantage to their white neighbors, and the resulting demoralization is a great factor in such high fatality in the early grades.

Considerable controversy rages in the present South over the level of Negro intelligence. Unhappily, most white southerners have the fixed idea that the Negro is intellectually inferior. It is popularly believed that his capacity to learn is limited, and that this limitation becomes more severe with advancing years. Some southerners continue to rely on the results of intelligence tests administered during World War I, which drew conclusions about the racial inferiority of the Negro. Objective testing and scientific sources since have raised doubt about the results of the World War I tests, and have questioned the full validity of conclusions based on their results. Differences between the races have been shown to lie rather in environmental and associational conditions. The Negro's backwardness would seem to rest not alone in his historical indifference to educational attendance but in the low level of instruction to which he has been subjected in the classroom by poorly trained teachers. The point of Negro inferiority was raised again recently after the Washington, D.C., schools were integrated. The key argument against this charge was the same one stated above. Supporters of the integration of Washington schools emphasized that the poor performance of Negro children could be laid to environmental and educational factors rather than any hereditary deficiencies.

In 1942, the Carnegie Foundation financed an intensive study of the race situation in the United States. As a matter of course, much of the burden of this study concerned the South. Gunnar Myrdal, the noted Swedish sociologist, was invited to direct the study. He came to America presumably free of any regional prejudices in the field of race relations. It is doubtful that he had more than an academic knowledge of the complex racial relationships in the United States. The two-volume study which resulted was the work of many people, and by the severest appraisal it is a provocative study. A distinguished southern historian said it is "the most complete study of American race relations." *An American Dilemma* has its weaknesses, which both author and collaborators acknowledged. It was meant largely to stimulate more specialized studies in areas closed to a general work. Two major conclusions of the book are that the race problem is national in scope and that the Negro problem in America is in fact a white man's problem.

In rendering their famous school decision in 1954, Supreme Court justices gave evidence that they had read the Myrdal volumes in search for a historical foundation for their opinion. Footnote 11 of the decision cited psychological and sociological studies. Immediately upon publication of the 1954 decision, extremists, some of whom had made a partial exploration of the field of sociology between the covers of Theodore Bilbo's *Take Your Choice,* attacked the Myrdal book for its supposed socialistic and even communistic implications. Leaving aside such unbalanced views, Myrdal's work has much to offer the conservative southerner, as well as everyone else in America. It is an excellent source for understanding the Negro's place in American society, and it offers an effective analysis of the dilemma in which the nation as a whole has found itself in dealing with its race problem. The bibliography in this work leads far into the hinterlands of monographic and local studies of the Negro, studies which make serious efforts to help the South gain an appreciation of the nature of its central social and historical theme.

In 1929, the distinguished southern historian Ulrich B. Phillips, a Georgia native, published a highly provocative article in the *American Historical Review* proclaiming slavery the central theme of ante-bellum southern history. Seventy-five years earlier, Frederick Law Olmsted arrived at this conclusion. Almost everything that Olmsted viewed firsthand in the South convinced him of this fact. Everything that Phillips and his fellow historians viewed in the documents presented the same lights and shadows of slave or Negro influence. Today, the observer of the modern South is left with the same conclusion that Olmsted, Phillips, and Myrdal reached; for the Negro is still a central figure in state legislation, social anxiety, educational progress, political fortunes, and intellectual approaches to southern history and life.

Just as southerners have relied too long upon their inherent knowledge of the Negro, they have failed to read objectively the vast amount of dependable materials on so important a chapter of southern history. They have been willing to dismiss Negro history as having little or no meaning, or as being intellectually dishonest, and thus have missed the danger signals which were given southern leaders decades ago. Booker T. Washington's eloquent Atlanta speech had expressed so well in homey metaphor what they, the southerners, wanted to believe. The next year the Supreme Court boosted the Washington sedative with Plessy v. Ferguson, and, again in 1927, Chief Justice William Howard Taft gave the Court's decision in Gum Long v. Rice. This case arose out of a dispute with the school board in Meridian, Mississippi, as to whether or not a child of Oriental parentage could attend a white school. The board placed the child in a Negro school over the protest of her parents. Thus with the words of the South's great Negro leader and two Supreme Court decisions behind them, southerners could take refuge behind their own interpretation of the separate but equal management of racial affairs.

Gum Long *v.* Rice came just before the depression. The South was over the worst of its fears as to how the Negro returning from World War I would react to conditions at home, fears which Howard Odum described as follows: "At the close of the war there was fear in the minds of some that the returning Negro soldiers might cause trouble between the races and that some steps should be taken to prevent it. This fear proved groundless. But in some sections of the so-called 'black belt' of the South, the interracial conditions were still very primitive and most deplorable. In certain remote counties in the Southwest it was found, for example, that thousands of Negroes were being held on the farms in a state of practical peonage."

The depression modified the old southern social system. The Negro's relationship to the land was radically changed. The young Negro was more subject to the depression than even his hard-pressed white neighbor, and he reacted more extremely. He found himself on the road away from the country and the traditional background of his ancestors. He even found himself moving away from the South itself. The vocational training which Booker T. Washington and most white leaders had advocated was now denied him, for manual training was enormously expensive and competent teachers almost unobtainable. Too, this area of training had become more attractive to white students who were themselves competing for non-farm jobs.

By force of circumstances the Negro in depression years was thrown back upon the less expensive resources of arts-and-sciences training. In this area he has made a creditable showing, and it is in this area that over the last twenty years he has come to study subject matter which has had a profound bearing upon his attitudes toward his present position in American democracy. Likewise, this fact has enabled leaders of his own race to mobilize Negro opinion more effectively than ever before in American history.

The Negro on the whole has shown aptitude in expressive arts such as music, art, languages, and writing. The fact that this particular change in educational approach occurred in the last two decades has produced one of the strange ironies in southern cultural history. Traditionally, the arts and sciences were areas of learning which few white people believed the Negro either would or could master. Even today southern die-hards refuse to recognize the Negro as capable of such understanding. For example, Judge Tom Brady bitterly criticized the Supreme Court for stating in the 1954 decision that many Negroes "have achieved outstanding success" in the arts and sciences. Judge Brady suggested that justices spend thirty days, "in August, mind you," in certain southern states and "associate intimately with the average Negro family." Then, in his opinion, the Court would recognize the foolishness of its statement.

An objective reading of the Supreme Court's decision reveals a sense on the part of that body of the inequities which have existed between the races in the field of education since 1870. Not even the most aroused southerner can view the South's social history through the objective lenses of statistics without becoming aware of this fact. Formerly he may have shrugged off this state of affairs with the notion that the Negro could not take an education or that he did not want it. In these barren years some individual Negroes demonstrated real capacity to succeed by the white man's standards of excellence, but, generally speaking, the Negro's forte was in carefree music, patience, folklore, and homey philosophy. But whatever the regional attitude has been historically, it did not escape Howard Odum's mature observation, and two decades ago he attempted to warn the South of an impending adverse court decision. "For one," he said, "the cumulative neglect of the southern states of Negro schools, and the South's failure to live up to its obligations to provide equal facilities for the two races, have compounded educational deficits beyond the reasonable limits of tolerance within the framework of constitutional mandates, democratic fairplay, and moral obligations."

Some of the inequities which exist in southern education may be beyond the region's immediate capacity to correct. Shifting population patterns on the one hand and community resistance to even a slight relocation of schools on the other have fostered inequalities which would not exist under more effective consolidation and reorganization. The loss of population in scores of south-

ern counties can hardly keep from affecting schools by any standard of measurement, and, since the Negro population in many
places is declining, the colored schools show greater losses. In
some instances so few Negroes live in many of the border or fringe
borderland counties that maintenance of a segregated colored
school is out of the question. In such instances colored pupils are
transported unbelievable distances, even across county lines, which
means they are often exhausted traveling back and forth to school.
Occasionally counties have paid boarding expenses of Negro students in distant high schools rather than admit them to the white
high schools. The Negro, however, has no corner on the shifting
of population and the necessity for relocation of schools and re-
allocation of funds.

The obvious discrimination against the Negro in public schools
frightened conservative southerners enough to bring about a
breakdown of some of the traditional barriers to tax resistance.
They knew, by help of the courts, that the time-worn argument
that whites paid a disproportionate per-capita amount of the taxes
would no longer serve as a protective device. They also saw that,
in the face of changing conditions in the South, the urban Negro
would be less complacent about accepting indifferent schools.
The rumblings at this point were audible enough for southern
leadership, facing a stern court test, to understand that a bigger
educational effort for the Negro was mandatory if segregation was
to be maintained. Already the South was spending a greater proportion of its income for schools than was any other major geographical region of the United States. The old tax sources, except
for higher and more equitable assessments of real property, were
quite thoroughly pre-empted by the Federal Government or by
the states for other purposes. Only one tax source remained which
promised enough income — a levy on retail sales. Under other and
less urgent conditions to have suggested a sales levy in most of
the southern states would have drowned the region in the tears
of politicians weeping for their poverty-stricken constituents.

A traditional southern contention died with the adoption of the
sales tax in the various states. No longer could it be said that the
Negro escaped his fiscal responsibility. A levy on retail sales gave
him a rather sizable stake in financing education, for he tends to
spend his wages as fast as he makes them for food and immediately

needed appliances and clothing. Thus, he has become a fairly fruitful tax source. Because of this fact the Negro now finds himself in a new fiscal relationship to the southern educational system.

Since 1948 the southern states with large Negro populations have engaged in programs which have led to sweeping improvements of Negro schools. Gaps between the two races have been narrowed, despite the fact that some informed sources have estimated that it would take a billion dollars to equalize educational opportunity for the two races. As mentioned earlier, in some states many of the gaps have been closed, especially in teacher qualifications and salaries. Negro teachers have been guaranteed tenure and the fringe benefits of pensions. One cannot help but be impressed with the good quality of new Negro school buildings, many of them models of modern school architecture. It is not unusual at all to see newer and maybe better Negro schools in some communities than those available to whites. The Negro is not only the beneficiary of a considerably expanded effort on his behalf, but he also benefits from the fact that American school-plant architecture has undergone vast improvements. The consolidation of large numbers of the one-room schools has resulted in greatly improved physical conditions of buildings, and has afforded Negro access to efficient school transportation.

Since 1945 the level of training of Negro teachers has moved upward. Today it is rapidly approaching, if not exceeding in some instances, that of white teachers. In the border areas Negro teachers can attend former all-white universities and colleges, or they can attend former all-Negro colleges. Teaching gives the average Negro instructor more social status among his people than is enjoyed by a white teacher. Pierce, Carmichael, Moore, and Drewery in *White and Negro Schools in the South* found that in Georgia, North Carolina, Tennessee, Texas, and Virginia, a larger proportion of white teachers than Negroes had less than two years of college training in 1952. With major consolidations of rural schools, the improvement of teacher salaries, and stricter certification rules, the quality of Negro teachers has been vastly improved.

Training accomplishments cannot be accepted as precise measurements of the real capability of the individual teacher to perform his duties behind the closed door of the classroom. Nevertheless, the Negro teacher in some states is still at a disadvantage in the matter of training. The color bar in state universities and colleges in six or seven of the southern states denies him access to local graduate schools. Yet there is a possibility that, despite this handicap, the Negro teacher may equalize qualitative training in a remarkably short time. It is not at all unlikely that a relatively higher type Negro is going into the teaching profession than is true in a portion of the white teaching force. The trained Negro in the present South has fewer opportunities to enter other professions or businesses than has the average trained white person, with the result that teaching is a major profession for the educated Negro.

Though improved qualifications of Negro teacher training is a genuinely constructive accomplishment, it contains the germ of possible tragedy for the future. If schools are desegregated in many areas, the Negro teacher may become a victim of prejudice both in the social community and in the industrial field, unless prevailing attitudes change radically. Industries moving south will have to show far more willingness than at present to alter the prevailing social pattern.

Conservative southerners are no doubt justified in seeing a threat to the regional *status quo* in both advanced and secondary college training for Negroes. As young Negroes have achieved higher levels of training, they have been projected more and more into the fields which have emphasized the history of American democracy and the democratic role of America among the nations of the world. As one highly intelligent southern Negro college president said to this author, it is frustrating indeed to be held academically responsible for the lessons of democracy in the classroom and yet to be laid woefully liable for its free practice on the outside. Such inequities are a major stimulus to Negro aggressiveness over equal rights. The segregationalist literature which has appeared in great quantity recently has made an egregious error in locating the mainspring of Negro dissatisfaction with his present educational status in the southern states. The enormous emphasis placed upon democracy in the war and postwar years, the manful efforts of the nation in the cold-war years to combat Communist propaganda, the widespread American informational services, the anti-

Communist crusade at home, and the emphasis placed upon democracy in the school curriculum go far to explain the changing Negro attitudes.

A publisher could scarcely expect to sell a textbook in the field of economics, political science, or history which did not in some way stress the democratic achievements of the American people. It is from the pages of these textbooks that white and black alike formulate their notions of a democratic society. As teachers become better prepared, and as an increasing number of Negro students enters the higher grades of secondary schools and goes on to college, pressures for opportunities for Negroes in American democratic society will become intense. One of the basic problems of the immediate future is how American society — and southern society in particular — still bound by traditions, can absorb a restless and well-trained part of the Negro population.

The existence of schools and the great efforts of the southern states to lessen inequalities force the region headlong into deciding what is to become of the end product of this improved educational system. It is clear that the South cannot maintain its traditional attitudes if it is to meet the challenge of better educational opportunities for its Negro youth. The issue places the whole social and economic structure of the modern South in a dilemma because of the new emphasis on education as an economic necessity.

The depression and World War II brought the Negro into a new set of relationships with his traditional background. The depression sent him to town and to areas outside the South to search for employment. Already the old agrarian system of the South was breaking down. In many instances, much of the race problem was largely drained away from the communities. What the depression left undone, the movement away from the farm is helping to finish. Few incidents in southern history have had such deep-seated effect upon the region's social life. Southern racial paternalism was largely destroyed. Only the lumber and pulpwood industries have maintained so close a control over laborers as the farm. Away from the farm the southern Negro has to live off his wages, earned in many instances in the employ of an impersonal corporation or company which supplies no "furnish" and has no other casual credit system. The breaking down of the old easy-going but ruinous relationships of the southern farm has come close to making meaningless clichés of much of what the southern white man thought and said about the Negro.

Living in town with the social problems accompanying his new form of life, the formerly rural Negro found more adequate communication with members of his own race. Often a higher cultural level accounted for changing attitudes and new forms of Negro aggressiveness. There is no way of knowing at the moment the full impact of World War II upon white-Negro relationships in the South. There was a revival of the fears which prevailed in World War I when the Interracial Commission was formed, that the Negro soldier would come back from the war an emancipated individual, and that he would set to work to destroy the traditional pattern of Negro-white relationships. Larger numbers of Negroes experienced combat service than ever before in American military history.

The young Negro in the postwar South found himself, like his white neighbor, in a changed personal relationship with his country. He faced new challenges which demanded personal courage and sacrifice, and a need for a more extended technical knowledge of things about him. Again, he was indoctrinated in the American democratic tradition in the various army training programs which placed major emphasis upon the American political system and way of life. This was really the basic objective of the war itself. There is no accurate measurement of what happened to the Negro's thinking during the war period. One indication was his changed approach to his educational problems. He sought remedy to the obvious inequities through both state and federal courts.

Before the war had ended, a group of moderately minded southern Negro leaders met in Durham, North Carolina, to draft a statement of principles by which their race could make social progress in the South. Their statement, prepared in 1942, bore the descriptive title, "A Basis for Inter-racial Co-operation and Development in the South." They said a new consideration of Negro education was mandatory if harmonious relations between the races were to prevail. This statement of principles asked first for equalization of educational opportunities which would eliminate the inequities revealed in some of the statistics cited above. They sought recognition of the fact that there was definite need for graduate and professional training on terms specified in the Lloyd Gaines case. This case in many ways was one of the most significant that led to the Brown v. Topeka decision. In 1938 Lloyd Gaines, a young Negro, brought suit seeking admission to the Law School of the University of Missouri. The state offered to pay his tuition to an outside school, or to establish a special law school for Negroes. He pleaded that offer of tuition to go outside Missouri was unacceptable, and that a "separate but equal" law school would not be equivalent to the work offered and prestige of the University of Missouri Law School. The Court held that opportunities available outside the state in no way satisfied the needs of a citizen within a state. "Manifestly," it said, "the obligation of the state to give the protection of equal laws can be performed only where its laws operate, that is, within its own jurisdiction."

In October 1942 the Durham statement was placed before a joint white-Negro conference in Atlanta. This group was told that the southern Negro was making an appeal frankly for educational equality, carrying out in fact the principles set forth in Plessy v. Ferguson. The Atlanta Conference made a clear response to the Durham Principles. "Their statement," said a conference resolution, "is so frank and courageous, so free from any suggestion of threat and ultimatum, and at the same time shows such good will, that we gladly agree to co-operate." Southern Negro leadership was commended for placing emphasis in their statement on racial discrimination in the administration of our laws. The Atlanta delegates said they were sensitive to the charge and admitted that it was essentially just. In a strong statement the Atlanta delegates observed that, "No southerner can logically dispute the fact that the Negro, as an American citizen, is entitled to his civil rights and economic opportunities."

In a subsequent meeting in Richmond, Negro and white leaders again came together in a joint conference. The group produced a forthright resolution in which they said, "In America, and particularly in the South, we face problems of readjustments to meet the demands of present and post-war conditions with reference to the Negro and the future development of a great region of the Nation. This, exclusive of the war, is the greatest crisis of the South and the Nation." The resolution took cognizance of the fact that the Negro was shifting cultural levels and that the postwar years would be a time when there would be great need for understanding and encouragement from his white neighbors. It was in this meeting that Dr. Gordon B. Hancock, Negro minister and sociologist, warned that the South could not afford to allow outside forces to extract from it certain gains. He pleaded with the conference to support southern Negro leadership then or otherwise the crusade for Negro rights would be directed from New York.

The Atlanta Covenant or Continuing Committee undertook to carry out the intent of the three conferences. The Southern Regional Council was formed and it undertook to bring about the necessary reforms that not only would retain the center of Negro leadership in Atlanta and the South but would begin a sane program of education. But charges of "nigger loving," and even Communism, scared away timid white support. The political demagogues unfairly distorted the work of both the Commission on Interracial Co-operation and the Southern Regional Council. The thwarting of this moderate Negro plea for equal opportunities was a costly error to the South's educational advancement. The South's refusal to meet the moderate challenges offered in the Durham Manifesto and to promote tolerant and objective purposes of the Southern Regional Council removed virtually the last chance for the principles of Plessy v. Ferguson to be applied to southern education.

By 1940 it was clearly evident to informed southerners that at last the issue of segregated schools would be taken to the courts. Already cases involving colleges and universities had either been decided or were before the courts. Extremists who had been opposed to any education for Negroes in years past now talked of trying to improve colored schools. By talking about "equal" opportunities sixty years later, they hoped they could still re-enforce the Plessy-Ferguson doctrine.

When four state-school cases reached the Supreme Court of the United States, docketed as Brown v. the Topeka School Board, there opened a new era of white-Negro relations in the South. Suits against the Virginia and South Carolina counties were based on lack of equal physical facilities and on the fact that segregation of the school system violated the Negro citizen's rights under the Fourteenth Amendment. This case brought squarely before the Court for the first time the issue of the constitutionality of the segregated public-school system. Again the South was being confronted by its age-old nemesis, the Fourteenth Amendment.

May 17, 1954, the Supreme Court through Chief Justice Earl Warren delivered its unanimous decision that segregation of children in schools on a racial basis in the defendant towns and counties was unconstitutional. In all but the Delaware case, a three-judge district court had subsequently denied the plaintiffs' relief under the separate-but-equal doctrine of Plessy v. Ferguson. Argument was first heard in 1952 before the Supreme Court and again in 1954. Central contentions of the argument were conditions surrounding the formulation and adoption of the Fourteenth Amendment and its subsequent history. This was especially true as it applied to educational development in nineteenth- and twentieth-century America. The Court reviewed briefly the progress of public education in the United States, in the South, and in the field of Negro education. Reviewing the feeble state of Negro education in 1868, the Court said, "Today in contrast, many Negroes have achieved outstanding success in the arts and sciences as well as in the business and professional world." Progress in American education had been phenomenal since the adoption of the Fourteenth Amendment. It was more complex in its organization and curriculum.

Reviewing court action in the field of education, the Court took cognizance of all the cases from Roberts v. City of Boston, to Sweatt v. Painter. Unlike conditions governing the latter case, it acknowledged the fact that rapid progress had been made in the field of equalization in the tangible areas, as well as in curriculum and teacher training and qualification, but, said the Court, "We must consider public education in the light of its full development and its present place in American life throughout the nation. Only in this way can it be determined if segregation in public schools deprives the plaintiffs of the equal protection of the laws." Although this particular sentence has often been quoted, it received less analytical attention than other parts of the decision. Here the Court led the two southern counties onto the boggiest ground. Any casual examination of statistical tables showed the region at a disadvantage with other areas, and the Negro at a disadvantage with the white student.

The Court then reviewed American educational history, taking into consideration the expansion of the system, its academic progress, and the advent of compulsory attendance of children in school under the laws of the various states. It likewise considered the importance of education in modern life. In the Kansas case the circuit judge had already analyzed the general psychological effects of segregation on the school-age child. Concluding its decision, the Supreme Court said, "Whatever may have been the extent of psychological knowledge at the time of Plessy vs. Ferguson, this finding is amply supported by modern authority. Any language in Plessy vs. Ferguson contrary to this finding is rejected." And so the separate-but-equal doctrine for the races of the South was overruled judicially.

The Court realized that it had taken a momentous step in reordering the social life of the nation, and especially the South. It had snatched out in a single grasp deeply rooted social customs and mores. Before the principles laid down in its decision could be applied, enormous adjustments would have to be made. The case was restored to the docket, and the Attorney General of the United States and the attorney generals of the several states were invited to file briefs before October 1, 1954, as friends of the Court, for rearguments of points four and five. These dealt with the questions of how best to implement the desegregation of schools in keeping with peculiar local conditions. In May 1955 the Court ordered the defendant counties to begin making reasonable progress toward desegregating their public schools.

The broader effects of the Supreme Court's decision are treated elsewhere. In the field of education it has wrought many changes and has also brought about an enormous statutory structure which surrounds the educational process with legal technicalities. The seventeen states and the District of Columbia have made varying responses to the mandate to desegregate their schools. The border states of Delaware, Maryland, Kentucky, Missouri, and Oklahoma have proceeded with some rapidity to carry out the Court's order. So has the District of Columbia. In January 1960 there were 6973 school districts in the seventeen states; of these 747 were desegregated. Out of a Negro enrollment of 3,039,135, or 23.5 per cent of the southern public school population, 522,719 pupils were enrolled in desegregated situations. Aside from the border states, integration has been occurring on at least a token basis in the

Old South states. Arkansas, Florida, Tennessee, Texas, Virginia, and North Carolina have desegregated schools. At the college level out of 195 formerly all white institutions of higher learning in these states, 124 were integrated.

Kentucky, as a border state, in many respects comes closest to representing a southern point of view. It is linked to the South by its folk origins, sentiments, social philosophy, and economic interests. A majority of its people might not have voluntarily chosen to integrate their public schools. Nevertheless integration has progressed in that state without incident, except for a brief furore in Clays, Sturgis, and Henderson. A private school was opened in Graves County, but its doors were closed within a year. After careful planning and preparation under the leadership of Dr. Omer Carmichael, Louisville not only desegregated its school system but it retained many of its Negro teachers. In Lexington token desegregation occurred without incident, and elsewhere in Kentucky the story was much the same.

Thus far integration of southern schools has not resulted in the unhappy incidents which segregationists have predicted. Wherever school boards, superintendents, and teachers have been allowed to reorganize their schools, changes have occurred without friction. Whether or not the Negro is better off sociologically and psychologically in desegregated schools is a matter which only time and mature study can determine. This much is certain: the Negro in the desegregated school shares with his white neighbor the fortunes of local education. If they are poor, both races suffer in like degree; if they are good, the two races enjoy equal opportunities to get an education.

XIII

"With All Deliberate Speed"

Touching the intellectual capacity of negroes: I was dining with a gentleman, when he asked the waiter — a lad of eighteen — to tell him what time it was. The boy, after studying the clock, replied incorrectly; and the gentleman said it was impossible for him to make the simple calculation necessary. He had promised to give him a dollar, a year ago, whenever he could tell the time by the clock; had taken a good deal of trouble to teach him, but he did not seem to make any progress. I have since met with another negro boy, having the same remarkable inability — both lads being intelligent, and learning easily in other respects: the first could read. I doubt if it is a general deficiency of the race; both boys had marked depressions where phrenologists locate the organ of calculation.

OLMSTED, A JOURNEY IN THE SEABOARD SLAVE STATES, p. 552

May 17, 1954, was a major date in southern history. Whether or not it will become as important as that of the Dred Scott decision depends on future events.

The ghost of federal intervention in southern public schools had hovered over the South since the Blair Bill was introduced in Congress in 1882. This bill proposed use of federal funds to equalize educational opportunities in the South, which meant the equalization of Negro and white educational opportunities. Proponents of the Blair legislation argued that, if the Negro were to receive education equal to that of the national public schools, more financial support was necessary. Arguments against the Blair Bill established a pattern against federal school support: it would bring federal intervention, would mix the races, and would destroy local educational autonomy.

In 1954 the impending Court decision hung over the South like the intense dread of an approaching tornado. Few people indeed doubted that the Negro in the modern South should have the best possible educational opportunity. He had been active in both military and economic efforts during the war, and his ignorance in moments of great national crisis made our defense of democracy more difficult. Many southerners acknowledged that the Negro was entitled to maximum educational opportunities, but believed that he should enjoy these in segregated schools. These people, including several governors, hoped that the Negro could be persuaded to adopt such a philosophy.

Publication of the Court's decision had these immediate effects on the South. The first was in the field of popular discussion; hardly any conversation, even the most casual one, could avoid the subject. The press reacted vigorously to the new mandate. Thousands of news stories, special columns, and other commentaries analyzed the Court's actions. Reporters moved about the South gathering thumbnail impressions of public reaction. An objective reporting service was organized in Nashville, Tennessee, to give a running summary of activities throughout the South. In the earlier phase of public reaction there was an air of anxious expectancy that something else was coming. If the expressed public mind of the first few weeks in the summer of 1954 had prevailed, the South's response to the decision might have been rather moderate. Once southerners had a moment to contemplate what had happened for the most part they adopted an attitude of watchful waiting. The Court itself had pointed the way for such reaction by having the case redocketed for reargument on two points. On the other hand it would have been unreasonable to suppose that a region which had lived with the race issue for so many decades, and which was now receiving so much publicity, would not suffer some kind of aftereffects.

There was quick and passionate response on the part of editors and politicians. The wide diversity of geography and social stratification in the South was clearly revealed in these public utterances. In the border and fringe areas there was actually some expression of relief that schools could now be integrated. Some school boards were relieved of the worry of trying to provide something approaching educational opportunity for a handful of Negro students in areas having sparse Negro populations. One chairman of a school board in such a community said his only concern with the Court decision was to find one or two good basketball players among the incoming students. If he could do this his worries were over.

In Kentucky, for instance, school officials were glad enough to see the Day Law, which was enacted in 1908 to prevent Berea College from admitting Negroes, become innocuous. Over the years this law had been both expensive and difficult to administrate. In valley and mountainous Virginia, in eastern Tennessee, and in western North Carolina there was little emotional concern over the prospects of desegregation. In a popular vote students in Lafollette, Tennessee, next door to Clinton, expressed a willingness to admit Negroes to their ranks. Curiously, more girls than boys favored integration.

Integrating the schools in the border region of the South involved few deep-seated emotional problems as compared with those of the old blackbelts or areas where slavery was most firmly established. Reconstruction had touched this part of the South more lightly than it had the more intense slave areas. Loyalties in the Civil War itself often favored maintenance of the Union. Negroes constituted a minor portion of the population, and generally they enjoyed somewhat better economic status than in the blackbelt. In the borderland the Negro had long exercised his right to vote, and in areas where the two major parties were active the balance of power was so delicate that the Negro, though in a definite minority, could sometimes determine the outcome of elections. Where there was a tendency for voters to drift from one party to the other, the Negro's voice in politics was greater. It was suicidal folly for politicians in those areas to irritate Negroes. A leading candidate for the United States Senate, who was also chairman of the Board of Trustees of the University of Kentucky, became agitated when it was proposed that the Board appeal the Johnson v. the University of Kentucky decision which had admitted Negroes to that institution.

However, such an attitude was exceptional. As one traveled toward the heartlands of the old slavery belt, reactions became more decisive. Both press comment and individual conversation indicated more resistant attitudes, yet, until the Court rendered the second part of its decision on May 31, 1955, there was willingness to wait to form firm convictions until after all the facts were in hand. Too, there was a hope that in its second decision the Court would see fit to leave the South some means of escaping the harsh fact of school integration. However, the Court cut off this escape in their 1955 decision.

In Alabama, State Senator Sam Engelhardt, representing the famous blackbelt county of Macon, where Negroes comprise 84.4 per cent of the population, presented bills in the Assembly to amend the state constitution so as to permit individuals to organize private schools to be supported with public funds and to permit the leasing of public school property for private use. This amendment was adopted by a vote of 128,545 to 80,777.

In Atlanta, the Georgia Assembly adopted resolutions creating a commission to be entrusted with the responsibility of satisfying both federal and state constitutional requirements. It also proposed amendment of the state constitution to permit the creation of private schools. Negroes accounted for approximately one-third of the school population, with distribution being heaviest in the old slave belt of eastern and middle Georgia and in the rapidly expanding urban centers. Like most southern states, Georgia had developed public schools after a long and arduous crusade. In mid-twentieth century the state was desperately short of classrooms and teachers. A shifting population of both whites and Negroes from the intensely rural areas, to towns and cities created a double-barreled crisis in both places. In many instances there were not enough students to maintain enrollments necessary for efficient high schools, and, in some instances, Negro schools were virtually without students. To halt the momentous public-school movement in Georgia and turn it over to private management was to halt a dynamic social movement that was so thoroughly interwoven with the fabric of Georgia society that it would perhaps create a bigger emotional storm than integration; certainly it would cause greater chaos and confusion. This approach is yet to be tested in concrete action.

The proposed amendment was opposed by the Georgia Parent Teachers Congress, the Georgia Educational Association, the Georgia Federation of Labor, the League of Woman Voters, and the United Church Women. In July 1958, the federal district court ordered the Atlanta School Board to submit a plan by December 1, 1959, for desegregating the city's schools. Immediately the city found itself caught between the federal court and the state legislature.

In Mississippi, Governor Hugh White undertook to maintain segregation on a voluntary basis. On July 30, 1954 he invited Negro educational leaders to his office in 1955 to discuss the school crisis. The meeting, however, did not occur until a tremendous amount of embittered press comment had been disseminated in the state. The Assembly and the twenty-five member Legislative Advisory Committee (created in 1954) had convinced the people that Mississippi would destroy its public schools rather than integrate the races. As a result, the meeting in the Governor's office was disappointing. Governor White had hoped a promise of equal facilities and staff advantages would satisfy the Negroes, but only one out of the ninety present favored the suggested plan, and one other spoke as partially favoring it. The others appeared to support Dr. R. T. M. Howard's contention that Mississippi adhere strictly to the Court decision.

Generally, Mississippi educators faced a serious crisis. They undoubtedly opposed any action which would injure public schools, even though they personally opposed integration. This meant that they opposed any constitutional amendment which would place the fate of the schools in the hands of a small group of politicians. History of public education in that state was one of deep sacrifice on the part of many courageous people. In 1950 Mississippi had the lowest per-capita income in the nation ($703), but it was twenty-seventh in effort to support public schools, and it was spending 2.7 per cent of its personal income for that purpose. In few states did public education have more fundamental meaning to the individual than in Mississippi, where economic opportunities in the traditional fields of employment were disappearing.

In calmer moments it was not unreasonable to believe that a vast majority of informed Mississippians would have abhorred the idea of adopting a constitutional amendment leading to possible destruction of the public schools. This decision was facing them in late summer 1954. In its regular session that year the Assembly anticipated an adverse Court decision and appropriated only enough funds for full operation of the schools for one year, and partial funds for the second part of the biennium. The school people were caught in a dilemma. They either had to support the "last resort" amendment to the state constitution or begin the next school year with insufficient funds. Without funds new buildings could not be constructed nor old ones repaired. Teachers could not be kept in the system, nor could new ones be employed. All necessary educational services would have to be curtailed.

The fact that Mississippi schools would be without funds was a distinct possibility. Governor White was specific in his ultimatum: if the special session of the legislature did not clear the legal way for the preparation and submission of a constitutional amendment making possible the destruction of the public school system as a last resort to prevent integration, and, then by equally as strong an implication, if the amendment were not adopted by the people, there would be no extraordinary session of the legislature to appropriate additional money for schools.

Both school people and politicians knew that special-interests groups in Mississippi, while favoring segregation, were opposed to increased taxes. These have traditionally frowned on taxes in that state. In February 1957 an extraordinary session of the legislature was called on the heels of an overwhelming victory for the constitutional amendment at the polls the preceding November. The legislature now faced the dual responsibility of making a second appropriation for continuing the public schools, and for providing additional revenue to equalize educational opportunities between the races and between the urban and rural areas. In 1955–56 the state had 799,662 educable children between the ages of six and twenty-one years. Of these, 367,388 were white and 431,857 were Negro. Negro average daily attendance was 214,649 as compared with 237,579 whites. Any appreciable change in the total enrollment and average daily attendance by themselves would alter significantly financial demands made on the state. This problem confronted the legislature in providing additional educational funds. Though Mississippi was losing Negro population at a rather appreciable rate, this loss did not relieve the state of the responsibility for equalizing its educational program.

When Governor White addressed the special session of the legislature about the desirability of amending the constitution, he voiced an opinion that was rapidly hardening into a fixed view in the Lower South. "An unanimous Court," he said, "saw fit to try to destroy every precedent of the past: it ignored the findings of fact of the trial courts, it usurped the legislative functions of the Congress specifically provided for in the 14th Amendment itself, and it embraced as the supreme law of the land the unsworn, personal theories of five or six sociologists, the chief of whom was a Swede [sic], Myrdall, who have never lived in the United States, much less in the South. . . . the people of Mississippi were shocked and stunned. There were no overt demonstrations, but I know I am correct in saying that their universal resolutions [are] not to abide by such an unreasonable decision if lawful means could be found by which to avoid it."

In raising additional money for schools, Mississippi legislators were to follow a fine line. To tax new industry at a time when every effort was being made to industrialize the state was out of the question, especially since Governor White was the main personal force behind the program to "balance agriculture with industry." Any threat of an increased tax on industry would frighten management into locating plants elsewhere. Industry was vital to Mississippi's future welfare, even though in other regions it may have adhered to policies opposed to segregation. Old tax sources were either overburdened or had developed tough protective techniques in their lobbying. The Assembly could increase the sales tax a penny, raise the levy on soft drinks and cigarettes, raise the excise on black-market whisky or on gasoline and oils, and collect a heavier severance tax on natural resources. Nearly all of these, except the $1,500,000 additional cigarette tax, were opposed by powerful interests. In concrete terms, equalizing educational opportunities for both races within a year or two would cost $44,000,-000, plus $118,000,000 for new buildings. The immediate cost for new school buildings for Negroes was estimated at $60,000,000. This meant that to maintain segregation by providing equal opportunities, an already discredited policy, the state of Mississippi faced mountainous costs.

While the legislature debated the issue of raising additional funds to equalize the schools, Negro leaders themselves debated what was best for the race. Rural weeklies carried stories of Negro arguments for separate-but-equal facilities. An influential Negro minister and publisher, Dr. H. H. Hume, expressed the belief that the Negro should accept voluntary segregation in exchange for improvement of his schools. On the other hand, Dr. R. T. M. Howard of Mound Bayou reiterated his view that the state should adhere strictly to the Court ruling.

Mississippians found raising money extremely difficult. Generally it was easier for officials in all the hard-core southern states to attack the Supreme Court for allowing itself to be brainwashed by sociologists and Communists and to magnify the horrors of segregation than it was to talk obstinate taxpayers into accepting higher levies. Emotionally, an overwhelming number of white southerners wished to maintain segregation, but they dreaded the extra tax burden involved. In not one of the states, however, was there appreciable opposition to the principle of equalizing educational opportunities between the races. People in Halifax County, Virginia, did express a desire to use accumulated building funds to improve white school buildings first. But when it came to considering integration there was almost no cost in freedom or better judgment which people were not willing to pay. The Mississippi legislature virtually removed all restrictions from the Legal Educational Advisory Committee and gave it life-and-death power of decision over the schools. This body was given power to summon witnesses before it by subpoena, and to examine evidence of violations of the principles of segregation.

In all the uproar over segregation there has appeared a consistent note of anxiety on the part of educational leadership that southern public schools not suffer disruption at a time when every effort should be made to keep abreast of modern educational demands. It is not hard to detect the anxiety of school officials at all levels. They have about all the responsibility they can manage without reckoning with a politically inspired crusade to throw the public-school system into chaos, if not eventually into abandon. In 1957 a southerner wrote that if a superintendent had in his files a plan by which he hoped to bring about orderly integration he hastened to destroy it.

While Governor White tried to solve the integration problem in Mississippi by equalizing aid to all public schools, Governor Luther Hodges proposed the same solution in North Carolina. On August 26, 1955, he appeared before a leadership conference of Negro teachers and outlined briefly the effects of the Supreme

Court decision on the future of public education in that state. He said either the Negro would volunteer to accept segregation or the public school system would be destroyed: "Let us realize with full knowledge that if we are not able to succeed in a program of voluntary separate school attendance, the state within the next year or so will be face to face with deciding the issue of whether it shall have some form of integrated public schools or shall abandon its public schools." Governor Hodges saw pressure from the outside as the greatest disservice done North Carolina in its history as a state, and saw Negro children as the greatest sufferers: "If that weapon [destruction of the public schools] is ever used in North Carolina, its results will be appalling in ignorance, poverty and bitterness. Generations of both races will suffer by it immeasurably, and it is likely the Negro citizen will suffer most."

Answering the Governor's plea for voluntary segregation, Negro teachers adopted resolutions rejecting the proposal, saying, "We heartily endorse the Supreme Court decision of May 17, 1954, and of May 31, 1955, as being just, courageous and timely. All good citizens have a solemn obligation to abide by the law. As professional educators, our obligations in this regard is even more impelling." Then saying what no doubt comes close to stating a unified Negro opinion in the South, the North Carolina teachers continued, "We do not now, nor have we ever subscribed to voluntary segregation, but as good citizens we have abided by segregation because it was the law of our state. Now that the Supreme Court has ruled that this law is in conflict with the Constitution of the United States it is our conviction that it is in conflict with our obligations as good citizens for us to advocate voluntary segregation."

An interesting sidelight on Governor Hodges's plea to the Negro teachers was a personal letter to him from Paul Green, the famous North Carolina playwright. He chided his old classmate with deserting the rich Aycock tradition which has meant so much in both North Carolina and southern public-school history. Hodges had turned his back on the kind of liberal leadership which Aycock had supplied, and he had spoken, not in "the voice of leadership and brave idealism but rather the old familiar message of an ancient and reactionary South."

Like Governor White, Governor Hodges soon learned about an

important development in white-Negro relations: No longer did the southern Negro come into the Governor's presence or into court as a suppliant defendant who waited for patriarchal justice to take its leisurely course. He now came as a militant plaintiff accompanied by a competent legal staff and apparently with enough funds to carry almost any number of issues all the way to the United States Supreme Court. If not arguing his case in court he could draft effective resolutions setting forth his views and position in clear forceful language. It was a breaking away from the old tradition where a few Negroes met a few white intellectuals in discussions of the educational needs of the two races, a fact which soon filtered down to local community leadership as well. Educational advancement has become the Negro's vital concern.

At the end of the first year following the Court's 1954 decision, three definite developments had occurred in the hard-core southern states. Plans had either been adopted or were being formulated to abandon the public schools, to permit the organization of private schools to be maintained by semi-public support, and to institute a scheme of student assignments. Political leadership in these states was solidly opposed to integration. There was a wide gap between what state officials were saying and the earlier attitudes of many local school boards. Those political officials who made such positive statements that they never would consent to mixing the races in the classrooms later tempered their remarks by saying their resistance would always be within the scope of the law.

School boards in major southern cities, and even many of those in smaller communities, adopted attitudes that the ruling of the Supreme Court was the law. In Norfolk, Virginia, the school board members said, "We intend without moral reservation, to uphold and abide by the laws of the land." The *Norfolk Journal and Guide* said, "That it is a simple, statesmanlike, democratic, and sensible declaration. It says in just fifteen words what anyone has to say who pretends to fulfill his citizenship duties as an American citizen." Much of the press pleaded in 1955 for sanity and patience in facing new social conditions outlined in the Court decision. From the very heart of the region in which argument over segregation was hottest, Ralph McGill of the *Atlanta Constitution* wrote, "What various state legislatures are doing, as they busy themselves with plans to carry on school segregation without legal compulsion, is admitting segregation by law is finished . . . either this year, next or within the next few to come. . . . As a matter of fact, segregation has been on its way out for a good long time and has been breaking down at the edges for more than a generation. . . . Two great forces have been at work on segregation and the problem of race. One is secular, the other religious. The Christian of today cannot help but wince at the full implications, and the jarring clash of his creed, with discrimination against any person of color. . . . Christianity cannot well afford to be on the wrong side of a moral force, as it was in some areas when it defended slavery."

Mr. McGill believed the secular forces of freedom would surely bring a lowering of discriminatory barriers, but when this came about there would be no social compunctions. Any law which a southern legislature might pass would of necessity be dealing with change in the South and not with the *status quo*. The fact that legislatures were dealing with the problem was evidence that their members also recognized that segregation was at an end, as a fact in law.

Three areas of opinion and action were quickly defined in the South after May 1954. The first of these was that of the public press. As has been said above, the press itself was aligned on both sides, with many papers still adhering to points of view dating back to the days of James K. Vardaman, Ben Tillman, Senator John Tyler Morgan of Alabama, and Thomas E. Watson of Georgia. The Supreme Court decision and its after effects have comprised the South's biggest news story since World War II. In fact no southern story since the Civil War has involved such deep regional emotions for so extended a time. In the past few years large numbers of aroused people have made countless and passionate statements. It has seemed that every southerner has wanted to be heard on the subject, and reporters have been present to hear them. Almost every week, especially during the opening of school terms, there have been incidents. Thus modern southern social history has been strung out from one incident to another like a sagging power line between poles. Each incident provokes a flood of news stories and a recurring storm of strong words and aroused passions.

In the realm of southern politics, the issue is cut to order. Instead of discussions of many positive issues before the South at this time of profound change, the ancient race issue is hammered to death. Almost every office-seeker feels compelled to reiterate his unrelenting desire for segregation of the schools. In some way he has to convince the voters that he is more segregationist than his opponents. Every candidate for governor or United States Senator has to convince voters that he can in some way save the South. Other vital southern issues which under other conditions would scream for discussion and decision have been obscured. It is safe to attack the Supreme Court, the National Association for the Advancement of Colored People (NAACP), "nigger lovers," both local and outsiders, sociologists, and meddlesome Yankees. None of these can talk back effectively or influence the outcome of an election. Characteristic of campaigns of this sort were those in Virginia, Alabama, South Carolina, Georgia, and Mississippi, where gubernatorial candidates fought their way into office by out-vowing their opponents on the public-school issue.

These feverish campaigns have at times caused confusion within the ranks of the segregationists. No doubt one of the most embarrassing political bobbles in this period was that which occurred in the Virginia campaign in October 1957. J. Lindsay Almond, Jr., enjoying the support of the powerful Byrd machine, appeared on a Sunday afternoon television program in Washington and was said to have admitted that holes would be hacked in Virginia's program of massive resistance. This admission was most damaging to the Virginia doctrine, "that in no school in any part of the Old Dominion shall Negro and white students sit down together." Mr. Almond said he was quoted out of context, but the press had access to recordings of the interview. Immediately Senator Harry Flood Byrd took to the stump, and in Leesburg the following Monday night he declared that Attorney General Herbert Brownell and the NAACP would never bring Virginians to their knees.

The position Mr. Almond was reported to have taken was almost precisely that of the Republican candidate Theodore R. Dalton. Dalton, though opposed to integration, advocated the North Carolina student-assignment plan which would admit Negroes to white schools and would breach the wall of massive resistance. To have admitted this position would have refuted

Senator Byrd's contention that Virginia was in fact the South's first line of resistance against integration. Quickly the television incident was smoothed over, and the campaign became one of rolling up the largest possible majority for the Democratic candidate.

Once in office some public officials have made sharp statements about the Supreme Court which have gained wide circulation. Senator James Eastland of Mississippi, on May 25, 1955, submitted a resolution to the Senate which was critical of the sources from which the Supreme Court drew its sociological materials. The resolution was aimed at Gunnar Myrdal and his book, *An American Dilemma.* He said the collaborating "so-called scholars and experts, who contributed to no less than 272 different articles and portions of the book, have been cited numerous times as members of communist and subversive organizations, and . . . Whereas the citation of the authorities clearly indicates a dangerous influence and control exerted on the Court by communist front pressure groups and other enemies of the American Republic and individual members thereof that it is inimical to the general welfare and best interest of the Republic."

Later the Federation for Constitutional Government with headquarters in New Orleans, distributed a double-spread leaflet quoting Senator Eastland as saying there was need for "A people's organization to fight the court, to fight the C.I.O., to fight the NAACP, and to fight all the conscienceless pressure groups who are attempting our destruction. We will mobilize public opinion. We will attempt to pledge candidates in advance as they attempt to pledge them." Senator Eastland viewed the fight as a great crusade. The South would enlist free enterprise and the medical profession of the country to aid it. He proposed a campaign to preserve "untainted racial heritage, their [unborn southerners'] culture, and the institution of the anglo-saxon race." Both the proposed senate resolution and the leaflet were given rather wide circulation in several of the lower southern states by the White Citizens Councils.

In Georgia, Attorney-General Eugene Cook addressed the fifty-fifth annual meeting of the Peace Officers Association of Georgia in 1955 on the subject of the subversive activities of the NAACP. Later this speech was reprinted as a pamphlet, and it too was distributed from the headquarters of the Association of Citizens Councils of Winona, Mississippi. Cook said the ugly truth about "the NAACP and its origins, aims and manipulations is so shocking as to stagger the imagination, but it is borne out by incontrovertible facts which can be established as matters of official records." He introduced abolitionism into his discussion by saying that some of the NAACP founders were direct descendants of abolitionists. He singled out Oswald Garrison Villard, Moorefield Storey, and Mary Ovington White. William E. Walling was called a Russian-trained southern scalawag journalist. In its current activities the NAACP was said to be engaged in fomenting racial strife, and of either being naïve or a willing Communist-front instrument for the destruction of American democracy.

A third group which has expressed sharp displeasure with the Court's decision is composed of a rather strange mixture of people. These are the old long-standing local enemies of public education. These are the opponents of taxes, as well as the illiterate elements of the population who have never been sympathetic to the cause of public schooling. Some personal and corporate interests have viewed education as a private enterprise venture, and such a point of view was actually expressed in the *Tarheel Banker*. Combined with the selfish interests and the illiterates are those highly mobile outsiders who stand ready to strike a mortal blow at public education anywhere in the country where it is left exposed to their attacks. They are calculating, and, maybe patient, where southerners are impulsive and emotional. Southerners seem to be willing to accept their assistance so long as they appear to be helping them to obtain their immediate objectives. Many of these camels are accepted inside the southern tent without southerners' knowing what baggage they bear.

In the last few years the South has encouraged a considerable number of opportunists who have used the emotional school issue as a springboard to public preferment. Otherwise many of them could not have attained influence and importance. The bottom rail has advanced upward at greater speed in this period than ever before in the South. Calm southerners who have taken a reflective look at the scene have detected a new type of leader who has come forward with only a negative approach to solve an exceedingly difficult southern problem. Not only does he thrive on aroused hate and emotions but he has skillfully injected an element of abject fear which all but paralyzes thinking and freedom in communities where he is heeded. Seldom before has the demagogue expressed his ideas over such broad areas with such effectiveness. He has used all the modern facilities of mass communication with rewarding results.

It would indeed be a rash observer who would contend that a good part of the South has begun to solve the problem of segregation with deliberate speed, or with any speed at all. An enormous amount of nervous energy has been expended in six or seven of the states to stay the day when schools and all other public facilities will be freed of racial restrictions. Progress, or lack of progress, can be measured in this instance with a fair degree of accuracy. A rather precise profile can be presented in terms of statistics. In June 1959 the *Southern School News* reported in its status analysis that there were 7677 school districts in the eighteen states involved; of these 2875 were bi-racial and 742 were segregated. There were 9,658,361 white children and 2,999,157 Negroes in the region, and of these, 2,261,513 white children and 447,022 Negroes were in integrated situations. Six states — Alabama, Florida, Georgia, Louisiana, Mississippi, and South Carolina — had no desegregated schools.

While a relatively small number of public-school districts in the South have moved toward integration, 202 publicly supported colleges in thirteen of the eighteen states now accept Negroes. In the legal field 160 school cases were decided by the courts between May 1954 and October 1955, and more than 200 pieces of legislation were passed by state legislatures. Added to this are more than a dozen resolutions which have called for all sorts of actions ranging from nullification by and interposition of the will of state governments against federal interference in school affairs to impeachment of the justices of the Supreme Court. A good portion of this legislation was threatened with sudden death by the Virginia decisions in 1959. In these decisions both the Virginia Supreme Court of Appeals and the special federal three-judge court held that the Virginia laws proposing to close the public schools which were integrated were unconstitutional. The three-judge federal court declared, "The Commonwealth of Virginia, having accepted and assumed the responsibility of maintaining and operating public schools, cannot act through one of its officers to close one or more public schools in the state solely by reason of the assignment to, or enrollment or presence in, that public school of children of different races or colors, and, at the same time, keep other public schools throughout the state open on a segregated basis. The 'equal protection' afforded to all persons and taxpayers is lacking in such a situation."

Violent outbursts have on several occasions greeted the fall opening of schools. Disturbances in Clinton and Nashville, Tennessee, at Hoxie and Little Rock, Arkansas, and at Clays, Sturgis, and Henderson, Kentucky, have refuted the extremist claims of living within the law. Outsiders in three or four cases contributed heavily to outbursts of passion. John Kasper was active in both Clinton and Nashville, and in both instances landed in court with stern results. The press reported that Governor Marvin Griffin of Georgia stimulated resistance in the Little Rock incident in a vigorous speech before the Arkansas Citizens Councils. There was no identifiable outside influence in the early revolt in Clays and Sturgis, but this influence arrived almost simultaneously with the state police and the state guard.

Against this domestic backdrop moves the great mass of well-meaning but deeply disturbed southerners who have neither taken time nor exercised the patience necessary to reach reflective conclusions of their problems. It is not unreasonable to believe that some of the cardinal sins of American education rest in the South's troubled backyard. Instead of regarding the social studies as a constructive force in American life they have brought the whole region under suspicion. Critics of the professional educator charge that there is a lack of knowledge of content matter, and that only on the basis of a curriculum organized around "solid content" courses can schools convey an understanding of our social and political structure. This problem confronts the educator at a time when the average southerner has a limited perspective and understanding of the social problems involved. It is hardly to be expected that an uninformed man will stand by and hear irate speakers all the way from United States senators to illiterate rabble-rousers charge the Supreme Court with being brainwashed by subversive forces without reacting vigorously.

Two things seem clear at this moment: first, the courts will continue to grind out bit by bit their interpretations of what is meant by deliberate speed; second, in many areas of the South the process of desegregating the schools is a thing of the distant future. For the South, faced as it is in places with closure of public schools, the answer lies in whether or not public opinion will accept token integration in order to maintain the school system. On the other side of the issue opponents of integration have expressed the belief that resistance is gaining nation-wide sanction.

In North Carolina, Alabama, and in Nashville, Tennessee, "deliberate speed" has seemed to mean either pupil placement by boards of education or desegregation by grades. The situation is different in Georgia. On December 15, 1959, Representative Frank Twitty, floor leader of the Georgia House of Representatives, was reported as saying no immediate legislation would be passed to permit token integration in Georgia. This came in response to Judge Frank Hopper's statement that he intended to give the legislature an opportunity to devise plans to meet the Court's previous order applying to the Atlanta schools. At this time the problem of integration of Atlanta's schools, already set in motion by the courts, is still unresolved.

XIV

The Central Theme

Very little candid, truthful, and unprejudiced public discussion has yet been had on this vexed subject of slavery. The extremists of the South esteem their opponents as madmen, or robbers; and invariably misrepresent, misunderstand, and consequently, entirely fail to meet their arguments. The extremists of the North esteem the slaveholders as robbers and tyrants, willfully and malevolently oppressive and cruel, but I suppose more has been done, to prevent reasonable views and judicious action, by those, both North and South, who have held moderate and more reasonable opinions, than by those of either of the extreme parties. I mean that, in the endeavor to suppress agitation, they have produced an unhealthy distrust, and an unsound and dangerous condition of the public mind. In the feverish effort to secure peace, they have forgotten, as is now apparent, the easiest lessons of history and disregarded the simplest demands of prudence. "Men," says Macaulay, "are never so likely to settle a question rightly, as when they discuss it freely." The principle is at the basis of free institutions. Its reverse is the apex of despotism. The attempt to suppress discussion has given advantage to the unterrified partisans on both sides, who assume to fight for truth and rights.

OLMSTED, A JOURNEY IN THE SEABOARD SLAVE STATES, pp. 177–8

If a modern Olmsted, Tocqueville, or Archer traveled through the present South he would hear observations southerners were making a century ago, and he doubtless would hear the same social philosophy given expression. Even in this period of transition from agriculture to industry, and from a predominantly rural society to an expanding urbanism, the Negro remains a central theme of southern life. When the modern southerner speaks so vehemently about maintaining the southern way of life, he is not talking about old economic or regional folk patterns, for these have almost vanished; he has in mind one specific subject — racial relations.

In another way the Negro influence in the South has made itself felt. In the last decade and a half not one session of a legislature in the ex-slave states has failed to give the Negro serious attention. In fact, so much attention has been given this subject that many times lawmakers have overlooked other vital legislation. Even special sessions of legislatures have been called to consider the subject. No one will ever know how much committee meetings, interstate conferences, and the communication of all sorts of political groups have cost the South in dollars and cents. If this were spent in combating tuberculosis it would go far to eradicate the disease.

In a less formal way the Negro theme has colored casual conversations. One can scarcely spend an evening in the South without hearing it discussed. Less well-informed persons inject it into conversations in the form of anxious questions. They reveal both their fears and their prejudices in these questions. Some discussions reflect lack of confidence in a large part of the southern population itself to maintain racial integrity. Newspapers, regional periodicals, religious and educational publications, books, pamphlets, and broadsides all reflect the deep concern of the South with the place of the Negro in regional society.

A visitor coming to the South for the first time might get the impression that a powerful minority of people in the region with strong leadership capacity was bringing about a social renaissance. He would look for the driving force in the new industrialism for an explanation. He might reason that a fresh wave of democracy following World War II and the responsibilities of free-world leadership by the United States had created this condition. A better informed individual might reach the conclusion that the South arrived at its present stage of racial dilemma at a most unfortunate moment in its history. Not only does it face the enormous challenges wrought by changes in its general economic structure, but also by changes in social and political conditions in many parts of the world. Although the arguments of southern Senators and the reactions of southerners generally are against the Court in this trying moment, the external pressures, whether from northern politicians, the organized Negro, regional critics in general, or from undefined sources, are infinitely greater. They stem from the vast struggle for survival of the free world itself. If the basis of the present racial confusion were purely regional, then the solutions would be less complex, but it is not. This fact depresses the southerner more than he is able to express.

It would indeed be a sad mistake to consider the race problem in the South purely in the light of its current painful state. Many people of course considered slavery a paradox in a democratic society. However, it was the fatal lack of planning for the rehabilitation of the ex-slave following the Civil War that produced one of America's major social tragedies. However humane and astute the Lincoln Administration was, it did not provide properly for the freedom of the Negro. Even the most ardent abolitionist crusaders failed to deal with this important and vital problem. The whole process of reconstruction in which the Negro was used as a social and political pawn was a further tragedy. After reconstruction ended, ambitious politicians made use of him. He was largely disenfranchised, for, then as now, southern politicians preferred to deal with the smallest number of voters rather than try to sway large masses.

The troubled South compounded the difficulty in the years after reconstruction by allowing the horrible practice of lynching to become widespread. It was not countless victims of rope and fagot who suffered but rather the South's honor, self-respect, and peace of mind. No community which ever experienced a lynching could then say that it was morally or spiritually better off the next day. The deeper the South got into the brutal practice, the guiltier became the regional conscience. The South was caught in a trap from which it had great difficulty extricating itself, for lynching brought down upon it bitter criticism from all parts of the world. Even southern morals and Christianity were challenged; in general the region was put very much on the defensive. Lynching bred fear of possible Negro retaliation, which in turn was one of the basic excuses for the practice. But, deeper was the fear of a breakdown of the Anglo-Saxon system of justice, which in the long run would affect white southerners even more than Negroes.

An almost negligible number of southerners either committed or condoned lynching, but it was not the guilty individual who stood convicted. The South as a region was adjudged guilty, guilty at the doors of the governors, the legislatures, the courts, and the law-enforcement officers. No clear-thinking southerner who stood beneath a swaying body suspended from the limb of a tree and read the dangling placard inscribed with bitter hatred could excuse the act. Lynching was a savage act in the light of every tenet of the Christian way of life, and of every principle of an established system of justice. Repeatedly southern representatives opposed federal anti-lynching legislation, not because they condoned the act, but because they realized their political future depended on such a stand. In a less selfish way they realized that such legislation would charge the South officially with sinning against the laws of humanity.

Gradually the South has stemmed the crime of lynching. Southerners emphasize this fact when they attempt to show how the South was making headway in solving its race problems even before 1954. But the South is not given such great credit for halting this practice, for people outside the region and elsewhere in the world have looked upon lynching as such a gross form of lawlessness and violence that it never should have been countenanced in the first place. And even today the practice has not been completely wiped out. The lynching of Mack Charles Parker at Poplarville, Mississippi, on April 26, 1959, shocked people everywhere. Newspapers carried the story emblazoned in bold headlines. The failure to bring the murderers to justice made non-southerners doubt the efficacy of southern progress in this area.

Changes wrought by World War II were of tremendous importance to the postwar South. Not only was the Negro called upon to do his part at home and in the armed forces, and not only was he told that he was a full beneficiary of the advantages of a democratic society in which he lived, but he was helped by the emotional racist campaign of Nazism, which the American government was actively combating. Parallel to this was the rising world resistance to colonialism unleashed by the war. This anti-colonial movement was directed not only against imperialism but against discrimination against minorities; indeed, the two were equated by the newly emergent powers. It has been the United States Government, not the South or a single state, which has had to answer these charges when they have been leveled against either the South or the nation as a whole. In answering these charges of discrimination and colonialism the Government has incurred the wrath of southern extremists as well as the gibes of the new nations which raised the issues. Thus the South finds itself suddenly caught in an international net which it had not known existed.

For the southern Negro the changing world situation has had deep implications. For the first time his position as a minority person has been emphasized, and he has found powerful world support from other minority groups, who have asked many embarrassing questions of a nation trying desperately hard to maintain a foreign policy which professes a point of view favorable to the protection of minority rights. Thus the cause of the southern Negro suddenly becomes a national issue involving the delicate balance of the United States before a free world.

On the local domestic scene one of the most confusing of all issues was the "place" of the Negro in southern society. His position in the regional social system was poorly defined from the beginning, but, as years passed, it became a more highly restrictive one. This was especially true as Jim Crow laws and folk customs forced him into a perpetual condition of retreat. Modern social relocation of the Negro in the South has helped shatter the old folk pattern, a fact which has done great violence to the old ways of life.

The issue of status is important in the South's present racial turmoil. Once the Negro's position was defined by a casual and indifferent social relationship with the white man which involved every aspect of his life. The white man seldom bothered to define the bounds of the Negro's place. In some instances they were broad, and in others they were extremely narrow, but whatever they were, they were exercised in day-to-day personal relationships. Once these were disrupted, the Negro turned to the federal courts and the Constitution for a more precise definition of his place, not in a community nor in relationships with specific white men, but in a democracy and a world society. The courts have been more specific in their definitions in this area than the old system could have ever tolerated. The old casualness has been destroyed, and in its place has been substituted the force of law and its interpretation.

Since 1945 there has been a systematic effort to lower discriminatory barriers in areas where Jim Crow laws bound the Negro's freedom of social action in the older South. The first important area in which this has been done is at the polls. Negro leadership knows full well that its toughest fight is to gain full and accepted rights to participate freely in politics in the South. The race has a long, bitter history behind it in the ordeal of exercising its right to vote. It knows the well-nigh insurmountable legal barriers which presently bar Negroes from the polls in some states, or the numerous clever subterfuges which can turn them out the side door without the ballot. Their great-grandfathers learned almost all of these things when they were victimized by both radical Republicans and defiant white southerners in the fight to control the southern vote during the reconstruction era.

The Negro remembers the bitter struggle over his voting franchise in those grim days of the subsequent Populist crusade. He knows intimately what Theodore G. Bilbo meant in Mississippi, in the first round in the courts over white primaries, when he said that if the circuit clerks of Mississippi did not know how to keep the Negroes from registering then he could show them. On the other hand southern politicians were not oblivious to the fact that admission of Negroes to the polls would bring their careers to abrupt ends. Doubtless the whole approach to the voters in the campaign in the South would be diametrically changed if the Negro voted. A good contrast is that between political campaigns in Kentucky and Georgia. A Kentucky politician shouting racial defiance from the stump would only be hastening his defeat. In September 1959 the two gubernatorial candidates in Kentucky were quick to shout "No!" to a Centre College student's question of whether or not they would favor closing the public schools rather than integrating them. This was in sharp contrast to attitudes expressed by candidates in the Georgia and Mississippi gubernatorial campaigns.

Sometime in the future the Negro, after a massive amount of civil rights legislation, commission investigation, platform writing by the two parties, and court action, will finally remove barriers to his voting. However, he has a tremendous handicap to overcome. First, the mass of southern Negroes must be educated at least to the extent that they can pass a moderate high school test in citizenship. It will not be sufficient defense for the Negro to point out that literally thousands of white voters fall far below the standards set for Negro voters, for it is he who is faced with the fight to gain the right to vote. One of the most difficult issues is the educational requirements for registration. There may be no objection to setting an educational requirement at a level in keeping with national educational attainment of the mass of the population, but if it is used for discriminatory purposes then it is being prostituted.

Before the Negro in general reaches the stage where he can exert an appreciable influence at the polls, he will have to generate enough interest among his people to get large numbers of them to undergo the exasperations of registering and then of appearing at the polls to cast their votes. The Negro not only shares the southern white man's apathy toward voting, but he suffers from an ingrained fear of white retribution toward "smart" Negroes who insist on voting.

An impartial observer in the present South could hardly fail to sense that it is only by gaining access to the polls that the Negro can hope to make more rapid progress as a free and competitive citizen. Desegregation of public schools is by comparison of secondary importance. Whether or not the schools are desegregated now or at some unforeseeable date in the future, however, does not mean that the Negro will stand still educationally. But until he gains full access to the polls and uses this right he obviously will stand still politically.

In erecting barriers to the Negro's registering and voting, extremist southerners are possibly doing more than any other Americans to hasten the day when he will vote. This was implicit in Governor John Battle's plea with the Alabama registration officials in December 1959 to deliver the Macon County voter records. For while public opinion in the nation might be somewhat reluctant to push desegregation of the public school system faster than wise and lasting adjustments can be made, hardly anyone outside the South would look favorably upon the attempt to keep free Americans away from the polls, no matter what their social or educational background. Repeatedly this argument was made in the civil rights debate in the United States Senate, both in 1957 and 1960. Senators who were not as emotionally aroused over the legal technicalities of the pending bill in 1957 as were some partisans on both sides of the great debate reiterated the point of view that the ballot must be kept free. Senator Edward Thye of Minnesota, for instance, in querying Senator John McClellan of Arkansas, said, "It is late Saturday afternoon, and here on the floor of the Senate my concern is that every American citizen shall have equal rights as a citizen. I care not of what race, color, or creed he may be. That is the first point. The first premise of my public service is to try to make possible that each one share in the blessedness of this government equally with all others." The right to vote has come to be considered an inherent right of a free people, and before the world court of public opinion Americans cannot refrain from accepting the proposition that all their people are free.

It is one of the anomalies of American politics that while the Negro, slave and free, has been a basic political issue in the South since the adoption of the Missouri Compromise in 1820, his vote has rarely had any real consequence, except during reconstruction. This has been especially true in areas where the Negro population has greatly outnumbered the white. Yet the Negro has disturbed both the polls and legislative halls as a troubled ghost of the American democratic system. He has never been present in spirit in greater and more disturbing force than in the great debate over civil rights in the United States Senate in the hot summer of 1957 and again in February 1960. In the lengthy debates, Senator Paul Douglas of Illinois accused Senator Russell Long of Louisiana, and southerners in general, of being victims of a Freudian guilt complex.

On July 13, Senator John McClellan discussed what might be considered one of the central issues so far as the southern opposition was concerned. He said, "This bill has been advanced primarily to affect the protection of voting rights. But this bill will affect a far wider field, and whether it is intentional or not, this bill would have a terrific impact on the problem of integrating the schools." Later he said, "Thus, under the doctrine of the Brown case, if a Negro could show that two or more persons conspired to refuse or prohibit or prevent his attendance at an integrated public school, he could sue either one of them or both of them for damages. That is the law, that is one of the results of the Supreme Court's decision in the Brown case." Senator McClellan believed that under the proposed act the Attorney General of the United States could file an application for an injunction at the opening of schools, and that, "on the first day of school, if the situation had not been taken care of, a number of fine citizens would either be subject to being brought into court and arbitrarily tried, fined, and sent to jail for contempt of such a court order."

In the debate the southerners presented long and legalistic discussions of the development of trial by jury. The better informed lawyers among them spent considerable time discussing the technicalities of contempt offenses against the law in equity. The earlier debates became so involved in historical and legal phraseology that the right to vote was almost overlooked. However, the nub of the whole debate, despite the offending Section III, which threatened removal in vote-denial cases of the right of trial by jury, was whether or not Negroes were allowed to exercise freely the right to vote in all of the southern states. If Negro rights were denied, would southern white juries, upon the presentation of such facts, find for the plaintiffs?

On July 8, 1957, in the midst of the first debate, Senator Richard B. Russell of Georgia was challenged on a C.B.S. public affairs program by a reporter, who wanted to know whether it was true that when an all-white jury was voting on the rights of a Negro voter, the latter had little chance of winning. Senator Russell replied, "Well, that's one of the common slanders that's been repeated against the South without a word of evidence to substantiate it. You have got a number of criminal statutes on your books now where it is made a violation of criminal law, punishable by imprisonment and fine to interfere with the voting rights of any citizen. Now the South is entitled to have at least some proof brought forward of this charge that it is repeatedly bandied that every southern white man is so irresponsible that he would forswear himself or perjure himself in a case involving a Negro citizen."

The Georgia senator further maintained that there was no difficulty involved in his home state about the Negro's voting. He said, "I deny the statement as to voting. At least, as far as the greater portion of the South is concerned, there is no real limitation or restriction on the rights of qualified Negroes to vote." The issue of this statement might center on a definition of the word "qualified." It was this point to which Senator Douglas addressed himself on July 26 when he published in the Congressional *Record* a summary of Negro voting in the South made by the Southern Regional Council. This did not take sharp issue with Senator Russell's statements, but it did discuss the arduous and disheartening course which Negroes in many southern counties had to pursue to become qualified voters, and their responsibilities for keeping their names on the voter rolls after they were registered.

In this connection, the editor of the Colfax *Chronicle* of Grant Parish, Louisiana, on October 12, 1956, made a rather astounding observation. He said that members of the local Citizens Council had re-examined the voter rolls and had removed the names of many Negro voters. The president of the local Council, W. J. B. Jones, was reported to have said that his group voted unanimously to purge Negro voters, and an estimate was made that 90 per cent of the Negro registrants were challenged. The *Chronicle*'s editor checked the first 100 white registrants' cards and found only one that would meet the exacting standards set for Negroes. He reported that not a single member of the Citizens Council committee had filled out his card correctly by the Council's standards.

Some states have used clever subterfuges to prevent the registration of Negro voters or to disqualify large blocks of voters once they are registered. In February 1959, the Associated Press reported that some Louisiana officials had plans under way to remove the names of over 100,000 people from the voting rolls of that state, but State Senator W. R. Rainach was reported as having said that, "Many would-be Negro voters would be eliminated for each white person affected." The device suggested would start with a long and complicated application form which applicants would be required to complete without help or benefit of notes and in their own handwriting. The second hurdle would be a request for applicants to interpret any section of the Louisiana or United States constitutions which the registrars might select, and the registrars in turn would judge whether or not applicants had interpreted the constitution correctly. Any mistake in form or fact would subject the applicant to disqualification and would prevent his name from being inscribed on the voting rolls. Future challengers would be empowered to scrutinize the applications of successful registrants for possible errors which had been overlooked. This sort of device is a ready-made one for arousing a widespread national opinion hostile to the South, and one which inevitably will lead to the enactment of sterner federal civil-rights legislation. The Commission on Civil Rights reported that the *Manual of Procedure for Registrars of Voters* carried a foreword which attacked the NAACP and its attempt to increase the registration of Negro voters. Its "Key to Victory" said, "We are in a life and death struggle with the Communists and the NAACP to maintain segregation and to preserve the liberties of our people. The impartial enforcement of our laws is the KEY TO VICTORY in this struggle."

In Georgia there was considerable reaction to the NAACP's threat to register three million Negro voters in the South. Numerous legislative means for preventing the registration of Negro voters have been proposed. If the present voter registration measures were strictly enforced, few people, white or black, educated or illiterate, would be able to register. In some instances registration laws do little more than suspend a legal axe over voters' heads. Individual applications can be reviewed as often in the future as challengers might wish to do so. Characteristic of some of this legislation was that outlined in 1957 by representative Peter Zack Geer of Colquitt County, Georgia. This proposal ultimately became the basis for the revised Georgia registration law. The law placed the right to vote largely in the field of social behavior. Prospective voters would be barred if they were parents of illegitimate children or parties to common-law marriages, or were accused of child abandonment or of possessing and transporting moonshine liquor, had failed to register or report for military service, had been adjudged guilty of bigamy, adultery, false swearing, or of committing a felony. Mr. Geer was said to have commented that 90 per cent of the adult Negroes of Georgia were guilty of adultery or bigamy, and 30 per cent were guilty of liquor violations. Besides these moral questions, applicants for voter registration would be asked thirty content questions which would range from, "What is the definition of a felony under Georgia Law?" to "What does the Constitution of the United States provide regarding the right of a citizen to vote?" A full answer to the latter question might incriminate the whole procedure.

The main feature of the Civil Rights Act of 1957 was the provision for the creation of a Commission on Civil Rights to "investigate allegations in writing as under oath or affirmation that certain citizens of the United States are being deprived of their right to vote and have that vote counted by reason of color, race, religion, or national origin." The Commission was instructed to collect information on vote discrimination, and to appraise the laws and policies of the Federal Government as to equal protection of the laws under the Constitution. Within two years the Commission was to report its findings and recommendations to the President and Congress. This Commission soon began holding hearings on alleged violations of voting rights in the South.

Judge Walter Geer of Colquitt County Superior Court threatened to jail Federal Bureau of Investigation agents and other federal investigators if they persisted in their efforts to examine voter records. Registrars and other voter officials were instructed not to allow federal investigators to see voting lists. Judge Geer said he believed the Terrell County suit, the first filed under the 1957 Civil Rights Act, was "arrogant, unwarranted, and highhanded."

A second case was filed against the registrars of Macon County, Alabama, and in turn against the State of Alabama in February 1959. In the Alabama case Judge Frank M. Johnson, Jr., held that the Federal Civil Rights Law was not broad enough to apply to the prosecution of a state for its violation. In the Terrell County case argued before Judge T. Hoys Davis, the court held that the law was so broad as to be considered unconstitutional. Thus two cases were sent to higher courts which took diametrically opposite points of view toward the effect of the Civil Rights Act of 1957.

The *Report* of the Civil Rights Commission in 1959 is an enlightening document which sets out much of the problem of removing barriers to voters in several of the southern states. In 1959 the Commission reported on three aspects of the problem of civil rights. These were voting, education and housing.

It found that to a large extent discrimination in these fields was of a racial nature. There was only one exception where vote denial was not "by reason of race or color." Heart of the Civil Rights Commission *Report* is the observation that "prejudice will not be cured by concentrating constantly on the discrimination. It may be cured, or reduced, or at least forgotten, if sights can be raised to new and challenging targets. Thus a curriculum designed to educate young Americans for this unfolding twentieth-century world, with better teachers and better schools, will go a long way to facilitate the transition of public education. Equal opportunity in housing will come more readily as part of a great program of urban reconstruction and regeneration. The right to vote will more easily be secured throughout the whole South if there are great issues on which people want to vote."

The Civil Rights Act of 1960 did not stir up quite as much furor in Congress, but at the same time it was far milder in the form passed by the House of Representatives than was the earlier act with its Point III section. The new law made three major provisions: (1) educational facilities in federal installations were to be desegregated; (2) bombings of schools and churches were made a federal offense; (3) in places where Negroes found it either too difficult or impossible to register, federal registrars would be appointed to register voters who wished to vote in federal elections. This law solves only a part of the registration problem, and actually does little toward insuring the right to vote. There is a tremendous gulf between being registered to vote and actually voting. The new law still leaves room for all sorts of intimidation and subterfuge.

Participation in the political affairs of the South is possibly one of the most important goals which the Negro might hope to achieve. His achievement of this goal, however, makes greater demands on him educationally than is made of the white man. He has to erase as many of the old prejudices against him as possible in the shortest time. The idea has persisted for generations, aided by a defective educational system, that he is incapable of making political decisions. Education is after all the only means by which he may hope to achieve his free political rights, or to compete in the race for industrial jobs in the South.

The new southern industrial employer cannot afford to tolerate ignorance and illiteracy among his employees. One mistake on the part of a laborer in a plant might consume a considerable block of profits, if not endanger the lives and property of the entire labor force and plant. Whatever industrial management's philosophy of wages might be, it is certainly not that of the old agricultural landlord. No allowances are made in a highly competitive business for the wastes and inefficiencies customary in the old way of life. The new southern industry, like industry everywhere, must concern itself with efficiency in production if it is to compete successfully in the market places.

The new southern industrialism has brought promise of greater change in the area of demands on labor than in any other field. Since the opening of the nineteenth century, the South has been content to accept an adverse ratio of culture and efficiency level from that maintained by people in some of the other sections of the country. Consequently southerners have long accepted the humiliation of unfavorable social and cultural statistics as a matter of course. They have shrugged off the great social imbalance by saying that the low position of the South in numerous standards of measurement was due to the large Negro population. But now that the new industry has made certain social and cultural demands on the South, the region can no longer afford to let this element of the population set a regional standard.

The southern Negro's economic condition has changed radically. He, in fact, has often to demonstrate a greater competence than a white applicant for a job in order to overcome racial prejudice against him. Thus education suddenly has become his fundamental means of moving from the old economic system into the new. Again the Negro's crusade for better opportunities has the support of a general world struggle to control men's minds. His cause is helped by the near panic at this point for advancing American educational efforts at all levels, and by the fact that national safety itself is involved in educational progress of all the American people. So for the southern Negro the equality of educational opportunity has far more meaning than the mere matter of social desegregation. It carries with it a heavier responsibility, and demands greater effort of him than of past generations of his race. He has to wipe away by achievement the fixed notion that he is incapable of meeting the challenge of the white man's society.

The modern Negro in the South is called upon to have enormous patience. Scarcely a month goes by that he does not see or hear himself abused by someone in the public press, on the radio, or in the handbills and pamphlets which peddle racial hatred. Every opening session of the public schools drags him before the public, and frequently he is labeled an inferior person incapable of improving himself. Charges are sometimes made that he is being misled by the Communists and Communist-front organizations. The charge of Communist infiltration into the NAACP has been disproved. In his book *Masters of Deceit*, FBI Director J. Edgar Hoover has a clear-cut statement on this issue.

In this era of change, with emotions running so high, it is difficult to assess with any degree of accuracy the full impact of the race issue on the region's future. Two facts, however, seem to stand out beyond reasonable challenge. The Negro has as secure a place in the history of the South as does the white man, and he is in the South to stay. It is true, of course, that large numbers of Negroes migrate annually to other sections of the country, but this does not mean that they are deserting the South as a race.

Southern cultural history bears the deep stamp of both slave and free Negro. Sectional economics have been largely conditioned by Negro labor, and regional humor and folk culture have been enriched by the imaginative language and customs of the Negro. Religious reactions have reflected the fact that the Negro too has a soul worthy of salvation. The physical organization of the early churches took this fact into consideration. In fact the whole moral code of the South was long ago shaped to include the Negro, if for no other reason than that of preserving law and order. In a more fundamental way southern white and Negro lives have developed a common interest, and the two races have a common regional sentimentality.

Many white southerners have long assumed that they have an inborn understanding of the Negro. It is a novel thing indeed that many white men are quick to declare that they understand the Negro, while it is a rare occasion when a Negro will boast that he understands the white man. In fact the Negro's precise knowledge of his white neighbors is perhaps many folds greater than is white understanding of the Negro. Oftentimes this constant protestation of understanding closely resembles whistling past a darkened social graveyard. The plain truth perhaps is that few or no white southerners truly understand their Negro neighbors. Often individuals claim knowledge of the race, but a closer examination reveals that it is based on little more than associations with Negroes on a single farm or with household servants.

Human understanding involves a large number of factors, including knowledge of personality traits and innermost emotions and a sharing of ideas and beliefs and troubles and disappointments. Above all, it means a thoroughgoing intellectual honesty must come into play. Southerners know that large numbers of Negroes nearly always put the best possible interpretation on situations when discussing issues with white people. They nearly always make less than a full statement of their innermost reactions toward their social problems and personal frustrations. Sometimes under certain conditions of extreme provocation a Negro will make an angry protest. But calm and dependable opinions can be had only when Negroes obtain enough education to permit them to share opinions and to discuss problems with objectivity and a degree of economic security. White southerners on the whole have been more garrulous and emotional, and they have freely revealed their feelings. The Negro on the other hand has been a victim of fear and has most often remained silent. To speak out of turn could mean serious consequences for him, maybe even loss of life.

Failure of free and full communication between whites and Negroes has become a deep social tragedy in the South. Since the days of slavery, the Negro's word against that of a white man has had little or no worth, and, partly because of this, Negroes have feared retributions of various sorts. By long tradition southern whites have generally remained away from Negro assemblies. Once slave and master shared a common communion in churches, but after the Civil War this ceased to be true. It is true that Negroes have stood on the outskirts of political gatherings and listened to political orations. They even gathered on the fringes of the Bilbo audiences to hear him excoriate their race in the bitterest of language. Even so, there has been much to Thomas

Nelson Page's contention that close friendships prevailed between southern whites and individual Negroes. Long years of peaceful associations at work and in community relationships document this fact. It is in this area that the present South must rebuild harmonious social relationships. Here is the place where the greatest immediate gains in the future have to be made. Lines of communication must be re-established, and the two races will have to approach their mutual problems with good faith and intellectual honesty. This places upon leadership of both races a rather heavy burden of allaying extremist emotions, of erasing old scars of disharmony, and of making compromises which will actually show that southerners can and will solve their problems democratically and equitably.

Nevertheless the deep underlying fear between the two races must be overcome. Few rural southerners over fifty years of age have not heard in their youth rumors that a race riot was imminent. Country newspapers of half a century ago carried hints of the prevailing anxieties in various communities over this fact. The pro-segregationist literature of the present also contains a tone of fear of the Negro. Possibly no negative fact between the two races is so thoroughly established as the white man's fear of the Negro sexual lust. Based upon strict objective facts of history, the fear should be the other way around, but no clearly defined and dependable notion seems to prevail either privately or in print as to how the Negro man might feel toward the white man's violation of the Negro woman.

It may be that the nearest statement of feeling of Negroes is to be found in a book published by the University of North Carolina Press entitled *What the Negro Wants*. Some of the essays in this book outline more clearly than ever before the Negro's position in regard to this ticklish aspect of southern social relationships. In his *Caste and Class in a Southern Town* John Dollard likewise discusses racial sexual relationships with a high degree of frankness and assurance. Many lynching victims between the years 1880 and 1915 bore placards strung about their necks proclaiming rape as a major cause for lynching. Dependable research, however, has disproved this contention. Murder and assault were the major provocations, but behind these crimes were the abject fears of the white South of the Negro.

This was a fear engendered in the region as early as the Denmark Vesey and Nat Turner rebellions.

Fears of race riots have largely disappeared over the years. When the last of the bitterest of the old political race-baiters like James K. Vardaman, Ben Tillman, and Thomas E. Watson passed on, much of this lurking fear was dissipated. It passed out with the halting of lynching, and with periodic threats of the passage of federal anti-lynching legislation. The explanation of this changing phase of southern social history no doubt lies more closely in the fact that the South is speaking less and less with its frontier voice and has seen great changes in its basic economic structure.

In the present South, the age-old fears are expressed differently. The charge that compliance with the 1954 Supreme Court decision would bring about a commingling and mongrelization of the races has a background in the old fears that resulted in frequent lynchings. Historically large numbers of white men have not been able to trust themselves in the presence of Negro women, and they appear to be certain that intimate and casual relationships in the classroom will rip away the racial barrier. Roy Wilkins, speaking for the NAACP on the television program "Meet the Press" in 1958, answered a question about mongrelization by saying that the presence of so large a number of mulattoes in American society indicates that concern over the mongrelization issue is fully two centuries too late.

If the southern white man has an inborn fear of the Negro, he also has deep suspicion of the intentions of northerners. Just as it has been said that many southerners like the individual Negro and fear the race, it may be said they are fond of the individual northerner and suspect his tribe. Southerners have difficulty in this modern age deciding who the Yankee is. Is he *Life, Time, Look,* and the other slick magazines? Is he nine members of the United States Supreme Court, the NAACP, Adam Clayton Powell, Senator Paul Douglas, Hubert Humphrey, G. Mennen Williams, or Henry and Clare Boothe Luce, or Mrs. Eleanor Roosevelt? Geographically the southerner has difficulty in locating the North. In his mind its centers are New York, Detroit, Chicago, and maybe Los Angeles. But it may be any place where criticism of the South originates. It might even be in Memphis, if such were the case. Possibly there is no physical line, but it is to be located more specifically in terms of emotions, social attitudes, and political reactions. It is the point where often blind prejudices shade off into a doctrinaire certainty of a single solution to the problems of the South.

Everywhere southerners seek to sort out the Yankees: in social gatherings, in business dealings, in politics, and in public discussions. A group of South Carolina high school boys returning from a brief training period at the Great Lakes Training Base asks a Delta Airlines stewardess almost pleadingly whether or not she is a Yankee. It is the eternal triangle of the Negro, the Yankee, and the southern conscience which causes emotional struggle over the age-old issue of the southern way of life.

The South cannot exist happily, if at all, without the nation, and the nation in turn is dependent upon the South. Somewhere calm and responsible leadership must prevail to solve the larger issues of the race problem. The South can ill afford to continue to waste its emotional energies and further expend its precious resources in the negative approaches used since 1954 without suffering irreparable damages. Extremists on both sides of the issue have yet to offer durable solutions to racial confusions. The solution lies almost solely in the area of the repeated and implied promises that the South can find the answers to its problems. The finding of these answers, however, places a heavy and positive responsibility upon both social and political leadership to take a careful look at the region's needs and then attempt to bring about solutions in the best of faith and by the sanest possible legislation. The challenge is even greater to everyday citizens, churchmen, newspaper editors, educators, and businessmen. Solutions, however, cannot be accomplished in an atmosphere of bitter denunciation, denial of the law, threatened economic and social boycott and retribution, or dynamitings and other forms of violence.

The negative approach to solving the South's racial issues has the pressure of history against it. On the positive side there is enough calm leadership and dignity in the South to face the current social issues without flinching. It can, of course, by patience and use of good judgment find the answers to all of the region's problems. They will not be simple answers easily arrived at, but they will set the foot of the South on the road to progress.

No one can write a prescription for solving so complex and ancient a problem as that which faces the South at the moment. It seems, however, reasonable to make some general assumptions. Southerners are unaccustomed to gauging the complexity of the race problems — and others as well — on the basis of a full statistical consideration. As a result, they more often than not lose perspective in viewing actual conditions. For instance, it has been the experience of the border areas where schools have been desegregated that Negroes have not flocked to integrated classes in overwhelming numbers. Actually little more than token registrations have occurred. Too, there is a sobering lesson in the fact that these desegregated schools, including Norfolk, Virginia, have been free of unhappy incidents. Where traditionally white universities and colleges have opened their classrooms to Negroes, remarkably small numbers have registered. The more accurate gauge is to be found in the enrollment of Negro colleges, and there is at present no indications that a reduction has or will occur at any time in the foreseeable future. Again, in the political area, the Negro has neither broken nor altered the political behavior pattern of a community where he has exercised his freedom to vote. There has been little if any bloc voting. Sometimes one would conclude from the arguments of the extremists that the Negro has a capacity for leadership and change which the white man does not possess. By the sheer matter of statistics the Negro, except in certain intensely colored areas of the old blackbelt, can hardly alter the political picture in the dire way predicted by the prophets of doom.

The South's economic and social life has been developed around the two races. Both have made major contributions to the region, and a calm and objective evaluation of these contributions offers a key to future peaceful relationships. To attempt to write off or belittle Negro contributions to southern culture would be akin to disowning the contributions of large segments of the white race itself. Here is a broad common ground for the two races to base a positive and mutual respect for the accomplishments of each other.

XV

The Dilemma

As the present policy so madly pursued has departed from the principles of Democracy and the old Democratic party, so that the words of Jefferson would now hang a man anywhere at the South, I do not much doubt that when reaction comes, the principles on which Jefferson desired to deal with slavery will be found eminently safe and profitable. There would still be extremist; there would be fanatics and fools; there would be great difference of opinion as to the ultimate destiny of the negro race, and as to the final disappearance of slavery, and difference of judgment among moderate men as to measures; but the common.sense of the South would be seconded by the common sense of the North, and would receive the respect of the world. . . .
    OLMSTED, A JOURNEY IN THE BACK COUNTRY, pp. 481–2

In my Mississippi county seat town I drove past a handsome grove which is now a city park. Here beneath the stately trees, James K. Vardaman harangued his red-necked constituents for hours. And they stood in rapt attention listening to his sonorous outpourings, nodding in approval, or growling in anger when he denounced their exploiters. Pacing the green pine plank stage mounted atop an eight-wheel log wagon, the Great White Father played the poor countryman's Hamlet. In a highly alliterative style of speaking, he swayed his audiences with the assured talent of a master tragedian. He gave his hearers both pathos and hate, never allowing them to lose sight of the Vardaman objectives of white supremacy and political triumph. He was quick in repartee and wise in the workings of the minds of farmers burdened with the perplexities of cotton economics. His issues were stated in sharp personal attacks on his enemies, real and imagined, against corporations which were as vague to his hearers as his allusions to Wall Street, and in promises of help for the common man burning to a crisp on a Mississippi hillside.

His was not a campaign of specifics anyway. Both he and his noisy supporters knew that a revolution would have to occur before either would find life easier. Vardaman could always attack the Negro with safety from the recriminations of opponents. His colorful speech was adapted to the forceful uttering of age-old clichés and bitter epithets. He knew his audience lived in fear of racial uprisings, and he could strike deep notes in his subtle references to lurking dangers.

Following in the old master's footsteps in this park came Theodore G. Bilbo to cut a host of political enemies down to size. This blue-eyed crusader in many ways played a miniature Falstaff who used self-pity and personal abuse skillfully. Planted hecklers in his audiences were in fact prompters who egged the old boy on to higher levels of attack and ridicule. But the performances of Bilbo, though fully as long-winded as Vardaman's, were never as monotonous. He never allowed *non sequiturs* to break his spell. There in the old park he outlined the wonderful scheme of building Mississippi better roads. Bricks would be made by convicts from the state's clay hillsides, and then fabricated, still by convicts, into model highways so that farmers and their families could go to market, to church, to a political rally, and even to hell on a decent road. When some doubting Thomas in the audience retorted that the bricks would wear out, Bilbo had a ready answer. The convicts would turn them over so they could wear out on the other side; then when they were worn out on that side, they would be turned bottoms up and worn thin from that angle. This involved intricacies of mind over matter, and no one in Bilbo's audiences seemed to want to solve the riddle of the revolving bricks, or ask why there were so many convicts to keep them turning. It was wonderful to stand there under the shade of the trees and hear the little man spin his clever web to trap red-neck voters.

Bilbo's flashing blue eyes swept the farmer audience as shrewdly as his hearers surveyed their cotton fields. From boyhood I listened to "The Man" lay his spleen on the particular line which currently agitated him. It was here that I heard him castigate Huey P. Long for encroaching on his Mississippi preserves with his Share-the-Wealth program. Bilbo knew there was little danger that Long would injure him, but here was an exposed and defenseless head to be beaten bloody without fear of political recriminations. He knew that he could kill the "Kingfish" politically with the people in that or any other grove in Mississippi by reciting the refrain that the secretaries of several Share-the-Wealth clubs in the state were "damned niggers."

Vardaman's and Bilbo's voices have been stilled, but their key issue, the race problem, still agitates the people of the South. The Supreme Court decision in 1954 touched off a wave of defensive groups in the South. Just as if the calendar had been put in reverse and the region had reverted to the period of reconstruction, the future of the southern way of life seemed hinged on a highly organized resistance to the Supreme Court and other outside attackers. Not even reconstruction itself brought about the formation of so many defensive groups. Among the twentieth-century resisters are the Federation of Constitutional Government, the Grass Roots League, Inc., the Virginia League, The Federation of Defenders of State Sovereignty and Individual Liberties, American State's Rights Association, The State's Rights Council of Georgia, Inc., The Society for the Preservation of State Government and Racial Integrity, White American, Inc., and the National Citizen's Protective Association. None, however, is so powerful as the White Citizens Council, or Citizens Council, which operates in several southern states.

The first Citizens Council was organized in Indianola, Mississippi, in 1954. A preliminary meeting was held on July 11, when fourteen men of the delta country met to discuss the South's educational future in the light of the recent Supreme Court decision. Leading spirits in this meeting were D. H. Hawkins and Robert Patterson. Later, at a public meeting of a hundred people in the Indianola city hall, the first Citizens Council was organized.

Patterson, a farmer and former football player at Mississippi State University, aroused over the possibility of the Supreme Court handing down a decision destroying segregation, had begun an active letter-writing campaign. It was his local effort, however, which got immediate results. Once the Citizens Council was organized, he became its secretary and organizer. He not only appeared in many counties to help organize new chapters, but from the Associate Citizens Council office in Winona he directed the mailing of pro-segregation material in the form of pamphlets, leaflets, and open letters. Senator James Eastland's speech and resolution to the United States Senate, Judge Tom P. Brady's *Black Monday*, Attorney General Eugene Cook's *The Ugly Truth About the NAACP*, Thomas E. Watson's *Equality, Can Man Improve on God?* and *The White Sentinel*, and many other pieces of literature of like nature were sent out from Winona.

The Citizens Council movement began in the delta blackbelt. Since this section was first settled, the land has been devoted intensively to the growing of cotton. Here large numbers of slaves were concentrated. After the Civil War, the freedman remained as a tenant farmer, and, indeed, there was a remarkable kinship between the master of slave days and the bossman after the war. In few other places in the United States have paternalism and its peculiar human controls been so vital to the social lives of people. To understand this fact is to appreciate the tremendous shock of the Supreme Court decision.

The Citizens Council movement, said an early folder, is "dedicated to the maintenance of peace, good order and domestic tranquility in our communities and in our state, to the preservation of state's rights." Four committees were established to deal with education and information, politics and elections, membership, legal and advisory matters. Their object was to help correct the grievances created by "nine political appointees." Readers of the prospectus were informed that their communities needed a Citizens Council just as they needed health and fire departments. If they had no immediate race problem, they could soon expect to have one, because the "NAACP, aided by alien influences, bloc-vote-seeking politicians and left-wing do-gooders will see that you have a problem in the near future." Washington, Jefferson, and Lincoln were called in to testify on the subject of segregation. With their backing, the Citizens Council chose to follow "the old paths of our founding fathers and [to] refuse to destroy ancient landmarks to appease anyone, even the internationalists. This integration scheme ties right in with the new, one world, one creed, one race philosophy fostered by ultra-idealists and international left-wingers." The organization proposed to pit 40 million white southerners against 200,000 members of the NAACP in a battle to the finish.

The Citizens Council organizations spread rapidly in several southern states. Early organizational meetings were secret, even organizers were sometimes unknown to early members. There prevailed a philosophy of keeping the Negro confused and guessing. As the Councils became more numerous and better established, they operated openly. It is doubtful, however, that a dissenting individual could have challenged statements made at meetings, or could have discussed dispassionately the race problem, or advocated doing nothing to prevent a peaceable settlement of the major issue. Speakers tended to be sensational and inflammatory, and, if their speeches were reported correctly in the local papers, they erred in facts of history and political science.

It would be difficult to document specifically any appreciable part of the charges that the Councils have generated economic and social reprisal against both white and colored people. There are bits of evidence, however, that this is true. Speakers, including Congressman John Bell Williams of Mississippi, have suggested economic pressures. It is now true that many people are afraid to discuss racial relations. If they do so in a liberal way and it becomes known, they are apt to be fired from their jobs. Persons who discuss conditions most often plead that what they say must not be repeated because they might lose both jobs and peace of mind. Ministers in some places have been visited by members of the local Council, who have sought to curb their remarks from the pulpit. One of the most disturbing means of intimidation is use of the anonymous telephone call. Businessmen and educators have been subjected to pressure both by letter and oral threats. Casual remarks, some made in jest, have jeopardized their authors. In many places in the South, tension and fear prevail, affecting everybody from the humblest individual to teacher, preacher, and public official.

In areas where the Council or kindred body is active, it would be political suicide for a candidate or public official to voice a contrary opinion. The Council prospectus says that one of the organization's objectives is screening candidates for office to see that none goes far who holds an independent point of view. If none of the things mentioned above could be charged against the Council, it could still be called to account for the tragic destruction of inter-racial communication in the South. There is in the organized point of view a self-defeating spirit of reaction, the tarnishing of a fine regional reputation for liberality and fair play, an irrational approach to the solution of complex and highly sensitive social problems, and a lowering of respect for constituted government. To this list might be added a deterrent to the full application of Christianity.

Organization of the Citizens Council has created one of the South's perplexing paradoxes. Repeatedly, the claim is made that the Supreme Court acted illegally and unconstitutionally in the 1954 decision. But how can the Court act illegally or unconstitutionally? Since 1789 the American political system has recognized the Court as the final arbiter of our law. If the issue is, as some claim, the failure of the Constitution to mention public education, then the answer is that it does not mention steamboats and railroads, public health, organized religion, or agricultural legislation, yet the Court has decided cases in all these areas. Economic boycott, coercion of candidates, and a defiance of the law of the land all refute the basic contention of the Council's legal and peaceful intent. It is the Council and not the Court which seems to be acting extra-legally.

Some of the earlier critics called the Citizens Council "Main Street Ku Klux Klans." At a Citizens Council rally in Selma, Alabama, in 1955 Congressman John Bell Williams denied this. He said the Councils were organized to give a direct answer to the NAACP's motto "The Negro shall be free by 1963." Such a thing, he said, would ruin the South's economic system.

Speaking at the same place in February 1955, Robert Patterson told his audience that the "integration monster creates the most serious crisis in the South since the Civil War. The people of the South have been complacent and apathetic for many years. Every battle we have lost has been by default. Some great philosopher once said, 'All that is necessary for the triumph of evil is for good men to do nothing,' and that certainly applies to us. . . . If 50,000,000 of us can't keep our race white, then we aren't fit to be white, and we won't be white very long. . . . Some people think we are the Ku Klux Klan. We're not. We don't cover our faces and we aren't baiting anybody. . . . In places like Chicago and Detroit they hate the Negro. Here the Negro is our friend. But we in Mississippi will never stand for the integration monster."

The editor of the Montgomery *Advertiser* listened to an earlier speech at Selma and appraised both the segregation monster and the furor of the moment. "At the White Citizens Council rally in Selma" he wrote, "a Mississippi circuit judge, Tom Brady, evidently a man without an intellectual problem in his head, urged impeachment of the United States Supreme Court and, thereafter, the election of judges rather than appointment . . . but what would be the circumstances if the justices were undergoing impeachment proceedings, or if they were on the stump campaigning for election? Obviously, the justices would be quickly vindicated in the first instance and would sweep in in the second. . . . The truth is, we southerners and our latter-day 'peculiar institution' of segregation are compressed into a fortress whose perimeter is shrinking along the border states, with defection within such states as Tennessee. Further the feeling in North Alabama is mild compared with that in South Alabama."

Organization of the Citizens Council resulted in two immediate reactions. The press, North and South, carried numerous news stories and editorial comments about the organization. Whatever denial the organizers made, a segment of the press regarded the Council as closely akin to the Ku Klux Klan. At the same time there was a rash of organizations advocating eternal segregation and castigating the Supreme Court. The Ku Klux Klan in its various revised forms was among them. Almost every organization published a prospectus stating its philosophy and attacking the enemies of the southern way of life.

From the beginning of the eighteenth century in the South, there has been much pamphleteering and publication of political organs and diatribes. For more than a century every election has produced an outpouring of handbills and political sheets. When one man set upon another with enough vigor to obscure all political issues he blasted away with defamatory handbills and pamphlets. There have been colorful moments when southern colonels hurled fiery pamphlets at each other instead of fists and bullets. The Talmadges of Georgia published the *Standard;* Bilbo in Mississippi patronized a weekly which spoke for him, and so did James K. Vardaman. But the flow of leaflets, pamphlets, booklets, cartoons, mimeographed letters, and printed material has thus far exceeded anything in southern history. These publications are so numerous and have originated in such diverse places that no one can be certain he has them collected. Many are cheaply printed and poorly written. The information is lurid, and they treat all kinds of sensitive subjects, from God's intent concerning segregation to race-mixing around various army posts and other unidentified places. Some photographic reproductions give the appearance of being faked.

In much of the current propaganda literature there is a biblical note. Once again the Scriptures are drawn upon to establish Negro inferiority. Ham's indiscretions are again misquoted to prove divine intentions that the Negro should be an inferior and subservient human being. But it was Noah, not God, who cursed the Canaanites, and not Ham personally.

While his white neighbors were organizing to circumvent court decisions and civil rights legislation, the Negro was diligent. Since 1900 he has organized the Negro Alliance, the National Council of Negro Women, the National Negro Youth Congress, the Southern Negro Youth Congress, the Urban League, the Congress of Racial Equality, and the National Association for the Advancement of Colored People. The latter organization has exerted the greatest influence on relations in the South.

The NAACP was organized in 1909 as an outgrowth of a race riot which occurred in Springfield, Illinois. The founders were white people, among them William English Walling, Mary Ovington White, Henry Moskowitz, and Oswald Garrison Villard. Almost immediately the new organization was merged with the liberal Negro Niagara Movement. This body adopted as a long-range objective the removal of discrimination against American Negro citizens. In 1940 the NAACP announced an eight-point program which sought anti-lynching legislation, destruction of peonage and share-cropper evils, enfranchisement of Negroes, abolition of discriminatory legal and criminal procedures based upon race and color, equitable distribution of educational funds, equal work and pay opportunities, and the right for Negroes to bargain collectively in labor unions.

Efforts by the NAACP to intensify its activities coincided with the outbreak of World War II. In these years it broadened its all-Negro base at the grass-roots level of its local branches, and it pounded away at its stated objectives in this time of great national stress and tension. The strength of the NAACP lies largely in the effectiveness of its local branches. Here, however, it faces trouble among its large potential Negro membership because it is an outside organization. This creates suspicion on the one hand and causes Negroes to be concerned with the attitudes of their white neighbors on the other. The local branches are charged with the responsibility of reporting racial discriminations. This practice has brought about reprisals by many southern states, which have attempted to disrupt the work of the organization by forcing local officials to make public membership lists. As a further barrier to NAACP activities several of the states have passed anti-barritry laws in efforts to prevent outside Negro lawyers from practicing in the state courts. So long as the NAACP branches continue to report discriminations, they stand as threats to the traditional southern race relationships.

At the national level the NAACP has been active in lobbying in Congress against discriminatory federal legislation. It has undoubtedly influenced major executive decisions where the Negro was concerned. The real strength of the organization, however, has been its ability to maintain able legal counsel and to take its grievances to the courts. In this way it has avoided radical and emotional crusades and has consistently gained its objectives by the orderly processes of court decisions.

Even the bitterest critic of the NAACP has to admire the effectiveness of its legal battles. The American system of law has favored the organization in its fight against discrimination. Despite its successes, though, the NAACP still has its weaknesses. It has never been able to maintain enough local branches to organize Negro opinion fully. No doubt it has been overzealous at times and in places and thus has irritated some of its friends and incurred needless ill-will. In a final analysis, however, the southern racial system could hardly be confronted by a more determined and resourceful foe.

While organizations were producing arguments and literature designed to scare southern people into active opposition to the Negro crusaders and the Supreme Court, southerners in Congress in 1956 produced the "Congressional Manifesto." Senators John Stennis of Mississippi, Richard B. Russell of Georgia, and Samuel J. Ervin, Jr. of North Carolina — three of the ablest and most intelligent men in the body — constituted a drafting committee. The final draft of the Manifesto, however, was the work of Senators Russell and J. Strom Thurmond of South Carolina. The original draft was said to have been so truculent in tone that Senators Spessard Holland and Price Daniels refused to sign it. Thus the phraseology of the document was softened.

Senator Harry Flood Byrd of Virginia was active in gaining support for the declaration. Seventy-seven congressmen and nineteen senators from eleven southern states signed the statement. The majority leader of the Senate, Lyndon B. Johnson, and the Speaker of the House, Sam Rayburn, were not asked to sign. Senators from the border states of Tennessee and Kentucky refused to sign, as did the entire House membership from Kentucky. Senator Estes Kefauver of Tennessee, then a presidential hopeful, refused to endorse the statement on the grounds that "the Supreme Court must be the final authority on constitutional questions. Its decision now is the law of the land and must be followed." In his opinion, chaos and confusion could only result from flaunting a ruling of the Court.

In the minds of the Manifesto's draftsmen, the Supreme Court had deserted the principles of the Constitution and had "substituted naked power for established law." Judges of the Court had abused their judicial powers and had "substituted their personal political and social ideas for the established law of the land." It said the principle of separate-but-equal facilities for the two races had become a part of the lives of the people, and now in rejecting it, the Court had "planted hatred and suspicion where there had been heretofore friendship and understanding." The signers expressed reliance on the fundamental law of the land, decried the Supreme Court's encroachment on state's rights, and commended the states which proposed to "resist forced integration by any lawful means." They proposed to resist judicial usurpation of power and to use "all lawful means to bring a reversal of this decision which is contrary to the Constitution, and to prevent the use of force in its implementation." Southerners were admonished not to be provoked into committing disorderly or lawless acts by agitators and troublemakers.

The Manifesto had no official sanction in Congress. It was presented as a resolution and there it rested. Like so much of this type of material which either gets before the Congress or into the *Congressional Record*, the Southern Manifesto appealed to the folks back home. No doubt it confirmed the opinions of people in eleven states that the Supreme Court had ignored the Constitution and that unidentified agitators were responsible for rising tensions. It also raised hopes that somewhere, somehow, someone would find a legal loophole through which the Court's decision might be either circumvented or reversed. Historians at some future date may have a better perspective from which to view the personalities and the activities which brought the Manifesto into existence. Certainly there is evidence already in sight that tremendous political pressures were exerted on southern members of Congress to sign it, whether they conscientiously believed in its principles or not. In another respect the Manifesto outlined the sensitive points in the basic emotional and legalistic dispute with the Court.

Implicit in the Congressional statement was the turmoil occurring in the state legislatures. It would not be possible for an objective historian to read this document in light of the charged atmosphere of the times, and especially in light of subsequent actions by many southerners in the great debate in the United States Senate over civil rights, without arriving at the conclusion that the Old South is passing. This would seem to be true even in the face of vigorous senatorial debate.

There can be little doubt but what the Congressional Manifesto indicated that most southern representatives felt more the compulsion of home opinion than hope that they could accomplish anything. They opened themselves to severe criticism from their colleagues in Congress and from the American people. They were even accused of bordering on sedition.

Legislators in the Lower South have searched for means to circumvent the Court decision. Scores of bills have reached the enrolling stage, and enormous amounts of energy, time, and money have been spent to interpose the will of the states against that of the Federal Government. In 1957, the Georgia General Assembly adopted resolutions seeking impeachment of the justices of the Supreme Court. Impeachment was asked on sixteen counts, the heart of which was giving aid and comfort to enemies of the United States by subverting the Constitution.

Out of all the ideas that have reached legislative halls, only three or four have been generally acceptable. To nullify the Supreme Court decision and yet live within the law and Constitution of the United States presents a paradox indeed. Proposals to abandon public schools rather than segregate them have been numerous. In several instances communities have actually experimented with private schools.

Hunting in the forest of legislative evasion is most unpromising since the great wall of massive resistance tumbled down in Virginia. Effect of the Court's ruling in Norfolk, Arlington, and Warren County cases early in 1959 can be gauged somewhat by the conclusions of the Board of Directors of the Little Rock Chamber of Commerce. After surveying the relationships between closing Central High School and the state of business, this board declared in March 1959: "In our opinion, the State of Virginia has exhausted every possible legal method a state can attempt to get around the Supreme Court decision and maintain a state-wide public-school system." Special committees in four or five states have been instructed to find ways if possible to evade the Court decision. In South Carolina, for instance, the Governor has been granted unusually broad powers to deal with the subject.

Virginia granted its governor more powers, and created two special legislative committees, one of which is called the Committee on Law Reform and Racial Activities. Georgia has its Educational Commission, created in 1953, which is composed of a group of state officials, and its purposes seem clearly to be that of finding ways to circumvent the intent of the decision of the Supreme Court.

Never before have legislators enjoyed more opportunity to make loud sounds in legislative halls to be heard back home.

Their proposals are highly newsworthy. Almost all proposed legislation, however harebrained, has been given publicity. Each legislator hopes his bill will be the magic one to thwart the Court. The Supreme Court decision was made to order as a campaign issue for southern politicians. There are few institutions which candidates can berate with more assurance that they will not anger voters than the Supreme Court. Both political campaign and legislative furor bespeak the sentiments of large blocs of voters, and they also explain one of the major reasons why the issue is kept alive.

There is, however, a body of moderate-minded people, who, though emotionally not in accord with the decision, wish to see the country's laws obeyed. But the group is largely inarticulate, for fear of economic and social reprisals and because, by and large, it has never enjoyed personal controversy. Moderates have spoken out, however, and much of what they have said has angered the extremists. Three prize-winning southern authors — William Faulkner, Robert Penn Warren, and Hodding Carter — have published their views on the region in national magazines, and all three have stimulated controversy.

William Faulkner published his comments in letters to the editors of *Life, Look,* and the Memphis *Commercial Appeal,* in several speeches, and in a brief paper read before the Southern Historical Association in Memphis. This latter paper was presented just after Faulkner had traveled abroad and had viewed the southern race problem from long-range perspective. He saw the grave dangers of creeping communism, and predicted that only England among the countries he visited would not become communist within a decade. If the Communists won so great a foothold, then America would be "strangled to extinction." He said that, if the South had given the Negro equal rights and opportunities "ninety or fifty or ten years ago, there would have been no Supreme Court decision."

In a subsequent interview with a *Commercial Appeal* reporter, Faulkner, thinking of the bitter things which had been said about him, said, "We accept insult and contumely and the risk of violence because we will not sit quietly by and see our native land, the South, not just Mississippi but all the South, wreck and ruin itself twice in less than a hundred years, over the Negro question."

Despite the enormous noise and reaction which gained so much publicity, there are moderates throughout the South. Several newspapers in the region have adopted realistic points of view. Among these are the Atlanta *Constitution,* and Louisville *Courier-Journal,* the Charlotte *Observer,* the Arkansas *Gazette,* the Raleigh *News and Observer,* and the Greenville *Delta Democrat-Times.* Editorials on racial and civil rights which have appeared in the *Courier-Journal* have been written by Weldon James, a South Carolinian. During the Little Rock school crisis, Harry Ashmore continually appealed for reason in the Arkansas *Gazette.*

Most outspoken in the lower South are Ralph McGill of the Atlanta *Constitution* and Jonathan Daniels of the *News and Observer.* They have exhibited enormous courage in both their editorials and their public speeches. Neither Daniels nor McGill has advocated an immediate end to the old southern way of life. As a matter of fact, both of them are regional sentimentalists, but they plead for a realistic and active approach to the South's racial problems, and have actively opposed extremist actions.

In the political field many southerners have demonstrated courage and a sense of reality in dealing with the South's problems. Several governors and members of congressional delegations have come to accept the Court's decision as a mandate and have instituted steps to conform. None, however, has displayed greater statesmanship than former Governor Leroy Collins of Florida. He is both highly literate and articulate. In his inaugural address in 1957 he told his listeners that they should first of all be honest in recognizing the realities of the South's position. Failure to do so would damage the moral welfare of their state. The decisions of the Supreme Court, he said, "are the law of the land. And this nation's strengths are bottomed upon the basic premise that ours is a land of law." He expressed belief that his people could find solutions for their problems, "if the white citizens face up to the fact that the Negro does not now have equal opportunities; that he is morally and legally entitled to progress more rapidly, and that a full good-faith effort should be made forthwith to help him move forward in the improvement of all his standards."

Three years later, Governor Collins addressed students at Princeton University. On this occasion he took a broad look at the modern South. The days of economic colonialism of the

South were ended, and the region was faced with the challenge of accepting its new position "as a part of the challenge of accepting its part of the main stream of national life, and the responsibilities that go with it." The region, he said, would grow in economic strength, but it had to grow in moral strength and dedication to the nation's goals. "If the South should wrap itself in a Confederate blanket," he said, "and consume itself in racial furor, it would surely miss its greatest opportunity for channeling into a wonderful future the products of change now taking place. And the South must face up to the further fact that it would also bury itself for decades to come." He believed that no longer should "advocates of racial and economic reaction — the very ones against whom we in the South have to struggle on a local and state level for every inch of progress we have made — be allowed to speak for the South, simply because they have made the loudest noise."

The McGills, Jameses, Danielses, Ashmores, Carters, and Collinses have never been accepted by the noisemakers. Yet the passage of every year and the impact of change and revolution in the modern southern way of life bring the people of the region closer to an acceptance of the realities with which these outspoken southerners have identified themselves. Back of these spokesmen there is growing a large body of moderate opinion which is coming to be a more meaningful force in the South.

In many respects the segregation controversy has been a boon to some southerners. Lawyers have had golden opportunities to attract public notice and to seek high office by vigorous attacks upon integrationists in and out of court. They have stoutly defended litigants in cases which clutter state and federal court dockets. For those crass lawyers who find cash more tangible than political glory, there are funds to pay counsel.

By the same token the national newspaper and magazine press has fed heavily on the racial story. This publicity has not only stirred up the issue in local situations but it has drawn attention to it elsewhere in the nation and abroad. It is difficult to make calm decisions on so delicate a social issue amidst all the noise. There is high drama in breaking old social customs, of bringing two races into new associations, if not into new conflicts. In the courtroom, legal counsel has presented exciting arguments. Extremists on both sides readily utter opinions of varying hues, and some even hint at acts of violence.

On the national scene *Life, Time, Look,* and the *Saturday Evening Post* have given generous coverage to the South and the race problem. In fact, *Life* now almost enjoys the contempt which slaveholders held for the *Liberator* and *Uncle Tom's Cabin.* R. Carter Pittman of Dalton, Georgia, attributed the success of the Luce publications to their fanning of sectional hatreds. "The South," he says, "is an ideal whipping boy because no magazine with national circulation is published in the South and most of her newspapers are owned by residents of the North — some as far north as Moscow. The South has nothing with which to fight back, except the ballot. Many of her congressmen had rather see their pictures in *Life* or *Time* than to see their constituents treated fairly. The people of the South have learned slowly. Now a splash in *Life* or *Time* is rapidly becoming the kiss of Judas for southern politicians."

The most zealous souls among the publicists, though, are the grass-roots authors — men of single purpose. They flood editorial desks with their passionate public letters. They have expressed unbridled anger, sectional pride, reviewed Confederate history, shouted invectives at one another, and have aired vehemently other personal views. They have submitted plans for reorganizing the Federal Government, for getting rid of the Supreme Court, for electing judges, and for making the people's wishes known instantly in Washington. These furious correspondents have brought into print a considerable volume of the most bizarre folk literature in American history.

In the constant survey of the southern scene two questions predominate: What effect does the great debate have on industry moving South? And, how soon will integration take place? The first of these questions can be answered in only a vague way. Many informed and responsible people are certain that the controversy does figure prominently in the location of new industries. It would hardly be reasonable to expect an industry depending on a national market to announce that it by-passed the South because of the race issue. No one can answer the second question except to say that every new court case, congressional act, and national political convention brings integration closer. The Delaware decision in July 1960 definitely shortened the time to be allowed by the courts to prepare for integration. Two facts are clear, however. There is woeful lack of knowledge on the part of many people as to the workings of constitutional government, and there is genuine fear in many parts of the South of the reactions of the emancipated Negro.

Today, an appreciable segment of southern white people is so emotionally aroused that it is doubtful that they can rationally appraise the issues raised by the Court decision. Their thinking is predominantly negative, and, because of changing conditions in many parts of the South, they have failed to communicate with Negro leadership. This is especially true where Negroes have left rural farm areas and congregated in urban communities. In larger towns, the Negro community has grown almost entirely away from the old agrarian pattern of paternalism. Where once the Negro appealed to a landlord for advice, he now has to turn elsewhere. The urban Negro has an impersonal employer, and his community has become more responsible socially. As a consequence, the federal courts, to a degree, have supplanted the old system of personal resort for the Negro.

Because communications between the races are blurred, it is difficult for the Negro to make known what he asks of his white neighbors. Nevertheless, there are eloquent spokesmen like Benjamin Mayes of Atlanta and others who are able to state clearly the objectives of their race. Negro views, like those of people in general, range from extreme conservatism to unthinking extremism. In a free society, for instance, Negroes find it hard to reconcile the consideration accorded peoples of color from other countries in our schools and public facilities with discriminations against Americans of color. Too, in this age when education is so necessary for a man to function efficiently in an industrial society he seeks equal opportunity free of racial restrictions.

In 1958, at Dallas, Texas, 112 Negro ministers gave a nine-point answer to what the Negro wants. In this statement the ministers said the Negro wants: (1) no special privilege, (2) to be respected as a person, (3) to live in a truly free society, (4) all services rendered on his behalf to be based upon deeper values than purely humanitarian philanthropy and paternalism, (5) the right to live and find free expression for his native endowments as an individual, (6) his differences neither to be ignored nor accentuated, (7) unity of equal terms, (8) unity in diversity, and (9) peace and harmony in an ordered society.

Negro leadership in general perhaps has not thought through its desires so carefully as have the Dallas ministers. Thus it is difficult to say specifically what it wants in the South except as these desires are expressed in court actions and pressure for the adoption of civil rights legislation. But uppermost would be equal educational-employment opportunities and free political expression. It wants, of course, to remove barriers from Negro enjoyment of public facilities of a free and ordered society. It is to be doubted that moderate Negro leadership is disturbed basically over the mere desegregation of public schools. Certainly this has not been a demonstrable fact in schools which have been desegregated in the border states. There is every indication that race problems in this country will be solved in so far as the American people accept the premises of the Dallas ministers.

Breakdown of communication between the two races has bred suspicion and a degree of hatred. Southerners in five or six hard-core states would be afraid to participate in mixed group discussions of race problems. Many active church laymen have found it increasingly difficult to hold joint meetings with Negroes, and some professional and scholarly societies have almost abandoned holding meetings in the South because of eternal disputes over allowing Negro members to attend sessions and to dine and lodge in hotels.

There is no record of the number of ministers who have engendered criticism because they have followed a practice extending into slavery times by visiting Negro churches and religious meetings. Malicious rumors and gossip are apt to tear to shreds the good name of any person found in communication with Negroes in a formal way. There would be threats by anonymous telephone calls and anonymous letters. There might even be a boycott of businesses and services. Ministers in many instances would lose members from their congregations, and there might be irate demands that they resign if they discussed the segregation issue from the pulpit.

The southern Negro is so severely limited in his own channels of communication that he has difficulty in approaching his problems with ease of mind and with the faith that he can accomplish much. His meetings, especially in rural communities, are suspect. If he distributed handbills and pamphlets giving his views, he might find himself in serious difficulty in some places. State Senator Sam Englehardt told a *Wall Street Journal* reporter in October 1957, in Alabama, "One nigger on my farm has been making some remarks — joking about Eisenhower and those federal troops [at Little Rock]. He'll be leaving soon. I'll see to that."

In a fundamental way the last few years have seen the South lose ground in an area that has little specific bearing on the race issue itself. Teachers, for instance, are sharply divided in their personal views. Yet the expression of a contrary view to that held in some communities, however moderate, could land an individual in the hands of a mob, or get his house dynamited. In Camden, South Carolina, in December 1956, Guy Hutchins, a high school bandmaster, was accused of making pro-integration statements and was beset by masked men. This incident threw the whole issue of local administration of justice into a snarl when the grand jury changed the charges to a lesser crime and remanded the case to a magistrate's court. In the same state, Professor Chester Travelstead of the University of South Carolina became the central figure in a controversy that led to his separation from the faculty because he was reported to have said, "It is my firm conviction that enforced segregation of the races in our public schools can no longer be justified on any basis — and should therefore be abolished as soon as possible."

The University of Mississippi found itself involved in a freedom of religion and speech controversy when it withdrew an invitation to the Reverend Alvin Kershaw to deliver some lectures in connection with its religious emphasis week. The minister had contributed a part of his winnings on a television program to the educational fund of the NAACP. This resulted in a burst of unfavorable publicity in the state; members of the legislature demanded that Mr. Kershaw not be allowed to speak; resolutions were presented to the Board of Trustees of Higher Education to bar him. Possibly the most far-reaching effect of the Kershaw incident was not the withdrawal of the invitation to speak, but the fact that in the future all lecturers brought to the state schools had to be carefully screened to make sure they would not "utter pronouncements contrary to Mississippi's way of life."

The real issues of freedom, however, are not necessarily those incidents which come to full bloom in headlines. There are the little intimidations of teachers. No teacher who ever appeared before a class and expressed a coherent idea has been free from either quotation or misquotation, and provocation is more often than not disturbing both to the student in the classroom and to his auditors at home who have received garbled accounts. In many areas teachers are denied, through fear, this most effective approach to stimulating teaching. On the other hand, students themselves introduce controversial subjects into classroom discussions and their teachers are named the authors. The effect this situation has on the South's drive for more and better teachers is catastrophic. Many southerners have undoubtedly been discouraged from entering teaching, and a considerable number of teachers, educated at enormous cost to southern taxpayers, have joined the migrants away from the region.

It is becoming increasingly difficult for authors of textbooks, publishers, and textbook commissions to find suitable books for adoption in some states. Unhappily, intellectual quality is not always a prime criterion for selecting a book. Books in many fields have to conform to concepts which textbook commissions and parents have of the meaning of the term "southern way of life." Already two social science textbooks, *Our Changing Social Order* and *Land of Freedom,* have been criticized in Georgia. These books may or may not be valid intellectually, but apparently they were judged by other standards. This anxiety about texts and points of view extends even to college classrooms. Instructors in some places in the South say they find it increasingly difficult to select texts which do not in some way deal with racial issues. Surprisingly, this is even true in the field of freshman English where instructors use supplementary readings. In one southern college a student inspired a mild witch-hunt against an orthodox text used in an English course by expressing his views to reporters.

Librarians in schools have to select books with greater concern for their emotional possibilities than ever before. A book criticizing the South, found on a library shelf in some places, might be professionally disastrous for a school librarian. This condition brings the South into conflict with one of its proudest political traditions. Southerners wonder whether the region's long record of freedom of thought and opposition to tyranny is not threatened by these new attitudes. There is the question whether the South is not turning its back on its traditional values. The region will need considerable learning and perspective on the part of a calm and thoughtful leadership to protect it. This is not a tradition which thrives in a state of aroused emotions, where ignorant men could do irreparable violence under the guise of preserving a way of life.

The question uppermost in the minds of thoughtful people in the South is whether or not the solution of the emotional race problem lies within the scope of gradualism. The borderland will soon integrate most of its schools — not easily and not always without incident, but it no doubt will be done. Great furor will prevail in the hard-core states, and hot verbal battles with some violent resistance will take place. Every indication seems to be that the struggle between Citizens Councils, the legislatures, and the NAACP will go on indefinitely. There are no present indications that the executive branch of the Federal Government will relent in its efforts to enforce the Court decision in resisting states, if the Eisenhower statement of August 18, 1958, and the civil rights planks in the two party platforms in 1960 are to be construed as central governmental policy.

Court tests will continue in an ever abundant crop of cases. Both the Federal Government and Negro leadership are committed against a policy of separate-but-equal gradualism, yet both policies may prevail for time to come in at least five states. On the other hand, and despite a firm declaration of "Never!" there are detectable notes of "Eventually!" in the angry chorus. Pressures from within and without the South have already become influential in bringing about observance of the Court ruling.

Already injury has been done to several southern school systems. The time and energy of administrative and instructional staffs have been wasted on formulating tests, in making surveys, and otherwise serving the campaign of resistance. At present, southern school personnel can hardly meet the normal challenges of the changing South without being annoyed and disrupted by the emotional disturbances of the race issue. In instances, some plans for expansion and modernizing school systems have been held in abeyance. In some states, Mississippi and Georgia for instance, school bonds on one occasion were temporarily removed from the market because investment agencies proposed increased interest rates in the face of the liabilities created by local tensions and threats to abandon public schools. But these are only minor irritations compared with the migration away from the South of competent teachers and the demoralization of the southern school system in this age of industrialization.

XVI

By Day a Pillar of Cloud
By Night a Pillar of Fire

A majority of the public houses of worship at the South are small, rude structures of logs, or rough boards, built by the united labor or contributions of the people of a large neighborhood or district country, and are used as places of assembly for all public purposes. Few of them have any regular clergymen, but preachers of different denominations go from one to another, sometimes in a defined rotation, or "circuit," so that they may be expected at each of their stations at regular intervals. A late report on the Southern Aid Society states that hardly one-fifth of the preachers are regularly educated for their business, and that "you would starve a host of them if you debarred them from seeking additional support for their families by worldly occupation." In one presbytery of the Presbyterian Church, which is, perhaps, the richest, and includes the most educated body of people of all the Southern Churches, there are twenty-one ministers whose wages are not over two hundred and fifty dollars each. The proportion of ministers, of all sorts, to people, is estimated at one to thirteen hundred (in free states it is estimated at one to nine hundred.) The report of the Society also states, that "within the limits of the United States religious destitution lies comparatively at the South and Southwest . . ."

OLMSTED, A JOURNEY IN THE SEABOARD SLAVE STATES, pp. 451–2

No institution in the modern South so clearly reflects conditions of regional life as the church. Though deep change is at once noticeable, there is still an underlying fact of historical continuity. In an era of change the church remains a central force in shaping social attitudes. To appraise the South without examining in

considerable detail the place of organized religion would be akin
to viewing a forest without singling out the trees.

In many ways the South has preached the New Testament and
lived by the narrower tenets of the Old. The rich historical and
personal nature of the Old Testament fitted ideally the needs of
a literal-minded and agrarian people who saw reflected in its
pages images of their own struggles. The wanderings and frustrations of the Hebrew people paralleled the social confusion of the
South. The story of man's beginnings, followed by bitter trials
and tribulations, outlined broad social forms. Much of testamen-
tary history detailed the rise of families where numerous patri-
archs gained status largely by their procreative achievements.
Family was man's primary responsibility, whether he be a Hebrew
father wandering in the rocky wastes of Sinai Plain or a southern
cotton farmer trudging a rocky hillside behind a plow.

There are highly cultivated people in the modern South who
contend with force that the study of Hebrew culture has basic
regional pertinency. Many of the gentler pastorals of the Psalmists
are often overlooked, except for their lilting rhetoric and the
promises which they make to people in moments of adversity and
sorrow. They hardly reflect the tempestuous course of crisis of
southern history. Yet in facing trials and tribulations, southerners
have turned to orthodox religion to gain strength to meet realities
of their lives.

Old South influences have retained a hold upon the modern
southern church. In politics and society, the rugged domination
of Protestantism has helped to color regional history. Only in
the last two decades have there been discernible departures from
the past. An era of economic revolution, coupled with the dis-
illusion brought by two world wars, had little influence on the
fundamental structure of the southern church.

In the 1920s bigots lashed out at science and liberalism in blind
fury. Unlearned and unlettered men put pressure on legislators
to do their bidding or lose the powerful rural vote. In their minds,
if universal education were to survive in the South it had to keep
hands off religious traditions and prejudices. The positiveness of
the Old Testament's account of man's origin was sufficient answer
to the Darwinists. Any upstart scientist who questioned the Book
of Genesis was certain to have trouble with his literal-minded

neighbors. There were no shadings, subtleties, or rationalizations between the Word of God and that of science.

This was a period of uprooted emotions in the South. Those who accepted a literal interpretation of the Scriptures succeeded only in making themselves utterly ridiculous to the outside world. Pressed for defensible answers to the new and troublesome questions raised by science, the literalists fell into their self-created abyss of speculative error. On the other hand, science itself existed on too shaky a foundation in the southern educational curriculum to escape injury at the hands of ill-prepared amateurs.

Noisy religious bigots and immature scientists both made themselves obnoxious. Neither enjoyed the security of position afforded by intellectual maturity. Most misguided of all the critics of the South was H. L. Mencken. His concentration on the failures of evangelical religion caused him to jump to conclusions that the South was an intellectually sterile "Sahara of the Bozart!" For most literate southerners his sharp gibes caused them to take a closer look at what was happening about them; for others it only provoked blind, animal fury.

Mencken and his fellow critics filled newspaper and periodical columns with stinging judgments which ignored the pertinent fact of regional change then occurring. They glibly labeled the South with derogatory terms without identifying the fundamental forces that were beginning to revolutionize the course of southern life. On the face of the record, the South, to them, nurtured both a stupid pulpit and a blind legislative hall where ignorant lawmakers sought to erase the indelible laws of nature. These critics little realized that the average rural southern legislator could easily be rushed into supporting legislation that would both satisfy the people back home and hold off the noisy lobbyists at the statehouse door. What did it matter if an intellectually stifling law were placed in the statute book? Already statute books everywhere bulged with the sinful indiscretions of other legislative sessions. A good way to bury a pesky issue was to pass a law. The law has long been the tomb of political problems, and politicians were able to accept the anti-evolution laws, because their enactment allowed them to go home to their constituents without criticism.

It is doubtful that a single legislator in a state which passed an anti-evolution bill really envisioned a culprit being brought to the bar of justice. Certainly no one in the Tennessee Legislature in 1924 foresaw the Scopes Trial with its resounding and embarrassing publicity. Though southern laws threatened ominous punishment in fine and imprisonment, they were little more than legislative bluster. When an offender was dragged before a judge in the Dayton courtroom in 1926 amidst a loud clatter of contending legal counsel and the shattering bombardment of sensational news stories, even legislators who had made the law were surprised.

Behind the anti-evolution bills were two significant facts which critics of the South overlooked. One of these was the pressure to promote emotional issues in order to divert legislative energies and time from curbing the activities of special interests. Railroads, for instance, knew the price of legislation which commanded them to improve some of their public services. The other fact was the rising influence of public education. It would have been impossible a decade before to have stirred up such a furor over the contradictions of science and religion, because too little science was being taught in the public schools to provoke a dispute.

The courageous stand of many southern ministers against the trumpetings of their fundamentalist colleagues was largely ignored by the sensation-hungry reporters who sifted the arid sands of the Bozartian desert. There were intelligent leaders who cried out against the excesses of the bigoted and the spineless legislator, but their voices were drowned in a flood of publicity of the ridiculous. These rumblings of the new order in the 1920s bear sharply upon the course of recent southern religious history. Today there is still a solid foundation of extreme fundamentalism in the South, but it would be difficult to enact into law its narrow religious concepts. Many ministers and legislators are no more enlightened now than they were in the 1920s, but they lack the quiescent support of the people which they had in that period.

Modernism has changed its coat; it now comes in the guise of social and cultural reform. The burden of modern religion is that of placing man in contemporary society rather than dealing with man's obscure origin. That he exists is a tangible enough fact, and his social needs and conflicts make an interest in his origin of secondary importance.

This is not to say that certain southern religious groups have ceased to fear modernism and its unemotional approach to human questions. Darwinism is as unacceptable in most places in the region today as it was in the 1890s and 1920s. But the fear that a modern social doctrine harbors a cynicism that will blight the warmly emotional individual responses which have characterized the religious experiences of the South is greater. In some undefinable way, in the minds of present-day fundamentalists the critical attitudes of the modernists have come to share the evil intent of the Communists.

Modernism has far broader implications for the southerner than mere religious ones. For two centuries the southern Protestant minister has largely refrained from participating in politics. The mundane affairs of campaigning and officeholding were left to the masses in the pews. The pulpit abhorred, often in discreet silence, the conscienceless, mudslinging, and unscrupulous manipulations of the politicians — even though occasionally a minister forsook the cloth to wallow in the same mire. In like manner, the pulpit largely refrained from direct action in social reform. The nineteenth-century term "social gospel" contained an implication that was alien to an individualistic agrarian society. Problems and sins were personal, not social. The proscriptions of the Hebrew scriptures reckoned in terms of individual commission of sin as well as organized societies sinning. The minister in the modern South can hardly concern himself with the new social emphases of religion without concerning himself with the social, economic, and political affairs of his community.

Beyond the traditional scope of the daily problems of economic society in the South lay the two larger issues of industrial labor in a rising urban America and the race problem. Organized labor was foreign to much of the region in the 1920s, and so was the present type of rising industrialism. There were, however, the combined forces of the city and the labor union which threatened orthodoxy and Protestantism. They both sheltered the foreign immigrant who brought with him either a strong attachment for the Catholic Church or was tainted with poisonous "foreign atheism."

Industrialism has stimulated some organization of labor, and there has been a slight increase in the number of Catholics who have come to the modern South. It has brought the disintegration of older neighborhoods where established churches have long gathered their flocks. Now the ancient fold of the church is in one place and the range of the flock in another. Many church spires which for generations have been landmarks in southern cities and towns now represent little more than the fact of change. Congregations have fled to the outer circles of expanding suburbia, and many a meeting of administrative church boards has been rocked on the breakers of impending change. Congregations have been torn asunder, and ancient church houses have either been toppled to make room for parking lots or stand, pigeon-stained and windowless, like architectural outcasts awaiting their final days of destruction. Too, the great mobility of southerners has sent some churches themselves scurrying away on wheels.

As significant as the facts of physical change are the new demands being made upon the established southern churches to serve new and differently stratified social classes. The influx of industrial management personnel has brought a new and aggressive type of church member to many old congregations. This new member is often unwilling to accept pokey southern attitudes. In some instances church leadership has slipped away from the native sons to rest in the hands of the newcomers. At the same time rural migrations of poor and uneducated countrymen to the towns and cities have created demands for less socially-minded and sophisticated churches to serve their spiritual needs and to satisfy their emotional hunger. The various pentecostal groups have enjoyed increases in membership. Characteristic of these is the rapidly maturing Church of God, which has its headquarters in Cleveland, Tennessee. This church, beginning in 1886 in the Unicoi Mountains, repeated the history of some of the older Protestant denominations in their colonial beginnings.

Failures of the older southern congregations to offer emotional satisfaction to the less well-educated and economically under-privileged groups in many instances caused them to lose ground with these people. Too, some of the older denominations became so concerned with social status that they moved away and left large numbers of their neighbors spiritually stranded. Ministerial salaries were increased by competition for their services, and congregations which once paid church obligations in produce were often left without preachers. The so-called "Holy-Roller," rocking humble church houses with his highly emotional sermons, shouting, holy dancing, and incoherent babbling has become a social outcast. It is all but impossible to conceive of this sweat-drenched child of God sitting in the sedate pews of a seminary-trained minister. The Pentecostals, rather than the Catholic Church, are at present making the deepest inroads in the statistical ranks of traditional southern church affiliation.

In the heart of every slum area and on the side of many country roads there are pentecostal churches of some new and unusual dispensation. Often the names of the churches express the particular type of inspiration which spurs their self-appointed ministers to battle sin. Members of these mushrooming institutions bear the most casual relationship to the church and make little or no real sacrifice to support it. They feel called upon to make impassioned confessions of sin and to undergo severe self-flagellations in atonement. Some of them handle snakes and dangerous chemicals, while others lapse into subconscious states of emotional exhaustion when God himself is said to speak through them in undecipherable tongues.

It is doubtful that any other part of the nation offers so fruitful a field for the roving evangelists as does the South. These casual men of the cloth hasten over the roads in modern cars which are plastered with stern admonitions to the sinful to repent before it is too late. They drag swaying trailers loaded with tents and folding chairs to enable them to set up their tabernacles wherever the field seems ripe for the harvest. The peripatetic revivalist and buxom female song leader have become as much a part of the southern scene as the motel and the barbecue stand. Closely allied to the itinerant evangelists are those tireless sinners who do public penance by erecting admonitory signs across the South, reminding speeding motorists, caught in hairpin curves, that they are about to face eternity with inadequate spiritual preparation.

More than a century ago several of the older southern churches pulled themselves away from national bodies rather than succumb to northern teachings against slavery. The northern religious philosophy threatened southern views, and the anti-slavery crusade condemned slaveholders for moral and spiritual wrongdoing. Clearly the will of the pew in this instance had brought the pulpit to time. Hundreds of books, pamphlets, and sermons expounded biblical justification for the course of the South. The Scriptures were combed for light and justification.

In many local congregations today there is remarkably little change in certain social attitudes from those that prevailed a century ago. Again there is fear of the northern church bodies, not alone because of their liberal racial attitudes, but because of their deviations from orthodoxy. The liberalism of the northern pulpit may be far more frightening than its racial views. Some of the northern view of religion to the great mass of southerners contains seeds of destruction for southern evangelism and conservatism. To large numbers of southerners, the northern point of view is dangerously sodden with alien socialism and lack of fundamentalism.

Theologically, an appreciable part of the southern ministry is able to deal with abstract modern philosophies without upsetting either themselves or their congregations. Many of them can even discuss so abstruse a subject as existentialism without arousing much dissent. However, there are still many southern ministers who hold tenaciously to narrow sectarian concepts of human behavior and sin. They then labor diligently to maintain their notions. The stern anti-social preacher has sometimes found the going tough through two world wars and the accompanying periods of readjustment. The old rural taboos of half a century ago are shattered by pleasure-seeking, emancipated, and mobile youth. In this age of rapidly changing tastes in popular music and the lowering of barriers between the sexes, the devil becomes a most agile adversary. A conservative North Carolina Baptist minister in 1957 not only aroused Wake Forest College students, but he brought reporters and photographers running to his door to give his crusade against dancing world-wide publicity. No longer is the fight for adherence to a strict code of personal conduct a matter between a minister and his congregation; it has become sensational enough to be given publicity. Dislike of publicity no doubt has chastened many a negative-minded bigot of the type who once enjoyed anonymity in pressuring an anti-evolution law through a state legislature.

Industry with its tremendous social and economic impact promises further to change the southern religious pattern. Where present-day industrialism has changed community organization, the pulpit finds itself in a ticklish situation between the older employer groups and their employees. Never before have southern churches had to deal with the broad problems of industrialization and its peculiar demands for an applied religion. Greater intensification of industry in the South undoubtedly will tend to bring Protestantism and Catholicism into sharper rivalry. The Catholic Church has under way a campaign to break the Protestant grip on the sprawling and rock-ribbed cotton belt. But it has to do battle first with an aggressive and traditional religious adversary and to overcome antagonisms aroused by church policies which tolerate liberal racial attitudes.

Modernism of a more subtle kind has crept into southern religious bodies. Consolidation of public schools has destroyed many older community centers. Industry and rising towns have brought changes in local social emphases, and churches are forced to accept new approaches to maintain their central places in communities. No longer are bi-monthly or weekly services enough. The progressive church conducts a social program that virtually keeps its doors standing open. Boards of elders, deacons, and stewards have come to look upon a church house in the same functional sense with which they regard a factory building. It has to be given a certain amount of use to justify its original cost. Social activities are now part of southern church programs, the practice of which would have brought censure in 1920.

A church without a modern kitchen of hotel proportions and a dining hall large enough to serve a banquet to Belshazzar is an antiquated institution. A stranger visiting a southern church could easily get the impression that a gorged stomach is a necessary part of the religious rite; in fact, he would have difficulty at times in knowing whether he was in a church house or an unusually convivial country club. Some churches even permit dancing in their recreation halls, and congregations work up almost as much enthusiasm over sandlot baseball and basketball teams as student bodies in school or college. Never before has the church been so active a part of the everyday lives of its members.

Diversified Sunday schools, training programs for youth, organizations of all sorts, drives, dinners, couples' clubs, brotherhoods, mission circles, and dozens of other church-centered activities engage members in social responsibilities which often lie more in the domain of public recreation and chambers of commerce than in the realm of the spirit. Because of this, many southern church plants have come to resemble small colleges. There is the chapel or auditorium, the Sunday school plant, recreational centers, administrative quarters. Staggering sums of money have been invested in these physical plants. In many instances church members are kept so busy participating in a multiplicity of church activities that they have little time to sin privately.

It is doubtful that the social community is reflected more in membership in a country or cotillion club than by membership in the "right" church. First of all, membership in a church of high social acceptance designates the social class to which one at least aspires to belong. Too, it places him in line to be recognized by acceptable people. A perceptive minister has remarked about the southern scene that membership in the Episcopal Church had much to offer in climbing the social ladder, and that affiliation with the Presbyterian Church is seldom a social liability. Further down the ladder are Methodists, Baptists, and Disciples of Christ who struggle between their responsibilities to the masses and their aspirations to rule the social roost. Many a man embarking upon a business career in the South has given as much attention to his church membership as to his preparations for business, and his time may have been equally well spent.

From time to time southern church bodies have recognized regional, social, and economic problems in their annual resolutions. In 1908 the Southern Baptist Convention first broke its ancient rule of refraining from officially participating in political affairs by encouraging its members to help create "a wholesome public opinion for making the criminal laws more certain. More prompt and more effective; so as to take away the reproach resting on civilization and religion by prevalence of crime and lynching; and so as to make the law respected and effective in all parts of our country." This represented a considerable reversal of attitudes for an organization which had refused vigorously and consistently to involve itself in political matters. In 1944, Dr. J. B. Weatherspoon, an important figure in the massive body of Southern Baptists, prompted a break in traditional barriers by recognizing that "Organized Christianity should be in the vanguard of leadership in grappling with social wrongs that harass the people to whom it preaches." In this same year the Convention converted its Social Service Commission into a Christian Life Commission, with Congressman Brooks Hays of Arkansas as its chairman. This change gave the Commission a broader social charge.

In another important respect individual Baptist churches and ministers found themselves departing from their traditional attitudes toward the state. For almost a half century prior to 1918 that denomination had campaigned energetically in local option elections to curb the sale and use of intoxicating liquors. Denominational members were active in campaigning for adoption of the Eighteenth Amendment, and since 1934 Baptist ministers have again fought the battles of local option. They have labored both at the community level and in the wings of the state houses to implore legislators to adopt dry legislation and to make the way of the brewer and distiller uneasy.

In avoiding entanglements with the state, southern Baptists have at times made considerable sacrifices. They have refused to accept Hill-Burton funds for hospital construction on the grounds that it would involve an unholy alliance between church and state. Not only have they refused public hospital funds, they have bitterly criticized other church bodies, particularly the Catholics, for accepting them. In 1957 the Southern Baptist Convention meeting in Chicago made clear its position by admonishing its people to repel all attempts by the political state to curb their freedom. They dared the "administrative, legislative or judicial" powers of government to lay the weight of a feather upon the conscience of any man in the realm of religion by privilege or penalty.

While Baptists wrestled with their notions of how the church should deal with the woes at their doorstep, other Protestant groups have proved less hesitant in discussing the social environment. Both Methodists and Presbyterians have learned the lessons of economics, political science, and sociology. If southern society were to function in conformity with Christian ideals, it had to readjust itself consistently to changing times and attitudes. Lynching, race confusion, murder, and crimes of every sort came within the purview of the church's watch care. Congregational and ministerial responses varied with educational experience. Where conferences and general assemblies dealt progressively with social issues, local ministers and congregations often ignored them as either being too secular or too explosive for discussion. Ministers in the South know how sensitive their congregations are, and they know also that it is not impossible for them to be discharged if they become too outspoken in their sermons. It is safe to speak of social sin in broad general terms; being specific could lead them into great trouble. At the same time they are called upon to exercise the utmost patience in order to accomplish positive good.

Southern religious bodies have always been conscious of the dangers of political corruption. Repeatedly conferences, synods, and conventions have resolved against the restrictive and corrupt political forces which would ultimately destroy religious freedom. And just as repeatedly local church members have supported politicians and measures aiming to curb freedom.

Southern Presbyterians, meeting in general assembly at Birmingham in 1957, showed they understood the dangers latent in the emotionalism arising out of racial tensions. They made an unusually forceful avowal of faith in individual freedom in a report entitled: "Freedom — The Christian Concept." The authors expressed the belief that "our technique then as churchmen is to place our personal freedom in the matrix of present conditions and encourage its growth into all areas of life. The experience of this personal freedom creates a healthy discontentment with every form of bondage, subtle or conspicuous." After an extensive definition of freedom in its varied applications to modern life, the report got to the base of a problem which has mightily troubled southerners in all denominations since 1900. "In this nation where Christianity and democracy are by-words," said the report, "it is unthinkable that a Christian should join himself to Klan or Council whose purpose is to gain its point by intimidation, reprisal, and violence, or that he should lift no voice of protest against those who appeal to prejudice to spread fear."

In some of their state synods southern Presbyterians have showed extraordinary courage in support of the strong Birmingham declaration. They have refused to be stampeded into softening their resolutions in spite of the possibility of bruising the feelings of individual members who might be tempted to trample freedom in "Klan or Council." These resolutions no doubt are powerful factors in curbing extremism in parts of the South. It is reasonably safe to say that were it not for these chastening expressions, there might be some areas in the present South where there would be a reversion to the social chaos of lynching. In this respect the southern religious bodies have exerted their most pronounced social influence. It cannot be said in truth that the churches of the South were active in stopping the brutality of lynching, or that they had any major hand in stopping it. But that is beside the point now. The church has helped develop a social and moral climate in the region which would make return to such barbarism well-nigh impossible, even though there are still instances when the subversion of justice blackens the pages of contemporary southern history. This is an area where the effectiveness of Christian social gospel promises to be more pronounced.

Every major church body in the South has made some pronouncement in agreement with the Supreme Court decision regarding segregation of the races in public schools. Whatever may be the feelings of individuals and local congregations on this subject, there is the knowledge that the church cannot function as a free body in a state of political anarchy. Also, as Ralph McGill of the Atlanta *Constitution* said in the weeks after the decision, the church cannot afford to come up on the wrong moral side of an issue, and observance of the civil law is a moral issue.

The Southern Baptist Convention, meeting in St. Louis in June 1954, was one of the first large religious bodies to adopt resolutions accepting the Supreme Court decision. In a five-part resolution that body was clear in its statement that race relations also involved religion and morals. It recognized the Court decision as harmonious with Christian principles of "equal justice and love for all men." The Court was commended for granting time in which to make adjustments; the people were urged to conduct themselves as Christians during the period; and there was an expression of confidence in the public-school system. Political leaders were enjoined to conduct themselves as statesmen so that "this crisis in our national history shall not be made the occasion for new and bitter prejudices." A. C. Miller wrote under the title, *Don't Blame the Supreme Court,* a leaflet to be distributed by the Christian Life Commission, a clear-cut statement of what the denomination's attitude should be: "These [race] issues must be met by Christian statesmanship on the basis of the scriptural teaching that every man is embraced in the love of God, and every man is included in the plan of God. In the light of these truths, legal segregation cannot be maintained." These are unusually strong statements coming from the major southern church body. They are in fact statements which run sharply counter to the views of the great mass of the membership of the denomination. So far, however, attempts in succeeding conventions to expunge the resolution from the minutes have been unsuccessful. So long as it remains, it stands as a powerful reminder for the southern Baptist conscience against any attempt of the church's members to thwart the laws of the nation.

In the same year of the decision of the Supreme Court, the *Church News* of the Episcopal Diocese of Mississippi discussed that church's views on the subject of the schools and segregation. Later this article was published in pamphlet form and distributed by the Department of Christian Social Relations. Equal educational opportunities are viewed as "a basic premise of Christian democracy." "There is no room for doubt in this discussion that the central issue involved in the Court's decision has to do with human beings. The great ethical principles of the New Testament proclaim the sanctity of the human personality as that which takes precedence over every other human consideration. Man, be he white or black, is made in the image of God. This is fundamental to the Biblical concept of the Fatherhood of God and the brotherhood of man. Our attitude toward the Supreme Court decision is, therefore, essentially a religious question, since it concerns what we really believe about God and his creations. It concerns what we believe ourselves to be in relation to other human beings."

In various ways the Methodist Conferences have spoken in favor of obeying the ruling of the Supreme Court. The Council of Bishops of the Methodist Church stated a positive attitude toward law and order. Earlier, in 1952, the church had adopted a broad and liberal social creed. In 1954 the Council of Bishops, meeting in Chicago, believed that "the Supreme Court recognized that such a ruling brought with it difficulties of enforcement, and therefore, made provisions for sufficient time to implement its decision. The declaration of the decision was made in the magnificent home of the Supreme Court in Washington, but the ultimate success of the ruling will be determined in the hearts of the people of the nation. Thus the church is furnished with an unequaled opportunity to provide leadership during this period in support of the principles involved in the action of the Court. We accept this responsibility, for one of the foundation stones of our faith is the belief that all men are brothers, equal in the sight of God. In that faith, we declare our support of the rulings of the Supreme Court."

On May 1, 1956, the General Conference of the Methodist Church condemned racial segregation, "by any method or practice." This decision, opening the doors of the church to full integration, was reached with a fervent display of unanimity. Delegates stood and cheered. The Reverend C. Cooper Bell of Lynchburg, Virginia, exclaimed, "God has been with us. He has worked a miracle!" Constitutional changes adopted by the General Conference, however, are a long way from getting the South Central Conference to ratify the abolition of the separate Central, or Negro, jurisdiction and its integration into the Methodist Church organization.

In 1957 two ministerial groups in the South made major pleas for moderation in the emotionalism aroused by the Supreme Court decision. Eighty Atlanta ministers signed a six-point statement which they hoped would stimulate a more rational consideration of the race issue than was being given it by the extremists. They considered "the issues which we face are not so simple, nor can they be resolved overnight. Because the questions which confront us are in many respects moral and spiritual as well as political, it is appropriate and necessary that men who occupy places of responsibility in the churches should not be silent concerning their convictions." The six points of the statement pleaded for maintenance of freedom of speech, obedience to laws, preservation of public schools, an end of racial hatred, communication between responsible leaders of the races, and an appeal to God for guidance.

While Atlanta ministers were preparing their statement, five South Carolina ministers were gathering materials for a booklet to be published under the title, *South Carolina Speaks*. They sought "people who will steer a course between the excesses of certain Citizens Councils on the one hand and extreme actions of the NAACP on the other hand." Their prospectus listed an eight-point statement of views which was similar to those included in the Atlanta documents. They sought contributions to their book from courageous persons of moderate views.

The prospectus of the South Carolina book was submitted to Governor George Bell Timmerman, who in turn released it to the press with his own interpretations. Generally, the statement received cautiously favorable responses. Nevertheless, one or two of the ministers promoting it had to resign, and some of the authors suffered harsh retribution at the hands of extremist neighbors.

Following up the Atlanta plea, 307 Atlanta ministers in 1958 made a more fervent plea for a calmer consideration of the race problem. Provoked into action by the bombing of schools and synagogues, the prospect of closing public schools in Georgia and elsewhere, the ministerial plea was embodied in three main points. They asked that a creative effort be made by state and community leaders to find solutions for their problems short of violence and school closings, that a bi-racial commission be appointed to consider racial matters, and that free and intelligent discussion of social issues be conducted in churches and synagogues. Those ministers living and working in a community where trouble might occur made a plea that local minds be permitted to work out in good faith the details of racial adjustment. But in any event they observed that "it is clearer now than ever before that we must obey the law."

The Roman Catholic Church has long held that "there is no segregation before God. There shall be none in the Church." This attitude, plus generous charitable work among Negroes, has aided Catholics in developing small congregations in strong Protestant communities. Parochial schools, as well as church services, have been racially integrated. All has not been smooth sailing for the church, however. Catholics in the Lower South are as conservative racially as their Protestant neighbors. In New Orleans and along the lower Mississippi there was resistance to lowering the racial barrier. But using the powerful whip of excommunication, many individual Catholics were brought to accept the Archbishop of New Orlean's ruling.

The attitudes of ministers and church bodies have no doubt had a sobering effect on extremist actions. Some of the Citizens Council leaders have found the voice of the church disturbing. Threats of dismissal of courageous ministers and even splits of churches at the synod and conference levels have failed to produce a comfortable silence for extremists to operate free of an annoying Christian conscience. A curious thing is happening in the South in this respect. The major southern churches more than a century ago broke away from their national bodies largely over the issue of slavery. The slaveholder was sufficiently influential to exert a deciding pressure on the actions of the ante-bellum churches. Today the individual finds himself at an embarrassing disadvantage within his own sectional church body. Church statements concerning the race issues brought about by the Supreme Court have given the segregation issue a moral implication, and the average dissenter finds it hard to be at moral variance with his church.

Some ministers and religious workers in several major denominations have found themselves in difficulty because of their expressed views on race problems in the South. Two Baptist ministers in Georgia were dismissed from their charges; one of them, Henry A. Buchanan of Shellman, scratched his and his wife's name from the church roll in the presence of his adversaries after a long and unhappy period in which Mr. Buchanan had preached several forthright sermons on the social problem following the Court decision. A similar case was that of Robert Blakely McNeill, who was dismissed from the Southeast Georgia presbytery in 1959. He had expressed a moderate attitude toward race relations in *Look* in 1957.

The Methodist Church has steered a circumspect course with its Central Jurisdiction, which has a membership of 395,000 Negroes. In viewing the race problem in his *Episcopal Message* to the Southeastern Jurisdictional Conference in July 1956, Bishop William Watkins in a guarded statement said: "We cannot rigidly maintain the customs of the dead past, nor dare we embrace the impatient idealism that attempts to solve the problems of race by refusing to take account of the limitations that confront us in an imperfect world. Instead, let us be open-minded, sane in judgments, Christian in our attitudes, constant in brotherly understanding and consideration, and ready to act as may in all good conscience appear best for the common good."

Every Southern Baptist Convention since 1955 has seen a minority group attempt to reverse that denomination's basic policy statement regarding the Supreme Court decision. Early in 1957 the Home Mission Board published a booklet of limited literary maturity but expressing racial views entitled *The Long Bridge*. The central theme of this mission study was Guy Bellamy's work with Negroes. The book gives a rather full and detailed account of the progress made in bridging the gap between white and Negro Christians of similar denominational.beliefs. In November of that year, Courts Redford, Executive Secretary of the Home Mission Board, issued a leaflet withdrawing *The Long Bridge* from mission study. Stocks of the books were recalled from Baptist book stores and churches were asked to return copies. He told Southern Baptists, "When preparation for the book was started in 1952 there was no indication that the promotion and study of such a book would incite divisive discussions or aggravate race tensions. Because of more recent developments, it now appears that this is an undesirable time to study the subject that in scores of societies and churches may be an occasion for bitter disagreement for harmful division." He might have added that courageously discussing sin would cause division in many societies and churches. Mr. Redford declared, "It is ever the purpose of the Board to promote harmony and co-operation in the denomination and in our churches, and furthermore, we earnestly desire to maintain the wonderful co-operation that we now have in the support and promotion of our Negro work." The Redford decision to withdraw *The Long Bridge* was reversed, however, and the book was again made available.

The South is solidly Protestant, and there are no present signs that it will ever be anything else. Catholics who promote expansion of their faith in the region must view the solid backbone of the old cotton belt with little else than frustration. Southern Protestantism is a powerful diffusion of social forces which defy assault.

Statistically, organized religion in the South reflects regional behavior. Church statistics for 1952, based upon the census for eleven southern states, excluding Maryland and Texas, estimate a population of 31,722,427, and there were 55,460 churches. They had a membership of 12,182,923, of which 10,063,271 were Protestants. Only in Louisiana were Protestants in a minority. South Carolina had a church membership of 847,440, of which 821,509 were Protestants. Mississippi, despite its old Latin population along the Gulf Coast, had 738,028 Protestants and only 55,553 Roman Catholics. Across the line in Louisiana, there were 858,295 Catholics and 568,784 Protestants. Protestant church membership ranged from 97.9 per cent in North Carolina to 39.5 in Louisiana. In all the other states except Kentucky and Florida, Protestants exceeded 90 per cent.

The South is perhaps the most intensively "churched" region in the country. There are indications that statistics fall short of truly reflecting this condition. In many instances regional church membership is a highly casual matter. In some respects it is passed on congenitally, whether or not the individual is formerly enrolled in a congregation. Actual accountable membership may be small as compared with a church's known constituency. The region averages approximately 3.5 churches per 10,000 population. North Carolina leads with its 8029 churches, Louisiana stands at the foot with only 3004 places of worship. Kentucky has 44.8 per cent of its population on church rolls, while only 31.3 per cent of the people of Arkansas are formal Christians. Approximately 36 per cent of southerners have joined a church, with more than 50 per cent of the white population in this category. Whites in Louisiana number 80 per cent church members, 61.9 in Mississippi, and 40.4 per cent in Arkansas. Established percentages, based on reportable church membership, indicate little more than a possible ratio of regional church affiliations. The large numbers of churches and the casualness with which some membership records are kept would account for discrepancies between reported statistics and the findings of the American Institute of Public Opinion poll.

No general statement could possibly give an adequate picture of Negro church membership. Hundreds of thousands of Negroes attend church and actively participate in worship services without being members of record in a church. The Statistical Division of the National Council of Churches makes no specific report on Negro church membership. These statistics are left out of the division's statistical reports because there is no information available. Some of the discrepancies between the races no doubt result from careless record-keeping, and part of it is due to the casualness of Negro church-joining. In Virginia in 1950, 20 per cent of the state's population was Negro, and 38.5 per cent of all Virginians were church members, but when Negroes were excluded from the count, church membership increased to 49.5 per cent of the population. In South Carolina exclusion of Negroes increased the ratio of church affiliation from approximately 40 to 60 per cent.

The Institute of Public Opinion analyzed religious attitudes in the nation. Southerners in the Southeastern Jurisdictional Conference of the Methodist Church revealed that 98 per cent of the people believed in God, 91 per cent accepted immortality as a firm hope, 81 per cent either belonged or had belonged to a church, a like number read the Bible, and the South led the nation in tithing.

The Southern Baptist denomination is in a majority in all eleven of the southern states except Louisiana and Virginia. In 1958 there were 9,207,758 Baptists enrolled in 31,297 southern congregations. In Virginia it has the largest individual membership. The second largest denomination is the Methodist Episcopal Church. The Presbyterian Church in the U.S. and the Disciples of Christ follow next in order, and there are some 200,000 members of the Church of Christ, Nazarenes, and Pentecostals.

The President of the Southern Baptist Convention, meeting in 1956 in Kansas City, charged delegates to establish 30,000 new churches by 1964; this meant doubling the denomination's congregations. There can be little doubt that many Baptist promoters are captivated by numbers. A critic from within the denomination wrote in the *Western Recorder*, a publication of the Kentucky Baptists, that "there is not one of the 30,000 churches affiliated with our Convention which does not have reason to be concerned about the numbers of its membership who manifest no evidence whatever of having committed themselves to Jesus Christ as Savior and Lord." He accused the Baptists of using "physical measurements in the determination of spiritual progress. Indeed it would be difficult to exaggerate the extent to which this particular phenomenon has dominated our thinking." Ministers, he said, evaluate their accomplishments in terms of budgets, Sunday school enrollments, value of church property, and new members.

Much Baptist megalomania gives an impression of unadulterated boosterism. The setting of a staggering goal of 30,000 new churches in less than a decade would seem to emphasize this fact. But the importance of the Southern Baptist denomination lies elsewhere so far as the internal social and religious affairs of the South are involved. By numerical dominance in the religious field it cannot escape assumption of a disproportionate share of responsibility for the moral response made by a large number of members to public issues. This body, which has more than a three-to-one edge in the southern church membership, cannot fail to realize it is capable of enormous influence in the shaping of public opinion.

Not a single southern issue, political or religious, has arisen in the last half-century which has not been influenced to some degree by Baptist attitudes. The congregational nature of this tremendous church body seldom acts in a congregational sense. Baptists generally are stubborn individualists. No set of officials, including those of the Southern Baptist Convention, speaks for all the membership. Some of it is economically poor and severely limited educationally. There are still ministers with little or no formal training whose perspectives are comparably restricted. All an individual needs to do to become an ordained practicing Baptist minister is to have an inspiration to preach and to find a congregation willing to listen to him. At the other end of the scale there is an able body of highly educated leaders who help to shape general Baptist policies and who administer colleges and seminaries. Members of congregations are becoming better educated, an uneducated minister is finding it increasingly difficult to find a congregation to serve. In 1939 Southern Baptists were invited to join the World Council of Churches, but the invitation was refused, partly because the Convention of Baptists has no ecclesiastical authority and partly because of the independence of the separate congregations. On the other hand, the Convention said, "We wish to do nothing that will imperil the growing spirit of co-operation on the part of our churches in the work of giving the gospel of Christ, as we understand it, to all men everywhere."

All the major denominations in the South maintain schools and colleges. Education, next to preaching the Gospel, is the first consideration of the churches. As late as the 1920s, desperate efforts were made to exercise thought control over curriculum, library, professor, and student. Any liberality of thought was a direct threat, not so much to the established social system as to orthodoxy. A youth who explored too far beyond the circumscribed boundaries of learning might not only be lost himself, he might lead others astray. One of the major changes in the southern religious picture has occurred in this area. Students are more sophisticated and more resistant to the old disciplines than were their fathers. Their perspectives are broader, and it would be difficult to stampede them emotionally. There are no fewer bigots than before, but they are now outnumbered by young rebels who shout bitter defiance at them. Even the seminaries have liberalized their teachings, some of them dangerously so in the eyes of the professional restrainers and thought controllers.

The Supreme Court decision of May 1954 created a staggering problem for southern churches. Because of its hold on the common people, the Baptist denomination was caught in confusion. Actually there are almost no Negro churches which are members of the Southern Baptist Convention. Negroes belong to the American Baptist Association or the National Baptist Convention of the U.S.A. There is little indication at the moment that the barriers of the Southern Baptist Convention will be lowered to admit Negroes. Two Nigerian students sent to Georgetown College in Kentucky by missionaries were admitted to membership in a white congregation.

The presence of Nigerians anywhere in the South would prove vexing to Baptists, or any other denomination. An important activity of southern churches has been missionary work, much of it in the African field. At Georgetown the Nigerians were at first asked to attend a Negro Baptist church, but pressure from students and faculty, in the face of much strife, paved the way to admit them to a white congregation. In affiliating with the church the colored students were asked to wear their native robes.

The Baptists are not alone in their problems. In several southern states Presbyterians have their conservatism challenged in the meeting of virtually every synod and assembly. One would have a hard time visualizing Negroes attending services of some congregations of this faith, yet there are Presbyterian congregations in the upper South where Negroes may be seated in Presbyterian pews. Methodists have suffered through equally tense discussions of social issues, and a constant threat of secession of splinter groups hangs over their southern jurisdictional conferences. The Pentecostal groups are just as conservative as the older denominations, and none of them accepts Negro members in integrated congregations. The Church of God of the Cleveland dispensation, for example, follows the segregated pattern.

The church and religion have deep spiritual meaning to the South. It is impossible to measure their meaning to individuals, or to apply a quantitative standard to personal commitments. The churches embody in their memberships every element of southern society, and their members and leaders represent myriads of points of view. Most church bodies have committed themselves to propositions regarding the social environment in which they exist, and have held to these commitments. The courage they have demonstrated as organized bodies has no doubt had a strong influence on the thinking and actions of individual members.

XVII

In the Image of the Future

Richmond, where I arrived a week later, somewhat surprised me by its
substance, show and gardens, and I was inclined to think that in com-
ing to it directly from New York and Philadelphia, I had been led to
rather underrate its quality at my first visit. There are only six towns,
having town-like character, in the slave states — New Orleans, Mobile,
Louisville, St. Louis, Charleston, and Richmond. Savannah, and all
other "places" having like it, in winter, a population for a town, are
simply overgrown villages in appearance, and in convenience; half the
streets tolerably good pastures, the other half intolerable cart roads;
the best mansions, clap-board, Americo-moresque cottages; the best
gardens in a setting of picket fence; the public squares mere camp
grounds, with weedy walks and sedge grass lawns; the majority of the
shops selling raisins, nailrods and nigger cloth, from the same counters
with silks, and school books and "bitters."
        OLMSTED, A JOURNEY IN THE BACK COUNTRY, pp. 279–80

The modern South stands astride the great divide. Behind it lies
both the nineteenth century and the first half of the twentieth,
eras marked by crisis and frustration. Essentially southern history has been marred by conflict: conflict between the sections;
between a predominantly agricultural society competing in a
rising industrial age; between political approaches and points of
view; between two races sharing a common regional heritage
and competing for economic survival on a common ground; and,
finally, conflicts engendered by defeat in a Civil War and the
impasse of a chaotic period of reconstruction. A region thus
caught in the travail of time has created many images by which it
has expressed both hopes and sentiments. Some of these have

been the deeply sentimental ones of the so-called "moonlight and roses" concept of better days in the past. Others have symbolized bitter racial friction, economic frustrations, and lost leadership and waste of human resources.

Whatever images the region has accepted, they have been familiar social landmarks in the past. One image which ranks high but undefined is the constant reverence for the southern heritage or southern way of life. Like every broad generalization this one makes a deep emotional appeal but gives a poorly defined sense of direction. Far too many southerners have accepted these generalities as images of regional peace and well-being without realizing that the South, like every other area of the world, lives in an era of deep-seated and fundamental change. Almost without realizing what they do, great masses of southern people have accepted forces which revolutionize their lives without understanding that they also destroy old images.

On Saturday, October 10, 1959, the metropolitan Atlanta area selected one of its citizens to represent this bulging community as a personal symbol of industrial well-being. Nominated as the millionth citizen was a young, well-educated, and fairly well-paid man named William Smith, originally from Rochester, New York. This millionth Atlantan was sent south as a sales executive for the Champion Paper and Fiber Company. Thus the modern South goes its way creating new images. Emotionally southern people are reluctant to desert the past, but the Atlanta Chamber of Commerce reconciles the selection of a young northern industrialist by saying, "Yankees get to be the most southern people in the world after a while here. First thing you know they're sitting under the magnolias wearing string ties and sipping mint juleps."

Image-making almost always involves some tragedy. For every new southern image that is created an old one is reduced in stature or destroyed. For more than a century, historians, statisticians, sociologists, and political reformers have viewed the South's march to the future largely within an atmosphere of crisis. Years of hard economic struggle both shortened regional vision and sharpened its temper. An intensely rural way of life not only experienced economic failures but nurtured a sensitivity toward urban society and urban economic and political controls.

If the present South faces a fundamental crisis, it is in the conflict between country and flourishing urban communities. Atlanta, New Orleans, Norfolk-Newport News, Memphis, Louisville, Miami, and Charlotte form spreading metropolitan complexes which grasp old rural communities in their tentacles. So do Birmingham, Mobile, Richmond, Charleston, Jacksonville, Savannah, Baton Rouge, Lynchburg, and Little Rock. These places, and scores of others, have outgrown their bounds since 1940. Every month the traditionally rural South is being forced deeper into retreat. Savannah, for instance, has within its metropolitan periphery an abundant supply of labor, but it also has access to labor resources in eight or more rural Georgia counties.

The old line "wool-hat" politician who perennially shouted his mighty defenses of the rural way of life to a responsive constituency now finds himself speaking more and more in a vacuum. His successors now glibly promise to bring new industries to the South and to serve their best interests when they arrive. There is a great gulf between yesterday's tirades of "Pitchfork Ben" Tillman and today's seductive messages of Governor Ernest F. Hollings of South Carolina. Across the Savannah there are indications that hairline cracks are developing in the tight county-unit system of voting which has so long given rural Georgians dominant political control. Elsewhere old political images are being defaced if not destroyed.

Southern governors meeting in Asheville, North Carolina, in October 1959, closed one long and revered chapter of southern history when they sought more adequate tariff protection for southern industrial goods. One can hardly imagine James Kimball Vardaman of Mississippi, John Tyler Morgan of Alabama, Thomas Watson of Georgia, and M. C. Butler of South Carolina giving voice to views that the Congress and President be urged "to consider at all times the protection of the national security and the domestic economy in decisions affecting the amount and extent of foreign imports." Southerners now identify themselves with northerners in resisting any competition that would threaten industry. A threat to domestic peace and safety in the South is a threat to future industrial expansion, and voices pleading for moderation can now be heard above the din of protesting extremists.

Early in 1957, William P. Engels, former chairman of the Committee of 100 which sought industrial plant locations for the Birmingham area, told his Alabama neighbors that lawless acts by the Ku Klux Klan and other hoodlums hampered their chances to secure new industries. *The Christian Science Monitor* reported Engels as saying, "We in Birmingham particularly must face up to our deficiencies and face them equally. The hoodlumism that has occurred in Birmingham in recent months has hit the headlines all over the country. This unfavorable publicity has overshadowed the splendid reputation we had built up over the last ten years for industrial and cultural progress. To my personal knowledge we have lost plants and other operations because of these events and the resulting publicity."

Elsewhere in the South industrial commissions and chambers of commerce voiced a similar point of view. The Little Rock crisis had noticeable effects on industrial expansion and on the maintenance of a climate conducive to the development of a hospitable industrial community. In some places the emergence of the Ku Klux Klan has no doubt damaged local hopes for new industry. Headlines which publicize southern violence might thwart an enormous amount of effort in securing new industry for the South. A story describing the bombing of a synagogue, a school, or a home or a lynching hardly induces boards of directors of·a northern manufacturing company to establish branch plants in such communities when other areas of the country are making equally strong bids for them.

The image of violence in the South can be costly. When the region was predominantly rural and agricultural, a lynching or a bombing did little economic damage. Today, when the South is courting industry, such outbreaks have a bearing on the future of a company's operation. The South as a whole perhaps has no greater amount of violence than other parts of the country, but the kinds of outbreak are more disturbing. Every new crime only lends force to the old image of lynching and disregard for established law.

The South's brightest hope for prosperous economic existence lies in the exploitation of its basic resources. Most important is a willing human resource anxious to sell muscle and brain to hasten the arrival of a new age. The region now bids fair to skip a full phase of American industrial history. Instead of debating states' rights and fighting back at political "Yankee strawmen," the southern governors at Asheville engaged in discussions of domestic use of atomic energy. Already installations in Tennessee, Kentucky, and South Carolina unmask a future of unlimited promise in this field. Atomic energy promises to thrust southerners forward in a mighty leap to lay claim to the last half of the twentieth century as a time of regional triumph. There is not now apparent either an emotionally aroused force or a resistant political crusade to stay plans to employ the atom to bring into being a new way of southern life.

Already the glass is clear as to the exploitation of human energy. The current rise of industry and the intoxicating promises of the atomic age have caught the South disastrously short in educational preparation. Before 1940 southerners found it easier to reconcile their lower educational achievements by saying they were good enough for a floundering rural society and to serve the professions. Too few southern educators prior to 1945 had thought constructively in terms of intense urbanization, or of the possible racial integration threat to the schools. Though arguments contended for better support of schools, and every educational survey showed the South hamstrung at the bottom of the statistical tables, educational leadership worked against great odds. From the beginning the image of southern education has been largely one of mediocrity and inadequacy.

New conditions in the South make the old human image as out of date and antiquated as that of the Yankee abolitionist and slave baron. If the South is ultimately to realize its promise, the new leadership will have to be soundly educated. Instead of a pink-cheeked colonel wearing a string tie, ruffled shirt, frock coat, and broad-brimmed planter's hat, the new southern human symbol will most likely be a less flamboyantly clad doctor of philosophy, who is a specialist in physics or business management. He will know more about atomic energy and corporate management than his aged prototype knew about slaves, staple crops, and cotton factors. If this new spokesman for the South is to be a trained scientist, the new southerner of necessity must be superior to his father in basic educational preparation in order to find profitable employment.

Again the Southern Governors' Conference reflected a realistic appreciation of the South's immediate condition. Governor J. Lindsay Almond, Jr., of Virginia, a realist, was elected its president. He made clear to his colleagues that the South must choose between allowing some integration and closing public schools. "We cannot secede from the Union," he said, "we cannot overthrow the Federal Government, and we cannot reverse a final decree of a federal court." On another occasion Governor Almond said, "And closing down the public schools means going back to the dark ages." This was indeed a clear voice of moderation in a gathering of southern governors. This body had just received a report from its committee on industrial development saying that southern labor is rapidly gaining skills and is becoming a greater drawing power for industry. This committee, headed by Governor Orval Faubus of Arkansas, made no suggested alternative if some states should close their public schools and further handicap their people in preparing themselves to compete for jobs in this new age.

There is still lacking in the South sufficient native capital to finance necessary industrial expansion. The region is still largely dependent on outside capital to finance the building and equipping of new plants. In this respect the South has made its least departure from the past. Almost every conversation, speech, or report is predicated on the fact that new industry must be brought in from the outside instead of being organized at home.

The South has been highly successful in the importation of industries. Between 1956 and July 1, 1959, 4448 new industrial plants were located in the South. Most of these were organized and managed by outside corporations. In 1956, there were 3971 banks with total liabilities and assets of $38,436,100,000 in the region. Of this amount $28,227,600,000 was deposited on demand. Southern assets represented a relatively small share of the national holdings of $250,763,000,000. This means that major financial control of industry still resides largely outside the South.

In 1929 southern personal income was derived largely from farming, service employment, and the older industries of lumbering, textiles, and mining. In eleven states it averaged $363. By 1956 it had increased to $1325 as compared with a national average income of $1940. In terms of gross income, southern farmers for 1956 received $3,855,000,000, as compared with an industrial income of $33,322,000,000 and with governmental disbursements of $9,861,000,000. These figures represent three interesting facts: Farm income is dropping phenomenally behind industrial and service incomes; government disbursements in the South are of sufficient importance to regional economy that the Federal Government is able to exert enormous pressure on the region; and there is a rising urbanism which is reshaping southern approaches to regional problems.

For more than a century the old cotton South struggled mightily with a lack of capital with which to set its economic house in order. The present South hardly struggles in the same way, partly because there is a greater proportion of native capital available, and partly because of the manner in which corporate capital originates in the American capitalistic system. This fact distinguishes the present moment from others in southern history. Before 1840, millions of rural southerners had literally no set margin of economic existence beyond which they could not survive. A small farm always provided a meager survival. This is no longer true for great masses of the population. The margin of survival in the present South is now measured largely in terms of cash-wage income and availability of industrial and public employment.

Although the South lacks both basic capital and control over that which finances industrial expansion in the region, southern economic thinking generally has moved close to that in the intensely industrial regions of the country. The actual political pattern may have changed little from that of 1920, but thinking within the political framework gives evidence of aligning itself with new economic conditions. Much of the casual conversation in the region centers upon the subject of capitalizing and managing industry. Every new expansion of industrial activity takes the South farther away from its past.

Physically the South is creating new images. Bulldozers and giant earth-movers gnaw away hillsides to create new industrial sites, airfields, and roads. Workmen with plastic and metal helmets thrust up new electric generating plants, atomic energy installations, and factory buildings. They personify the new southern industrial image. It is hard, for instance, to imagine the South

Carolina Industrial Commission restraining itself in an advertising section in the *New York Times* so far as not to show an antebellum Charleston home or parade the state's truly beautiful women in crinoline, or to ignore the Yankee menace, the NAACP, and General William T. Sherman. The new South Carolina image has not a single magnolia blossom on it; it is that of an electrical worker looking into the sky at an encircling manufacturing-company plane and shouting, "We thought you would be coming soon." It is also that of two sophisticated men who have withdrawn from the polo games at Aiken to discuss the state's industrial promise. In this advertising, South Carolina is indeed promising to depart from its past.

The Norfolk and Western Railroad enlarges the new southern image by proclaiming that southern labor is capable of high productivity, stays on the job, assumes citizenship responsibility, is young, vigorous, and responsive to training. Where Atlanta chose a young northern company man as its millionth metropolitan area citizen, the rest of the South has as its new personal symbol of economic revolution a native son dressed in overalls who is anxious to earn cash wages in an industrial plant.

While industrial workers hail arriving company planes, the modern South ponders another question. How long can it continue to exert major political influences in shaping national legislation? Only the passage of time itself can answer this question. There is an enormous chasm between southern representatives making their influence felt in Washington and individual southerners expressing their political choices at the polls. Of the 102,743,000 Americans twenty-one years of age or older in 1956, 19,684,000 were southerners. In the first primary elections for governors between 1954 and 1956, 5,570,000 voters went to the polls, or less than one-third of the voting-age population. Any appreciable increase in the total number of persons voting would have a bearing on the old political approaches. It is in this area that both urbanization and industrialization may well serve to change the nature of southern politics. To date, voter apathy has been more in evidence in the South than the rest of the country. In primary elections in 1954, only 228,000 Virginians went to the polls, as compared with 666,000 voters in Wisconsin.

Efforts are being made to stimulate greater Negro participation in southern politics. The greater the resistance to this move, the more certain it is that the traditional political image will be revised. It would not take an appreciable number of Negro registrants in Mississippi, for instance, to threaten the state's political system with change. Out of a potential voting population of 1,100,000 in 1955, only 44,000 persons voted in the first gubernatorial primary. Much of this discrepancy is represented by a long history of racial discrimination, but tragically much of it reflects low educational attainment and failure to motivate properly the people to participate in the elementary democratic process of voting. Current southern political leadership well understands that any effective federal civil-rights legislation would threaten its survival. But even more promising of political revolution is the fact that southern industrial labor will come to have a greater stake in political decisions as it begins to feel the direct economic impact of legislation and political control.

Of more immediate concern in many parts of the South is the survival of the public-school system in the face of the threatened integration of the two races in common classrooms. It is doubtful that the forces which opened the crusade to lower the barriers of educational discrimination between the two races really foresaw that the South would be caught in one of its most strategic moments of economic transition. An increasing number of responsible southerners have emphasized the fact that the modern South cannot prosper without making a maximum effort to improve its schools. Actions to close public schools have already provoked militant pressure groups to keep them open. In May 1959, Louis B. Pendleton of Richmond, Virginia, told members of the Sumter, South Carolina, Citizens Council, "Getting out of the public school business isn't easy to do. When the time comes in South Carolina, I trust you will be united, but do not be surprised at the so-called segregationists who suddenly become enthusiastic and active in 'Save-Our-Schools' organizations." In Little Rock, the Women's Emergency Committee for Public Schools demonstrated how effective such organizations can be. This action hardly involves the issue segregation versus integration; it is aimed at ensuring that young southerners will not be denied educational opportunity in their vital early years. When integration of Negro and white children will take place in the public schools in several southern states is at the moment beyond the guess of the most rash prophet. Governor J. Lindsay Almond, Jr., may indeed be correct in visualizing token integration as the minimum price for preserving public schools without disruption.

Whatever the outcome of the integration crisis, the fact that better education has become a necessary image for the South is important. Before the South can realize economic success, it has clearly to meet the challenge of educational maturity. The old southern image of culture was largely one of graciousness and gentility. Now it is intimately associated with economic welfare. Never before has the region had to define so specifically the details of its educational values. In the cold practical terms of educational maturity, the southern cultural heritage has assumed a new depth.

This was inherent in the statement of Governor S. Ernest Vandiver of Georgia in January 1961. Faced with the stern decision of closing the University of Georgia or permitting at least token integration upon direct court order, he and his advisers made the latter choice. The *New York Times* reported him as saying to a joint session of the legislature, "The crisis is upon us. I must tell you quite frankly that a failure to resolve it will blight our state. Like a cancerous growth, it will devour progress — consuming all in its path — pitting friend against friend — demoralizing all that is good — stifling the economic growth of the state — and denying the youth of Georgia their proper educational opportunity."

Racial integration is a highly relative condition which involves far more complex economic and social situations than mere classroom associations of white and Negro children. It may be that this is actually the least significant aspect of present efforts to abolish discriminatory racial barriers. The rise of a new southern economy has in it the necessary force to destroy many traditional discriminations. A rising scale of personal income affects white and Negro alike, and the Negro with cash in hand has become a welcome customer in all kinds of stores in many southern cities. Merchants in highly competitive situations can hardly afford to drive away customers who have only to cross the street to enrich their competitors. Department stores catering to women no longer close their floors to Negro women. In other areas barriers have been lowered. As the Negro has moved to town he has entered into an entirely different relationship with his white business and professional neighbors. He now appears in the new image of a cash customer.

Places of amusement, public recreation facilities, public transportation, and cultural institutions are gradually being opened to everybody. Negro passengers share common waiting rooms in the Atlanta airport where they were barred once in a similar situation in nearby railway and bus station waiting rooms. No one but the most unrelenting diehard resister can really believe that the southern Negro in the mass will be kept away from the polls much longer by legal technicalities. In another positive manner, it would be erroneous to assume that the Negro has lost ground educationally since 1945. On the contrary, and despite educational deficiencies of his schools, he has made some of his most solid educational gains in the history of his race in the South, even if he has made slow progress in removing discriminatory barriers. Except in cases of extreme actions in places like Little Rock and Warren and Prince Edward counties in Virginia, where public schools were closed, he can rejoice in much better educational opportunities and even hope for further improvement. As more southern colleges and universities make their classrooms free of racial restrictions, the Negro will have an opportunity to make even faster educational gains.

During these years of change the southerner finds himself faced with new approaches to solving the race problems. In 1956 Montgomery, Alabama, Negroes undertook to erase racial discrimination on the city bus system by refusing to ride the buses. In a sustained period of passive resistance they underwent considerable personal hardship to accomplish their objective. This strike was widely publicized and no doubt was effective in consolidating considerable public opinion in the nation in favor of the Negro's position.

A personal protest voice raised in the Montgomery strike was that of the Reverend Martin Luther King. Preaching non-violence, he came to speak to a national audience for an appreciable segment of Negro opinion. Passive resistance was difficult to deal with because there were no overt violations of law. Nevertheless, Dr. King has often found himself involved in the general racial argument in the South and elsewhere. In October 1960 he was arrested in Atlanta for participating in a sit-down strike in a department store in violation of a Georgia anti-trespass law which forbids persons to remain on the premises of a business after they have been asked to leave.

In all the history of racial adjustment in the South few incidents have been more disturbing than the so-called "sit-in strikes." This crusade against racial discrimination at lunch counters struck at a highly vulnerable point in the pattern of racial discrimination. Department store managers welcomed Negro trade in all other departments of their stores, but maintained segregated lunch counters. The sit-in strikes were stimulated partly by the Congress of Racial Equality and partly by Negro and white college students. In March 1960, four students from the North Carolina Agricultural and Technical College, led by 18-year-old Ezell Blair sought service at the lunch counter in the F. W. Woolworth Store in Greensboro and were refused. By mid-summer stores in nine or ten southern cities had desegregated their lunch counters. In Charlotte, North Carolina, the Mayor's Friendly Relations Committee, with Dr. John R. Cunningham, President of Davidson College, as chairman, carried on long discussions with local businessmen. In July the Committee was able to announce racial bans in the stores would be removed.

Almost at the moment Dr. Cunningham and his committee were reporting agreement in Charlotte, the Platform Committee of the Democratic party was presenting to the country a civil-rights plank condoning the sit-down activities. In their protests against the civil-rights proposal, southerners argued that to favor the strikes was to condone lawless invasion. of private property. They did not, however, contend that entry into a store to make a purchase from a department other than a food counter was such an invasion.

In leaving the country, the southern Negro is rapidly changing his own image. First he finds himself caught in the vacuous eye of the great centrifugal force of suburbia expanding out from old town centers. The impenetrable wall of suburban communities largely confines the Negro to older submarginal areas. Here he is rapidly exchanging the old sex-hunger image of the days when lynching was rampant for that of modern day urban violence. This is a social area where he is experiencing his greatest test as a responsible citizen. He is faced with the problem of preventing the occurrence of violence under conditions which are often highly conducive to rising criminality. Under the leadership of the Reverend Martin Luther King and students of the sit-down movement, the Negro attempts to create an image of passive resistance. Beyond this the Southern Christian Leadership Conference is undertaking to stimulate the Negro to become an active and responsive citizen at the polls.

Though the new image of the southern urban-dwelling Negro has not fully revealed itself, two facts are already clearly discernible. First, he has left the South in appreciable numbers. In 1950 the percentage of non-white emigrants from Alabama, Georgia, Louisiana, Mississippi, and South Carolina, and the non-white emigrants outside the South was larger for southern states than the comparable percentage of whites. Of the Negro emigrants who had moved from the state of their birth, 72.6 per cent lived outside the South. Specific population figures are not available for 1960, but the increase in the Negro population in several states reflects the trend of a movement away from the South. The Negro population in the five original northwestern states of Ohio, Indiana, Illinois, Michigan, and Wisconsin increased from 930,450 in 1930 to 1,803,698 in 1950. Five southern states — Louisiana, Arkansas, Alabama, Mississippi, and Georgia — for the same period showed an increase only from 4,280,466 to 4,337,-940. There is every reason to believe that the discrepancy between these figures has increased since 1950. Second, emigration of the Negro population has changed two parts of the old regional-Negro image. The Negro is now largely a town-dweller, and the race problem has lost much of its old rural form. Too, it is now national in scope not regional. No longer, except in some parts of the old blackbelts, is there a predominantly Negro population in the South. The percentage gap between the races is being constantly widened. There can be little doubt but what the final decisions in lowering racial barriers will be made in the towns and cities.

Nothing in the South is left untouched by change. Since the first pioneers broke their way into the great stretches of virgin land, moonshining has been a popular activity. The only thing the moonshiner had to fear was the nosy revenue officer. Today he faces a new fear. A Licensed Beverage Bureau survey reveals to him that he and his fellow brewers poured 55,000,000 gallons of illicit whisky onto the national market. Eleven southern states supplied an important portion of this burgeoning stream. No longer, however, do hillbilly distillers make moonshine liquor through the week to enliven the courthouse loafers on Saturday. Moonshining, like industrialization generally, depends upon an "outside" market. Only 14 per cent of southern moonshine is said to be produced by the old type distiller. The survey says, "In the South moonshining is becoming a 'big time' racket as syndicate operators move in." Historically, moonshiners shot it out with revenuers in the woods, but now the syndicate runners in powerful automobiles on improved southern roads hauling approximately 40,000,000 gallons of wildcat whisky a year give a new meaning to this traditional battle.

In a final analysis the South's adjustment to its new age lies largely in its ability to reconcile its past to the future. The temper in which this is done will determine the course of the region in the latter half of this century. Presently the word moderation is in ill-repute in places. Governor Ross R. Barnett of Mississippi told a Citizens' Council audience in Jackson on September 8, 1959, that, "these 'moderates' we've been hearing so much about are nothing more than southern burglars. They want to rob us of our priceless heritage, and they tell us that we shouldn't complain, as long as they steal it a little bit at a time." There is a wide gap between this view and that expressed by Leroy Collins and J. Lindsay Almond, Jr. In fact, there is a broad chasm between it and the actions of the Southern Governors' Conference. Colgate Darden, Jr., former Governor of Virginia and former president of that state's university, has expressed the view that "self-discipline and moderation at the council table" holds a solution for the South's basic problems.

Moderation is an inherent part of the best of the southern tradition. It has long symbolized the South's honor and dignity. The very heart of the regional heritage is hospitality, graciousness, Christianity, and humaneness, all of these embedded in moderation. The great Jeffersonian tradition of liberalism rests upon a foundation of law and civil obedience. General Robert

E. Lee further personified a spirit of moderation and dignity in the hard years following Appomattox. These are images which the South cherishes. An injury to any of these tarnishes the honor of the South itself. For this reason, if for no other, the South cannot tolerate the Ku Klux Klan; the schoolhouse, religious community, and synagogue bombers; or any other extremist groups who stampede the region into ignoring law and order, or who create an image of violence and injustice.

Spokesmen for the South in the nineteenth century were eloquent in their outpourings, whether it be for expansion of slavery or expansion of industry. Henry W. Grady and his zealous contemporaries understood the necessity of balancing an agrarian economy with industry. They, however, little realized that the future would bring with it moral and social responsibilities which would reach down to the very basis of regional economic existence. At this point in the twentieth century the mature southerner tends to view the future with a fair degree of optimism. Though statistical tables still warn that the South has far to go to accomplish both social and economic security, there is reason to hope for improvement. How successful the South is in laying claim to the latter half of this century will depend in large measure on how sound its people make positive educational, economic, and moral decisions. The details at present are confused and complex. Regional prejudices and pressures often obscure changes which are occurring. Nevertheless, much of the course of the South into the future is already charted, and that course gives every evidence of leading the region away from many of the old and familiar ways of the past. How much of the past the South of the future preserves will depend on what standard of values it adopts in this period of change.

XVIII

The Way of the Transgressor

A decade and a half has passed since the Supreme Court handed down its Brown *v.* School Board decision. It is now possible to make an appraisal of its effect upon the South. The question as to whether the region has made any effort to comply fully with the intent of the decision can be answered with a resounding No! Nevertheless changes have occurred in the South since 1954 which few if any southerners believed possible even within a quarter- or a half-century. But these changes are not all the result of the famous education decision nor are some of them in any way related to it. The decision did, however, shock southerners into awareness that their traditional patterns of life could no longer be sustained.

It has taken almost two decades for most southern legislatures to become convinced that they are powerless to interpose the will of the states by one means or another between their citizens and the power of the Federal Government. Never in American history have so many laws been placed on statute books with such rapidity and such ill-consideration. Conversely, in no other period in American legislative history has so much statutory dross been nullified by state and federal court decisions. It can be said at last that hardly a southerner today believes there is the slightest possibility that a state legislature can circumvent the mandates of the courts. No matter how angry individuals may become, or how many "Impeach Earl Warren" signs are erected along the highways, the fact remains that federal district and circuit courts have been able to nullify most of the evasive legislation passed by southern legislatures.

Passage of civil rights acts by Congress in 1964 and 1966 removed once and for all the legal barriers against those legally qualified to exercise fully their right to vote. Despite this, there are still pockets of bitter-end resistance to Negroes' voting in parts of the black belts in South Carolina, Mississippi, Alabama, Georgia, and Louisiana. Such resistance is, however, increasingly being challenged by federal authorities and is feeling the pressure of public opinion. The Civil Rights Commission's report on voting in Mississippi (1966) was a stinging exposé of petty, spiteful discriminations in three highly rural (old plantation) counties. Neither the report nor the presence of federal registrars completely ended intimidation or discrimination, but they did shatter the old political procedures of "closed" voting. Too, the state was placed in a precarious situation both before the courts and in areas where urban Negro voters held either a balance of power or were in the majority.

Baker *v.* Carr (1962), which was brought before the Supreme Court by *writ of certiorari* from the District Court of Middle Tennessee, promised greater changes in state patterns of voting and office-seeking than perhaps any other single act in this century. The Supreme Court remanded the issue of local reapportionment of the respective district courts. First, the decision struck hard at the old "manageable" districting of the states for both state legislative and congressional representation. Following this decision district federal judges, in carrying out the mandate of the Supreme Court, threatened in several cases to redistrict the states if state legislators did not make reasonable and equitable divisions based upon voter concentrations. No court or any other power can in fact tempt state legislators to neglect local political interests entirely, and no doubt much of the redistricting represents the influences of new political pressures.

The revolutionary court decision represented more than a judicial concern for the sanctity of the ballot. Urban political demands have come to be of the utmost importance in the past two decades in the South. At last the old agrarian-plantation tradition totters on the brink of the grave. In every state, with the possible exceptions of Mississippi and Arkansas, the power of political decision has come to rest more and more with urban voters. Even Georgia with its historic county unit system saw Baker *v.* Carr ease the rural grip on that state; it was evident there would be increasing urban predominance in political affairs. This despite the fact that voters in the gubernatorial election in 1966 elected a governor who represented a militant segregationist point of view and who gained a good portion of his strength from rural counties.

As revolutionary as Baker v. Carr was, there is now doubt whether in many parts of the South the urban centers have actually won a victory. In the movement from the farm large masses of voters have stopped on halfway ground in suburban communities. These promise to be almost as big a threat to the intensely urban community as the rural southerner was a quarter of a century ago.

Thus politically the South, now approaching the final quarter of the twentieth century, has to concern itself with two new forces. First is the urban voter, whose political decisions will be influenced largely by demands of an urban-industrial community, and who will in no wise be inclined to heed the siren call of the past. Second, the concentration of Negro population predominately in urban centers will remove it almost completely from the traditional forms of intimidations practiced by white men. The kind of discriminatory practices used in rural areas are all but impossible at urban polling places, especially when such acts would take place under the scrutiny of the urban press. Far more important than this is the fact that the young urban Negro tends to be a political activist, or to be periodically under the influence of organized activist groups. In time more and more Negroes will find their way into elective offices. In the general election in 1967 a Negro was elected to the Louisiana legislature from the 20th New Orleans House District. In Mississippi, Negroes won election to local offices, and Robert G. Clark of Holmes County was elected to the state legislature. Dr. W. Ferguson Reid of Richmond, Virginia, was elected to the General Assembly, and Mrs. Georgia Davis of Louisville was elected to the Kentucky Senate.

No one can now predict what kind of partisan allegiances southerners will form. In presidential elections they have forsaken the past either by supporting Republican nominees or by casting protest votes for splinter party candidates. Supporters of such splinter candidates have no real hope, of course, that their candidate will garner more than a token number of the national electoral votes. They do, however, hold to the hope that at some future time the national presidential election will wind up ultimately in the House of Representatives, where southern congressmen will find themselves in fortunate trading positions, if there is a protest candidate, such as George Wallace of Alabama, whom the congressmen can support. They can then trade such support to the national party or candidate willing to go easy on civil rights or to back other southern interests. In the election of governors, congressmen, and senators, the South has not made a radical departure from the traditional Democratic party alignment. This has produced a paradox. For while there has been opposition to Democratic presidential candidates, most national, state, and local Democratic office-seekers have kept voter loyalties by pledging to support the *status quo*.

It may be that industrialization and urbanization will bring about a genuine, clearly defined two-party system in the South. There is already evidence that political responses by southerners reflect their economic interests. If the Republican party hopes to gain major support from the newly enfranchised Negro, it will have to promulgate liberal racial attitudes which in turn will alienate a good bloc of the white vote it recently has gained. But its future development may depend on exactly such a course. It is difficult at this moment to predict the political course of the South in the immediate future. There are some guidelines, though. Some gubernatorial administrations have already reflected an awareness of changing conditions. For instance, Governor Terry Sanford of North Carolina, Carl Sanders of Georgia, Bert Combs and Edward T. Breathitt of Kentucky, and Buford Ellington of Tennessee have all moved with the times. There have been other cases, however, where governors have either attempted to hold the line against these changes or have even attempted to turn the calendar back.

A cynic examining the record of racial relations in the South since 1954 would note that few fundamental changes in attitudes and behavior patterns have occurred. But progress, and even phenomenal progress, has been made in some sectors. In many instances, however, what has seemed to be change has been largely a shifting of social and racial groups within the region itself rather than the solution of long-existing problems.

The southern school system is perhaps the best place to examine the degree of change that has taken place. To begin with, the attempted desegregation of the schools has created such a massive body of judicial decision. It has often not been clear from the decisions themselves as to what might properly be termed "All deliberate speed" in carrying out desegregation provisions or what could be called a reasonable expression of serious intent on the part of state and public school officials to conform to the mandate of the United States Supreme Court.

The Civil Rights Act of 1964 contained two sections which spelled out clearly the intent of the Congress on this matter. Unfortunately Section 401 of Title IV contained an apparent contradiction in its approach toward the transportation of students between schools to establish a racial balance in a community. Title VI provided for the withdrawal of federal funds from school districts that fail to comply with conditions for desegregating their schools. Enforcement of Title VI, however, involved several difficulties. First, Congress failed to provide adequate money to establish an enforcing agency. Second, the responsibility for administering the title provisions was placed under the Office of Education in the federal Department of Health, Education, and Welfare. This body was not organized for such a purpose, nor did it have the qualified staff, even if it had the authority to carry out such a staggering assignment with vigor and efficiency.

In 1965 the Office of Education assumed that state school officials would now proceed to carry out the intent of the Civil Rights Act of 1964. This proved to be a serious miscalculation. No appreciable dent was made in either desegregation or in the abolition of the dual school systems in many southern states. To add to the Office's difficulties, Congress in 1966 cut the budget of the Office of Education from support of a proposed 348 staff members to 278. Thus the enforcement body, already inadequately organized for such a task, was left hopelessly understaffed.

Starting in 1965, the Office of Education issued deadline dates on which school officials must either file satisfactory plans for compliance with both the mandate of the courts and Title VI of the Civil Rights Act of 1964 or be denied federal funds. In 1965 and again in 1966 the Commissioner's office prepared and issued guideline specifications for desegregation of schools and for ending the dual school system.

The appearance of the guidelines and of the compliance officers in the southern states introduced a new phase of resistance. Actually the guidelines were quite moderate. They prescribed little more than the exercise of "freedom of choice" programs or "tokenism" for most local school districts. Certainly they only slightly affected the central problem of dual schools and segregation. Immediately, however, the guidelines and agents of the Office of the Education Commissioner were attacked as being impractical and oppressive. In South Carolina, Louisiana, Georgia, Alabama, and Mississippi especially, there were loud protests. State superintendents of public instruction and other state officials went to Washington to call on southern congressional delegations to protest the high-handedness of the Office of Education, and its offensive agents and guidelines. They argued that the agents the Commissioner sent into the South were inexperienced and arbitrary. These protests even reached the White House. South Carolina entered suit in the federal court for relief. On December 29, 1966, the United States Fifth Circuit Appeals Court in New Orleans ruled in the cases of Louisiana and Alabama that the guidelines were reasonable, that the dual system of schools was unacceptable, and that freedom of choice and gradualism must now give way to the opening of all schools to pupils with proper grade qualifications.

The Court informed Louisiana and Alabama school officials that although it was not bound by rules prescribed by the Office of Education, the guidelines "are substantially the same as the Court's standards." Specifically the two states were ordered to desegregate classrooms, faculties, and staffs by the opening of the 1967–68 school year. In April 1967, the Supreme Court further rejected efforts of six southern states to delay compliance with the court mandate beyond the following school opening in the fall of 1968. On October 9, 1967, the Supreme Court refused to review a decision of the Fifth United States Circuit Court which in fact ordered sweeping desegregation in the six southern states. In handing down its mandate the Court said, "Now after 12 years of snail's pace progress toward school desegregation, the courts are entering a new era. The clock has ticked the last tick of tokenism and delay in the name of 'deliberate speed.'" It likewise said that school officials could no longer stave off desegregation by resorting to "freedom of choice" plans which did not free Negro children and parents of intimidation.

The Court in this latter decision followed a fine but subtle line. Southern school officials had argued that they should not be pushed into desegregating the southern schools when northern schools escaped compliance in the same areas. There was, as the Court and some newspaper editors said, a distinct difference between the two approaches. In Cincinnati, for instance, segregation resulted *de facto;* in the southern states, where vestiges of the old system were firmly rooted in deliberate and aggressive policies of discrimination, desegregation was in fact *de jure.*

At the time the Fifth United States Circuit Court handed down its sweeping decision applying directly to the schools of Louisiana and Alabama, Governor Lurleen Wallace called a meeting in Montgomery of the governors of Georgia, Alabama, Mississippi, and Louisiana to find some way to circumvent the Office of Education's guidelines. Governor Lester Maddox of Georgia was quoted by the *Atlanta Constitution* as saying the Health, Education, and Welfare instructions were "un-American, ungodly, and even criminal." In sharp contrast, Governor John J. McKeithan of Louisiana said, "I don't expect to stand in the schoolhouse door in open defiance of the federal law, although I might disagree with it. We've adopted a policy in Louisiana of obeying the law."

In May 1967, the Fifth Circuit Court further placed the Alabama school system under mandate to desegregate its educational program immediately, and in July ruled that the Department of Health, Education, and Welfare could not cut off federal funds for non-compliance with the guidelines without court approval. In issuing its original program for compliance, the United States Office of Education set a percentage formula which would be indicative of a sincere step toward desegregation, and which could be accepted as satisfactory conformity. The percentages were highly flexible, but the Office of Education suggested 8 to 10 per cent to begin with and a possible doubling of this amount the next year.

In 1965–66 the states having lower than 4 per cent conformity were Alabama, Georgia, Mississippi, Louisiana, and South Carolina. Alabama had 0.43 per cent, Louisiana 0.69 per cent, and Mississippi 0.59 per cent. Around the border, compliance ranged from almost complete desegregation in Kentucky to generous conformity in North Carolina, Tennessee, Texas, and Virginia. On the opening of school in 1966 the Southern Regional Conference undertook, with the assistance of experienced newspaper reporters and other reliable observers, to determine the degree of compliance with the court mandate and with Title VI of the Civil Rights Act. It reported a range from 2 per cent in Mississippi to 5.7 per cent in Georgia. All of the ranges in six states were well below the suggested percentage of the guideline instructions.

Thus in 1967, thirteen years after Brown v. School Board, these facts seem clear: There has been remarkably little actual desegregation in six states, and throughout the South there have been varying degrees of foot-dragging on desegregation of faculties and staffs. There is a contradiction, though microscopic it may be, between Title IV and Title VI of the Civil Rights Act of 1964. The United States Office of Education is poorly equipped to act as an enforcement agency. The powerful southern congressional delegation has been effective in halting enforcement of the guidelines, and the economy measures in education by the President and Congress late in 1967 have made this handicap more serious.

It remains to be seen whether the remand order by the United States Supreme Court to the Fifth United States Circuit for compliance is successful or not. With the number of judicial decisions there is a confusion of mandates in many instances. In November 1967, Peter Libassin, director of the Office of Civil Rights for the Department of Health, Education, and Welfare, said he believed most school districts could complete the process of desegregation within two years, and set September 1969 for the final date of full compliance. This he said was only a shift in emphasis from numbers and percentages to establishing a plan for eliminating the dual school system of the South. He followed the

Court in ruling out the freedom of choice plan. In Georgia, for instance, forty-eight school systems faced the 1969 deadline. Elsewhere in the South even more systems were involved in the order.

On December 5, 1967, the United States Supreme Court affirmed the March decision of the three-judge order that Alabama desegregate its schools immediately. This brought the reply from Governor Lurleen Wallace that "the people are ultimately going to change the effect" of the ruling. She called the ruling "part of a master plan being pushed and sponsored by the enemies of our constitution to nationalize our schools." Governor Wallace's husband said that in ordering that the governor and other state officials "take affirmative action to disestablish all state-enforced or encouraged public school segregation and to eliminate the effects of past . . . discriminations" the Court would "in effect, destroy neighborhood schools." Here he referred to the fact that it would be necessary to bus children considerable distances to equalize the racial composition of schools. This latter ruling applied to the 99 school systems involved in the March 22 court decree. Beyond this it closed the last avenue of legal delay in carrying out the mandate laid down in Brown v. School Board.

An impartial observer viewing the badly muddled situation in the summer of 1967 could not have helped but feel that what today's South needs is not so much desegregation *per se* as a fulfillment of the earlier Plessy v. Ferguson principle of equality of standards and opportunity.

While the greater part of the political furore regarding education has centered on compliance with federal law over desegregating student bodies and faculties, the South's monumental advance has been in the improvement of all its educational standards. Since the end of World War II the southern states, like the rest of the nation, have been forced to face up to the need for universal education to meet the heavy demands made by an increasingly technical, industrial, and urban society. In the postwar South more and more jobs have required a high level of education of the most diversified sort. Almost monthly the number of such positions is multiplied with industrial expansion in the region. Education has had to progress to meet these demands.

Tragically in many southern states the bitter fight to delay desegregation of schools has done irreparable harm to achieving higher standards of educational achievements. For instance, in at least six states administrators and teachers have spent a disproportionate amount of time trying to formulate compliance formulas that would satisfy both themselves and the technical requirements of guideline demands and have not concentrated on excellence in education. Governors and legislators have wasted their energies and talents formulating and enacting negative legislation and making public statements while southern youth has cried out for positive educational leadership. Some governors have, legislatively at least, stood in "schoolhouse doors" to turn back Negro students when their states' educational systems were at the bottom of national levels of excellence.

Two statistical areas will reveal the weakness of southern secondary educational effort. The median high school in the South, as reported in *High Schools in the South: A Fact Book,* Division of Surveys and Field Services Center for Southern Educational Studies, does not provide a sufficiently wide curriculum; also, too many instructors are assigned to classes outside the fields of their major college preparation. Thirty per cent of the South's high school pupils are enrolled in schools which offer fewer than fifty courses. Seventy-five per cent of the high schools, which involved 900,000 pupils, offer fewer than forty courses. It is in this area that the region faces its most serious challenges. Whether white or black, many southerners are being inadequately prepared to take productive places in the region's modern industrial society. Both races have ample reason to raise criticisms of gross inequalities.

In supporting its schools, the South has lived by a curious kind of a myth. There is a long tradition of frugal support for education, and it is hard for many states to break with the past. It is true that the southern states have remained historically near the bottom of the national scale in personal income. In 1965 average personal income in no southern state equalled the national average of $2724. The range was from $1566 in Mississippi to $2420 in Florida. The national average for percentage of personal income devoted to education was 4.4 per cent. In Mississippi it was 5 per cent, South Carolina 5.1 per cent, and in Kentucky 4 per cent, but nine other southern states ranked at the bottom of the list of revenue receipts per pupil. These ranged from $315

in Alabama to $500 in Florida, compared with a national average
of $560. In areas of general revenue income Alabama and South
Carolina collected $140.20 and $140.60 from general taxes per
pupil, and $28.38 and $32.96 per student in property taxes. The
relatively low assessment of property in all the southern states
partially explains the lower levels of educational support.

In two areas the South makes a particularly favorable showing:
percentage of revenue collected spent on elementary and secondary schools. All the states are above the national average of
40 per cent, and range from 43.2 per cent in Virginia to 71.9 per
cent in North Carolina. While the national average of federal
aid to elementary and secondary schools in 1965 was 3.8 per cent
of total support, in the South the range was from 4 per cent in
Tennessee to 9.2 per cent in Arkansas. In Alabama, it was 7.9
per cent, and in Mississippi 8.2 per cent. Thus the Federal Government makes a comparatively heavy investment in public education in the South.

If southerners have been made highly conscious of the role of
secondary education in their society since 1954, they have perhaps become equally conscious of the need for improving their
efforts at university and college levels. In 1964, there were in the
South 537 colleges and universities with full-time enrollment of
1,157,501 students, as compared with a national enrollment of
5,526,350. Thus the rise in ratio of persons seeking higher education in the South is an entirely satisfactory one. Too, much of the
quality of university and college enrollment shows an improvement over that in the South of a decade and a half ago. Since
1945 every university in the South has set out to make major
improvements in its academic standards and to expand its general
program. Within the past decade it is possible that some universities have received more financial support than they were
ready and able to spend prudently. There has been a scramble
to build up library holdings and faculties, and administrations
have increasingly talked in terms of research and publication.
Some administrations have become so bold as to use the terms
"great" and "excellent" in describing their schools.

Again in comparison with efforts made in the past this pride
seems proper. In a more objective measure, however, such as the
national survey of individual departments offering graduate work,

no southern university was in the list of first ten, and few departments were mentioned in the top twenty. Better showings were made in the "good" and "adequate" categories. This report confirmed earlier criticisms made by Dean W. Gordon Whaley of the Graduate School in the University of Texas that the South still had to achieve much higher standards to be competitive with institutions in the East and Middle West.

In further objective measure, the Hayward Keniston or national graduate departmental report, no southern university was listed among the first ten, and few departments were among the first twenty. Better showings were made in the "good" and "excellent" categories. In 1966 Allan M. Cartter's searching report for the American Council on Education examined thirty fields of study in more than 100 institutions, and no southern university was listed among the top twenty.

Otis A. Singletary, a former chancellor of the University of North Carolina at Greensboro, in an address before southern historians in Atlanta in November 1967, said that graduate students rank the southern schools as lowest on their list of choices. He said "prejudice, piety, and politics" were largely responsible for this condition. He referred, of course, to religious fundamentalism, racial bias, and political interference with schools and colleges. There still remain the speaker ban law in the statute books of North Carolina, the Johns Committee in Florida, and the shadows of George C. Wallace and Ross Barnett still linger in Alabama and Mississippi. Two old ghosts of the past have stirred a bit in the past two years. A young teacher, dismissed in April 1967, in Jacksboro, Tennessee, for teaching evolution, was later reinstated, but not until the incident had caused considerable public furore. The Tennessee legislature refused to remove the evolution law from the statutes, and officially at least the state still maintains it. In Arkansas the evolution law of that state faces an ultimate court test. The fact that these archaic laws are still a part of the official attitudes of two southern states casts gloom over the future of higher education. Thus it is with considerable justification that Mr. Singletary observed in his Atlanta speech, "These repeated violations of institutional autonomy and/or academic freedom have helped to create an atmosphere that is fundamentally hostile to the development of institutions of quality and have, thereby, made it extremely difficult to attract and hold outstanding faculty members." In a more optimistic vein, Rupert B. Vance has said, "The region began its advance with a campaign for universal education; it is now in the process of shifting to an emphasis on excellence in education."

There was in the Keniston report also an intimation that within a short time some southern graduate departments would be vastly improved by growing maturity and better support. This seemed to be indicated in several universities. More southern scholars are attracting attention by their research and published works. The location of several atomic energy centers, the work with missiles, and solar exploration have made heavy demands on southern scientists from several disciplines. The new field of computer utilization has become as important in the South as in the rest of the country. The important petrochemical and synthetics industries have expanded and have greatly increased the need for chemists, engineers, and physicists, and the expansion of other types of industries has strained the regional resources to supply the technicians that are needed.

If industrial specialists' insight into future needs can be relied upon, the South will undergo great expansion in all its specialized industrial fields. For it is estimated that within a decade and a half the American per-capita paper consumption will jump from 495 pounds to 675 pounds, and by 1990 this latter figure will be almost doubled; at the same time the national population will be vastly increased. Oil and gas consumption will grow more than 60 per cent in a decade, and so will the consumption of synthetic materials; consumption of water, minerals, and electrical power will skyrocket.

There is a contradiction in southern culture at present. While extremists on either side of the race issue create a political and social furore over issues which should have been resolved long ago, the new and demanding South of technology, revised industrial and commercial approaches, and intense scientific specialization goes on expanding as if the other aspects of southern life were wholly unrelated to it. It seems a preposterous irony of history that a state like Alabama should have such a bitter and stifling struggle over the issue of quality of public education when the state also houses so sophisticated an activity as the

Redstone Arsenal. In Georgia, where there is such an important and sensitive an industrial and financial center as Atlanta, a desperate struggle is going on in parts of the state to turn back the clock.

The South faces an even more profound revolution in the ways of the farmer and his life than the one it has already endured. The President's Commission on Food and Fibre reported in May 1967 that federal efforts in the form of subsidies, price supports, and crop controls have tended to help only the farmer with an adequate sized farm unit, technological know-how, and capital and managerial ability. The traditional subsistence family farm faces a perpetual state of poverty. No clearer obituary could be written to the traditional southern agricultural system than these words of the Commission: "If ultimately, the excess capacity were eliminated, agriculture would employ only those people, acres and dollars that could earn a return comparable to what they would earn in other industries. At that time there would be no need for government programs of income supplement or supply adjustment." What the Commission was saying specifically was that too many people are trying to live on a national farm income which is wholly inadequate for them.

The nature of the new southern agriculture was outlined in the February 1967 issue of the *Progressive Farmer*. Editorial writers drawing on materials prepared by Charles R. Pugh and Hugh L. Liner of the North Carolina State University Extension Service predicted that by the mid-1970s the South would lead the nation in increase in farm size and mechanization, and would compete head-on with midwestern farmers in growing soy beans and feed grains. It would lose its low cost laborers, and develop further specialization in livestock and poultry production.

This prophecy is not too far-fetched for southern farming. In the remarkably short interval between 1959 and 1964 average farm acreage increased from 220.9 acres to 256 acres. Farm units in these years declined from 2,209,227 to 1,571,608. More significant was the fact that 8 per cent of the farms in the South produced more than 50 per cent of the saleable products, and 16 per cent of the farms grossed $10,000, an increase in five years of 4.4 per cent.

Early in November 1967 the United States Department of

Agriculture reported both a rise in average farm values and a rise in farm indebtedness. Farmers were borrowing to increase their mechanization and to enlarge their landholdings. In Kentucky, an agricultural economist reported that a farm analysis for a selected group of farmers on fertile soil ran from a gross of 42 per cent on 317 acres to 56 per cent on 1500 acres. In five years in Henderson County the average size farms increased about thirty acres a year, or from 530 to 690 acres. Capital investment rose from $225,000 to $332,000.

In the *Progressive Farmer*'s table of farm products that would experience increased demands within the next decade the newer crops of the region showed the largest growth. Significantly cotton was next to the lowest on the list. Grains and meat products, except pork, were predicted to head the list of production. The Department of Agriculture economists did not list tobacco at all as a major crop of the future.

Clearly the South has experienced at least three decades of revolution, and no part of this revolution had been more important than the mechanization of agriculture and the shifting emphases on types of crops. The effects of this change are phenomenal and far-reaching. First, the purchase of machines has necessitated a revision of agricultural capitalization, which has become more complex as more sophisticated machines are purchased to handle specialized crops. Already the southern farm has increased phenomenally in size, but beyond this is the fact that since 1950 major farming has been concentrated more and more upon level fertile lands capable of returning a high yield under intensive mechanized conditions. The South is still in a pioneering stage in the use of improved seed stocks, chemical fertilizers, pre-emergent weed controls, and plant defoliants. These all promise appreciable increase in production. There has, however, risen a serious question as to whether or not plant scientists have actually found answers to stabilizing improved plant types. Can progress in this field be sustained, or is there danger or serious degeneracy and reversion? More than ever agricultural scientists have to bring themselves not only to make progress, but to hold the ground they have gained since 1940.

Poor lands which once sustained a considerable part of the

southern population are now largely out of cultivation, and are either growing pasture grasses or trees for various wood industry uses. The large wood-using corporations have moved into the red hill cotton belt and converted millions of acres of pine lands to their original and virginal uses. Weyerhauser, Georgia-Pacific, Continental Can Company, Bowater, Crown-Zellerbach, and insurance companies compete vigorously for purchase of this grade of land. Within the past decade a new product has been added to those already being produced in the South. Now yellow pine plywood is being manufactured for external use. As glues resistant to moisture have been perfected, this industry has begun to compete with that of the Northwest.

The central productive part of the southern farm and land history has thus come full circle. The plantation in a new form has come back into its own. But there are no tenants, no mules, no furnishing stores and lien notes, no boss men, and nobody singing slave songs. Every passing year sees a greater flow of higher priced products going to market, and a rising flood of emigrants going away from the land. It is not possible to be precise as to what proportion of farm tenants or little farmers have left the land since 1950, but something more than 60 per cent have departed. Most of those who now remain face eventual displacement.

Farm production as such has not dropped off, nor has farm income shrunk. The older categories of income have been revised radically. The wage factor in farm production has undergone considerable increase due to the mobility of farm labor and minimum wage laws. In 1966 the South averaged $0.91 an hour as compared with $1.26 for the nation. As the South has closed this gap and increased the rate of mechanization there has been an increased demand for higher capability on the part of the laborer. This fact has tended to suspend large numbers of people in a limbo between the farm and urban areas; they are too inefficient and numerous to follow their lifelong vocations and not skilled enough to find employment in industry. In an article in the *New York Times Magazine* in June 1967, Robert Sherrill wrote, "The same people who were considered 'good ol' darkies' a few years ago are now considered deadwood hardly worth keeping alive."

In this specific instance the author was referring to Negroes who had been put off of Mississippi delta cotton plantations, and who found themselves on the verge of starvation.

Dr. Raymond M. Wheeler of Charlotte, North Carolina, a member of the medical team sent to Mississippi by the Field Foundation early in 1967, said, "We can only describe as shocking — even to a group of physicians whose daily confrontation with disease and suffering" hardens them to such things — the conditions they found. Senator James O. Eastland, a delta plantation operator, denied the findings of this group. Dr. Wheeler asked Eastland to come "with me into the vast farm lands of the Delta and I will show you the children of whom we have spoken. I will show you their bright eyes and innocent faces, their shriveled arms and swollen bellies, their sickness and pain and fear and misery of their parents." Congressman Jamie Whitten branded this as monstrous nonsense, and told Secretary of Agriculture Orville Freeman, "There's nobody in Mississippi who can't raise $2 a month . . ." with which to purchase food stamps.

Even more biting was the charge made by civil rights leaders in four Mississippi delta counties. They said that the mechanization of the farms and the minimum wage boost offered the plantation operators excuses for turning a Negro voting majority into a minority. Representative Joseph Y. Resnick of New York, in the committee hearings on conditions in Mississippi, said, "There is no question in my mind that the state of Mississippi is engaged in a deliberate conspiracy to starve Negroes out of the state," and he accused Governor Paul Johnson of being "the real culprit." Governor Johnson in turn claimed the report on hunger and malnutrition was "politically inspired."

The one fact that clearly emerges from this exchange is that southern agriculture has moved sharply away from its traditional past. Angry guardians of the southern way of life in the 1950s failed to see clearly that its very foundation was being undermined by machines and the application of the newer scientific discoveries to production of goods, and not by judges and legislators. It is a profound irony that some of the most articulate defenders of the old regime were themselves helping to hasten the revolution.

While revolution has occurred on the southern farm, there has been a comparable rise in urban centers. There is growing realization that the South will have to reckon with these many industrial challenges in the future. Racial and political prejudices, hindered southerners from viewing the South's problems in their proper, modern perspectives. Since the 1880s many isolated southern voices have been raised in behalf of educating the Negro adequately to take his proper place in the region's economic system. In the latter half of the twentieth century a tremendous shift in the condition of the Negro's economic and social place in the South has occurred. Heavy migration away from certain areas continues, but the tide away from the South itself is ebbing. There has even been some backward flow of emigrants. Riots and general chaos in large northern and eastern cities revealed that those places were not havens of peaceful refuge for rural southern Negroes. Yet Negroes in many parts of the South are hard-pressed to find employment.

The unemployment of Negroes may have made racial extremists feel confirmed in their contentions that the Negro was incapable of holding jobs other than elementary ones on the farm and in service industries. This was not so. Negroes have been successfully employed in many of the new industries. The full implication of the employment situation is, however, one of unrest and possible social explosion. It contains the same frustration, desperation, and germ of revolt which characterized the riots in Detroit, Los Angeles, Newark, and Wichita. This proved to be so in a fair degree in Atlanta, Jacksonville, St. Augustine, and Winston-Salem. What the mass of southerners has overlooked in the late twentieth-century Negro revolt is the fact that, unlike the equalitarian Negro efforts in the past, this one has a strong element of formative change.

In a purely economic way the South stands to suffer serious loss from the inability of much of the Negro population, as well as of the white, to find employment in the new industry because of a lack of training and skill. This cuts two ways: the region loses a productive source of human energy, and is further burdened by a chronic problem of public relief. Officials in Alabama, Mississippi, and South Carolina were accused of refusing to meet costs of public relief in the form of surplus commodities and food stamps because of their adverse reactions to racial considerations and federal legislation.

The adult Negro or white could not be greatly helped by being exposed to traditional forms of schooling. His most urgent need is for the simplest kind of vocational training. Although most of the southern states have established vocational schools or supported special training classes, these are too few and inadequate to meet the needs of this period of physical relocation of large portions of the southern population. The Southern Governors' Conference in October 1967 took cognizance of this need. The governors went further in discussing this subject and admitted that educational standards in Negro colleges had to be improved. Governor Mills E. Godwin, Jr., of Virginia told his colleagues, "If we fail to realize the situation as it now exists we are doing nothing more than perpetuating an inferior brand of education for young Negroes in the South. I think a visit to almost any of these schools would show that their standards are well below those of our white institutions." The governors had in mind the kinds of explosion which occurred in Shaw University at Columbia, South Carolina. In May of 1967, students struck against what they claimed were poor academic standards. In the fall semester of that year students at Grambling College in Louisiana revolted against the school's overemphasis on athletics and its poor academic program.

Much of the South in this age of rising industry has found itself confronted with problems of such a nature that its leadership at educational and governmental levels has been sorely challenged if not actually proved inadequate. This condition is further aggravated by the fact that in its great transitional period a considerable portion of the South's population is caught in a vacuum. While farmers in certain areas may be pleased that machines are replacing Negroes, this situation does not relieve the urban South or the nation at large of a serious social responsibility. Speaking in Lubbock, Texas, in October 1967, Sargent Shriver of the Office of Economic Opportunity said, "The federal war on poverty is Mississippi's third leading industry. It passed cotton growing last year." He also said, "Although Mississippi congressmen continually vote against the war on poverty, the state is one of the most favored recipients of federal aid to the poor." By early fall 1967, twenty-three integrated Community Action Programs had been established in the state.

More serious than immediate charges of hunger and discrimination against helpless people was the more inhumane fact that thousands of people have been made economically sterile through no fault of their own. A generation of southerners of both races has been caught by the processes of change in a situation that would be difficult to handle, even if such intense racial animosity did not exist. The chances for violence or intensified racial antagonism are obvious.

Whatever chance there is for the solution of its deep-seated social problems, the South today stands on the verge of urban secularization. Modern southerners emotionally and educationally equipped to meet the challenges of the new age have quickly adjusted to the impersonal environment of suburbia. They also are learning what it means to be part of a bigger world caught in an era of violent social change and revolt. Realistically they have come face to face with social and economic problems which are no longer regional in origin or significance. If southerners grow restive over local conditions, they quickly realize that men around the globe share their anxieties. More fundamentally, thoughtful southerners realize that what was considered a distinctive regional culture in the past was in large measure a combination of provincialism and racism. As these two conditions have been ameliorated by the passage of time, the South has lost many characteristics which set it apart in the past. There are informed southerners who now say that, if it were not for the lingering race problem, the modern South could not otherwise be distinguished from most other parts of the United States.

Equally as important has been the impact of the social and physical sciences upon the South. Immediately following 1954 extremists chastised the United States Supreme Court for citing the works of social scientists in bolstering its decision to overturn the doctrine of "separate but equal" public facilities in public education. Already, however, historians, newsmen, educators, and social scientists had turned southerners' thoughts inwardly upon their problems. Every phase of change demanded some insight into elementary behavioral responses. The migration of people from rural to urban communities alone casts the southern approach to the future into new contexts. So did the rising challenge of institutional improvement and expansion. Internal forces within the southern population were in themselves enough to necessitate a searching re-examination of human relations.

In an age when the physical sciences have come to play such a vital role in the shaping of national and international policies, it would be folly for southerners now to seek refuge behind regional isolation. If for no other reason, the press, the automobile, airplane, television, and radio have helped gather the region together more tightly. Exploitation of regional petroleum, coal, minerals, timber, and water resources yearly thrust the South further away from its past.

Almost three decades after World War II there is a new perspective on the value of southern resources. In the first place there has never been in southern economic history such an enormous release of human energy as at present. Because of educational and environmental conditioning, better medical care, and mechanical amplification the South is now four or five times more productive per unit of human labor. In older fields of economy application of scientific knowledge gained in the field of conservation and forest and water management has brought a re-evaluation in economic planning. Beyond this further scientific advances in the perfection and utilization of harvesting and processing machines of all sorts will have to occur. More and more southern lands are now being turned to supplying modern industrial demand, and as this happens the region is forced into new social patterns.

Where once most southerners thought of industrial expansion taking place within a quarter of a century, modern southerners are having to adjust to thinking in terms of annual or bi-annual change. In October 1967, the *Wall Street Journal* announced that Mississippi was issuing $130,000,000 worth of public bonds to finance modernization and expansion of ship-building facilities in Pascagoula. This was almost a national record for public support of such a project. No one can guess the effect such a venture will have on the old ways of life in this agricultural state.

A modern factory rising out of worn-out cotton land, and which produces clocks by the hundreds and thousands has supplanted the cotton which once grew on the site. Hundreds of women who attend machines which stamp out parts, and who assemble all sorts of gadgets contrasts vividly to the southern woman pictured by the old orators in their flowery tributes to southern womanhood. A woman dressed in "stretch pants" and driving a machine on a hustling assembly line is a contradiction to the storied contented farm wife in her rocking chair reading the scriptures before the family hearth.

An orator picturing for an audience at the turn of the nineteenth century the honest farmer who was master of a happy homestead would be wholly irrelevant today. Most farmers have either moved to town, or, perhaps, more of them have been caught halfway between town and country in mushrooming communities. The old weatherbeaten and unboxed houses, some of which still stand, are rapidly falling into decay. Most of them, however, have been swept out of existence by bulldozers to make room for modern brick or stone-veneered houses with spacious carports, large picture windows, and backyard patios. Rural water lines deliver an abundance of water into kitchens and bathrooms, and even to lawns. The washtub and pot have disappeared, and the old springs and wells are abandoned. The change of work shifts in local industrial plants fill southern roads with suburban laborers rushing home to shop in chain stores clustered in malls. At home they give more attention to lawns, while away their time before television sets, and become great spectators of sports. Town and city fathers looking forward to days of even greater expansion have pushed metropolitan boundaries deep into the heartlands of the old rural South.

In thousands of southern communities, centers of social and economic activities have shifted since 1940. This has been especially true of the continuous process of school consolidation. Children, white and Negro, are hauled into centrally located schools, and town and county schools have been merged. This is true despite the fact that there are small, understaffed, and inefficient schools still functioning. The modern, centralized school has erased most of the old inequities which existed between town and country. It remains to be seen, however, whether they will also destroy barriers of racial prejudices and discrimination. The southern school is now largely engaged in training urban youth to adapt themselves to the new southern way of life, even to preparing southerners to adapt the standardizations of national life.

No single incident in modern southern history has been more significant in destroying ancient southern images than the construction of modern superhighways, and especially the great inter-state roads. By 1968 enough links of these roads have been completed to indicate the influence they will ultimately have on the region. This indicates that an enormous amount of intra- and inter-regional travel is taking place. The last vestiges of the frontier in the South are being wiped away. Communities which were isolated and backward places two decades ago are now industrial sites, or they have melted back into the woods.

In the latter part of the twentieth century there is little reason to doubt that the South is emerging rapidly from its past on many fronts. It makes little difference in an over-all view whether or not southern per-capita income equals the national average at the moment, or whether the rate of industrial expansion is comparable to that in other parts of the nation. Per-capita income will in time be increased because of the industry already in the region, and industrial expansion will continue if the present American prosperity prevails. Southerners are also much more aware of the importance that per-capita income and industrial progress have in their daily lives. The modern South seems to have become subjected to generous amount of economic determinism. This no doubt is true. Hundreds of thousands of southerners whose fathers thought in terms of cotton and tobacco prices, the costs of fertilizers, and farm mortgages now speak in terms of bank clearings, wage scales, export-import balances, and management-labor relations.

But the clouds of stubborn resistance to change have not all cleared away in the South. There are still pockets of violence such as those in Philadelphia and Jackson, Mississippi. There have been bombings, burnings, and shootings which have stemmed from racial hatreds. It is indeed a strange contradiction that in a rapidly expanding modern city such as Jackson a bomb would be exploded against a religious worker's house because he had concerned himself with the plight of people caught in the travail of change. Such cowardly acts shake the southerner's faith in the future. Public officials, church leaders, educators, and citizens are all answerable for such affronts to human dignity in the South. It matters little indeed that there are hundreds of thousands of good people who abhor what the Ku Klux Klan, the Americans for the Preservation of the White Race, the Citizens Councils, and like groups have countenanced in ignoring the laws of the land. So long as men peddle hatred of any sort, or resort to bombs and torches to destroy churches, synagogues, and homes because religious and civil rights workers crusade for free ballots and equal opportunities of underprivileged people, the South will be bound down by its violent past.

Today the political reactions of the South are so badly confused by sectional, national, and international issues that it is impossible to say positively what may be the alignments of the future. In December 1967 the Ku Klux Klan was distributing matchbooks bearing the legend "Draft George Wallace for President." Inside was a coupon to be filled out by persons seeking membership in the order: "If you are a native-born loyal United States Citizen, 21 years old, a White Gentile Person of Temperate Habits, of Protestant Faith, and believe in White Supremacy and Americanism."

More assuring, however, is the fact that much of the old pattern has been broken. Whether Baker *v.* Carr achieves its full purpose or not, urban southerners will not react in the same way as their rural forebears. The Negro has already had some influence, but he labors against tremendous odds. Not until the establishment of a Negro middle class which is able to participate fully in the economic and political affairs of the region without being intimidated or managed will the Negro have achieved full freedom from the past. From a broader perspective southern political alignments promise to be largely those of urban industrial America in general. Whether the labels are the traditional ones or not is already immaterial. The forces which motivate the modern South in the last decades of the twentieth century will reflect the degree of the region's emergence into a new age of national, social, economic, and political conformity.

A team of economists and educators commissioned by the Twentieth Century Fund to study economic conditions in the modern South, and especially those pertaining to the Negro's place in the region, gave a warning to the South in October 1967.

Dr. James G. Maddox of North Carolina State University said, "The South is the fastest developing of the country's and the world's developing regions. . . . Indications are that southern incomes will continue to rise as the balance shifts from low-wage to high-wage industries, that the rising new industries will attract other industries as buyers or suppliers of manufactured goods and that the quality of the labor force will continue to improve." If the region is to utilize its human energy to the fullest, all of its people will have to be prepared to serve the new industry. Because of lack of education and industrial experience, and the discrimination against him, the Negro still faces a grim future, and may find his solution in emigration from the South. The most effective utilization of its human resource still remains the central challenge of the South in this era. Political and economic realignments will by force of circumstance take care of themselves as time passes and conditions change.

The present South speaks with two voices, and these are more often than not in sharp conflict. Extremists keep up a refrain of bitter denunciation of the Supreme Court and meddlesome outside influences which would reshape the southern pattern of life. The voices of the New South pleading for industrial expansion and a reshaping of the regional economic patterns in the image of the industrial nation make themselves heard clearly above the sound and the fury of emotionalism. The conflict between these two voices increases every year, and the one which comes to predominate will largely shape the South's economic and political decisions in the future. An atmosphere of social peace and moderation offers the modern South its most positive means of competition in this age of declining agriculture.

Selected Bibliography

BOOKS

Ashmore, Harry, *An Epitaph for Dixie*, New York, 1957.

————, ed., *The Negro and the Schools*, Chapel Hill, 1954.

Barnes, W. W., *The Southern Baptist Convention, 1845–1953*, Nashville, 1954.

Barrett, Russell, *Integration at Ole Miss.*, Chicago, 1965.

Bilbo, Theodore G., *Take Your Choice, Separation or Mongrelization*, Poplarville, Miss., 1947.

Blaustein, Albert P., and Clarence C. Ferguson, Jr., *Desegregation and the Law, The Meaning and Effect of the School Segregation Cases*, New Brunswick, N.J., 1957.

Brady, Judge Tom P., *Black Monday*, Brookhaven, Miss., 1954.

Brewton, John E. (Dir)., *Higher Education in Mississippi*, Jackson, 1954.

Carmichael, Omer, and Weldon James, *The Louisville Story*, New York, 1957.

Changing Patterns in the New South, Atlanta, 1955.

Clark, Thomas D. and Albert D. Kirwan, *The South Since Appomattox, A Century of Regional Change*, New York, 1967.

Collins, Charles Wallace, *Whither the Solid South?*, New Orleans, 1947.

Dabbs, James McBride, *The Southern Heritage*, New York, 1958.

————, *Who Speaks for the South?*, New York, 1964.

Dabney, C. W., *Universal Education in the South*, 2 vols., Chapel Hill, 1936.

Dahir, James, *Region Building Community Lessons from the Tennessee Valley*, New York, 1955.

Debnam, W. E., *My Old Kentucky Home, Good Night*, Raleigh, 1955.

————, *Weep No More, My Lady*, Raleigh, 1953.

Dykeman, Wilma, and James Stokely, *Neither Black Nor White*, New York, 1957.

Efferson, John Norman, *The Production and Marketing of Rice*, New Orleans, 1952.

Eleazer, J. M., *Our Land Is Our Life, Conservation of South Carolina's Natural Resources*, Columbia, 1955.

Fulmer, John Leonard, *Agricultural Progress in the Cotton Belt Since 1920*, Chapel Hill, 1936.

Grady, Henry W., *The New South*, New York, 1890.

Grantham, Dewey, ed., *The South and the Sectional Image*, New York, 1967.

Hero, Alfred O., Jr., *The Southerner and World Affairs*, Baton Rouge, 1965.

Highsaw, Robert B., ed., *The Deep South in Transition*, Tuscaloosa, 1964.

Holley, Joseph Winthrop, *You Can't Build a Chimney from the Top*, New York, 1948.

Hoover, Calvin B., and Ben U. Ratchford, *Economic Resources and Policies of the South*, New York, 1951.

Johnson, Charles S., and others, *The Collapse of Cotton Tenantry*, Chapel Hill, 1953.

Johnson, John L., *Income in Kentucky*, Lexington, 1955.

King, Martin Luther, Jr., *Stride Toward Freedom*, New York, 1958.

Lilienthal, David E., *TVA, Democracy on the March*, New York, 1944.

Logan, Rayford, and others, *What the Negro Wants*, Chapel Hill, 1944.

McGill, Ralph, *The South and the Southerner*, Boston, 1963.

McKean, Keith F., *Cross Currents in the South*, Denver, 1960.

McKinney, John C. and Edgar T. Thompson, ed., *The South in Continuity and Change*, Durham, 1965.

Maclachlan, John M. and Joseph Floyd, *This Changing South*, Gainesville, Fla., 1956.

Meredith, James H., *Three Years in Mississippi*, Bloomington, 1966.

Mims, Edwin, *The Advancing South: Stories of Progress and Reaction*, New York, 1927.

Morris, Willie, ed., *The South Today, 100 Years after Appomattox*, New York, 1965.

Myrdal, Gunnar, *An American Dilemma, The Negro Problem and Modern Democracy*, 2 vols., New York, 1944.

Odum, Howard W., *Race and Rumor of Race*, Chapel Hill, 1943.

———, *Southern Regions of the United States*, Chapel Hill, 1936.

Owsley, Frank L., *Plain Folk of the Old South*, Baton Rouge, 1949.

Pierce, Truman M., James Kincheloe, Edgar R. Moore, Galen N. Drewry, and Bennie E. Carmichael, *White and Negro Schools in the South, An Analysis of Biracial Education*, Englewood Cliffs, N.J., 1956.

Ransome, John Crowe, and others, *I'll Take My Stand,* New York, 1930.

Raper, Arthur, *Tenants of the Almighty,* New York, 1943.

Sapp, Phyllis, *The Long Bridge,* Atlanta, 1957.

Shoemaker, Don, ed., *With All Deliberate Speed, Segregation-Desegregation, in Southern Schools,* New York, 1959.

Silver, James, *Mississippi: The Closed Society,* New York, 1964.

Simpson, George Lee, *The Cokers of Carolina,* Chapel Hill, 1955.

Sindler, Allan P., ed., *Changes in the Contemporary South,* Durham, 1963.

Swanson, Ernest W., and John A. Griffith, *Public Education in the South Today and Tomorrow,* Chapel Hill, 1955.

These Are Our Lives, As Told by the people and Written by Members of the Federal Writers' Project, Chapel Hill, 1939.

Thompson, Ernest Trice, *The Changing South and the Presbyterian Church in the United States,* Richmond, 1950.

Vance, Rupert B. (with Nadia Danilevsky), *All These People,* Chapel Hill, 1945.

————, *Human Factors in Cotton Culture,* Chapel Hill, 1929.

————, *Human Geography of the South, A Study in Regional Resources and Human Adequacy,* Chapel Hill, 1932.

————, and Nicholas J. Demerath, eds., *The Urban South,* Chapel Hill, 1954.

Walker, Rufus K. (compiler), *Rice,* Baton Rouge, 1954.

Warren, Robert Penn, *Segregation, The Inner Conflict in the South,* New York, 1956.

Watters, Pat and Reese Cleghorn, *Climbing Jacob's Ladder, The Arrival of Negroes in Southern Politics,* New York, 1967.

Weltner, Charles Longstreet, *Southerner,* New York, 1966.

Williams, Robin M., Jr., and Margaret W. Ryan, eds., *Schools in Transition,* Chapel Hill, 1954.

Woofter, T. J., Jr., *Landlord and Tenant on the Cotton Plantation,* Washington, D.C., 1936.

————, *Southern Race Progress, The Wavering Color Line,* Washington, D.C., 1957.

Ziegler, Benjamin Munn, *Desegregation and the Supreme Court,* New York, 1958.

Zinn, Howard, *The Southern Mystique,* New York, 1964.

PERIODICALS AND NEWSPAPERS

The Atlanta Constitution, 1930–60.
The Atlanta Journal, 1930–60.
The Christian Science Monitor, Boston, 1945–60.
Harper's Magazine, Vol. 214, New York, 1957.
Life, New York, 1940–60.
Look, New York, 1940–60.
The Louisville Courier-Journal, 1931–60.
New South, Atlanta, 1945–59.
The New York Times, 1930–60.
The Progressive Farmer, Raleigh and Memphis, 1935–60.
The Richmond Times-Dispatch, 1945–60.
Saturday Evening Post, Philadelphia, 1940–60.
South, The News Magazine of Dixie, Birmingham, 1935–58.
Southern School News, Nashville, 1955–60.
State, Columbia, South Carolina, 1931–60.
The Virginian, Vols. I–III, Newport News, 1955–58.
The Washington Post, 1945–60.
Western Recorder, Louisville, 1936–60.
The White Sentinel, Vols. V–VI, St. Louis, 1955.

AGRICULTURE

(PAMPHLETS AND BULLETINS)

Advisory Council on the Virginia Economy, Labor Resources and Labor Income in Virginia, Richmond, 1953.
Agriculture of Greenville, Oconee, and Sumter Counties, Clemson, 1958.
Agriculture of South Carolina, Clemson, 1958.
Alabama Agriculture, Its Characteristics and Farming Areas, Auburn, 1953.
Alabama Agriculture, Its Resources and Their Use, Montgomery, 1952.
Alabama Agricultural Statistics, Clemson, 1954.
Alabama Annual Agricultural Report, Montgomery, 1951–52, 1952–53.
Alexander, E. D., and others, *Small Grains in Georgia,* Athens, 1952.
Alexander, W. M., *Farm Ownership in Louisiana,* Baton Rouge, 1945.
Alfalfa Production in Georgia, Athens, 1954.
Aull, G. H., *Rural Landholdings in South Carolina,* Clemson, 1940.
———, *Some Economic Characteristics of Owner-Operated Farms in South Carolina,* Clemson, 1938.
———, and J. M. Stepp, *The Postwar Outlook in an Agricultural-Industrial Area,* Clemson, 1945.
Ballinger, Roy A., *The Taxation System of Virginia,* Blacksburg, 1931.

Barlow, F. D., *Soybean Production in the Louisiana-Mississippi Delta Area*, Baton Rouge, 1943.

Barlow, Frank D. Jr., and Leo J. Fenske, *Cost Utilization of Power Equipment on Farms in the Mississippi River Delta Cotton Area of Louisiana*, Baton Rouge, 1947.

Base Book of Mississippi Agriculture, 1866–1953, Jackson, 1955.

Beef Production in South Mississippi, Starkville, 1954.

Bickley, Dan W., *Marketing Information Available to the Livestock Industry in the Southern Region*, Clemson, 1959.

Blackstone, H., and others, *Food Habits of Consumer Groups in Small Alabama Towns that Affect Farmers' Markets*, Auburn, 1942.

Boonstra, C. A., *Part-Time Farming in Rural-Industrial Areas of Louisiana*, Baton Rouge, 1941.

Bryant, H. F., and others, *Kentucky Agricultural Statistics*, Frankfort, 1956.

Butler, Charles P., *Some Economic Effects of Cotton Acreage Diversions in the Piedmont Areas of Georgia and South Carolina, 1953–1955*, Clemson, 1956.

Butler, Charles P., and D. E. Crawford, *Farm Power Utilization and Cost on "Very Large" Farms in the South Carolina Piedmont*, Clemson, 1948.

Butler, Charles P., and Harold L. Streetman, *Economics of Mechanical Cotton Picking in South Carolina*, Clemson, 1952.

Campbell, R. C., and others, *Nutritive Values of Native Plants on Forest Range in Central Louisiana*, Baton Rouge, 1954.

Casso, Henry J., and Martin D. Woodin, *Marketing Practices of Livestock Producers in Louisiana*, Baton Rouge, 1953.

Chilton, S. J. P., *Rice Yields in Areas Improved by Application of Fertilizer*, Baton Rouge, 1944.

Clapp, Gordon, *Farms, Fertilizers, and Munitions*, Knoxville, 1954.

———, "The Purpose of TVA Fertilizer," *National Fertilizer Review*, reprint, Washington, D.C., 1952.

Coastal Bermuda for Grazing, Hay and Silage, Clemson, 1955.

Collings, G. H., and P. H. Montgomery, *Land Resource Areas in South Carolina*, Clemson, 1957.

Colwell, W. E., *Some Crop Potentialities in North Carolina*, Raleigh, n.d.

Commercial Broiler Production in South Carolina, Clemson, 1949.

Commercial Fertilizers Inspected and Analyzed in the State of Georgia, 1951–1952, Atlanta, 1953.

Cotton Statistics, Circular 82, South Carolina, Clemson, 1951.

Development of Agriculture's Human Resources, Washington, D.C., 1955.

Dickens, Dorothy, *Changing Patterns of Food Preparation of Small Town Families in Mississippi*, Starkville, 1945.

———, *The Home-Produced Food Supply of Non-Owner Farm Families, Some Factors Associated with It*, Starkville, 1954.

———, *A Nutritional Investigation of Negro Tenants in the Yazoo-Mississippi Delta*, Starkville, 1928.

————, *A Study of Food Habits of White People in Two Contrasting Areas of Mississippi*, Starkville, 1927.

An Economic Appraisal of Beef Cattle & Production in N. E. and Central Mississippi, Starkville, 1953.

Economics of Supplemental Irrigation in South Carolina, Clemson, 1958.

Edwards, A. D., *Population in Relation to Resources and Employment Opportunities in South Carolina*, Clemson, 1945.

Family Food Consumption in Three Types of Farming Areas of the South, Southern Co-operative Series Bulletin, 7, 1950.

Farm Family Diets in the Lower Coastal Plains of South Carolina, Clemson, 1930.

Farm Land Ownership in the Southeast, Pub. 4, S.E. Regional Land Tenure Committee, Clemson, 1949.

Farm Mechanization in the Upland Areas of Mississippi, Starkville, 1949.

Fenske, Leo J., and Frank D. Barlow, Jr., *Tractors on Upland Farms in North Louisiana*, Baton Rouge, 1945.

Fletcher, Paul L., *Costs of Marketing Virginia Livestock*, Blacksburg, 1933.

Folweiler, A. D., *Forest Land Ownership in Louisiana*, Baton Rouge, 1944.

Garrison, Robert H., and others, *A Study of Small Grain Planted by South Carolina Farmers*, Clemson, 1958.

Gee, Wilson, *The Qualitative Nature of Rural Depopulation in Santuc Township, South Carolina, 1900–1930*, Clemson, 1933.

Gibson, W. L., *An Economic Land Classification of Halifax County*, Blacksburg, Va., 1943.

————, *Good Pastures — Your Cheapest Feed*, Blacksburg, Va., 1954.

————, *Grassland Farming, Chemical Weed Control*, Baton Rouge, 1954.

Harris, H. E., and others, *Grassland Farming on Cutover Pineland of West Louisiana*, Baton Rouge, 1952.

Hodge, W. H., and C. O. Erlanson, *Plant Introduction as a Federal Service to Agriculture*, Beltsville, Maryland, n.d.

Horne, M. K., and others, *Price and Future of U. S. Cotton*, National Cotton Council of America, Memphis, 1958.

How Alabama Farmers Buy and Sell Livestock, Auburn, 1952.

Indexes of Agricultural Production in South Carolina, Clemson, 1951.

Johnson, J. R., *Soybeans in Georgia*, Athens, 1954.

Jones, Lewis W., "Share Dairying: New Tenancy Patterns for the South," reprint from *Rural Sociology*, vol. 17, no. 4, Dec. 1952.

Kinard, Joe D., and M. J. Peterson, *A Farm Business Study of the Six Mile Area of Pickens County, South Carolina, 1940*, Clemson, 1942.

Kundzu Culture and Uses in Georgia, Athens, 1950.

Livestock Marketing Agencies in Alabama, Auburn, 1952.

Love, H. M., and W. H. Scofield, *Virginia Farm Real Estate Trends in Seven Counties during 1941–1945*, Blacksburg, 1946.

Low Income Farm People, USDA, Washington, D.C., 1955.

Lyon, Gale H., *Commercial Chick Hatcheries in South Carolina*, Clemson, 1951.

SELECTED BIBLIOGRAPHY

Malphrus, Lewis D., *Livestock Auction Operations in South Carolina*, Clemson, 1958.

Miles, J. F., and V. Minichew, *Broiler Production in South Carolina*, Clemson, 1954.

Montgomery, J. P., *Agricultural Statistics for Louisiana, 1909–1953*, Baton Rouge, 1954.

———, *Louisiana Farm Products*, Baton Rouge, 1953.

Montgomery, J. P., and S. L. Bryan, *Agricultural Statistics for Louisiana, 1909–1949*, Baton Rouge, 1950.

Moschette, Dorothy and others, *Nutritional Status of Pre-adolescent Boys and Girls in Selected Areas of Louisiana*, Baton Rouge, 1954.

Moser, Ada, *Food Habits of South Carolina Farm Families*, Clemson, 1942.

———, *Menu Patterns and Food Preferences in South Carolina*, Clemson, 1953.

———, *Use of Food by Farm Families in the Tobacco Farming Area of South Carolina*, Clemson, 1953.

Owen, C. R., *Improvements of Native Dallis Grass in Louisiana*, Baton Rouge, 1951.

Parker, J. Reid, and G. H. Aull, *Farm Marketing of Saw Timber and Pulpwood in a Selected Area of South Carolina*, Clemson, 1953.

Pastures of Georgia, Athens, 1952.

Peterson, W. H., and G. H. Aull, *The Composition of Farm Income in South Carolina*, Clemson, 1952.

———, *Land Utilization and Agricultural Adustment in Edgefield County, South Carolina*, Clemson, 1944.

———, *A Pattern of Agricultural Production in South Carolina after the War*, Clemson, 1945.

Pitchford, C. W., *A Graphic Summary of Agricultural Change in South Carolina*, Clemson, 1954.

The Poultry Industry in South Carolina, Clemson, 1953.

Richey, Frederick D., *Hybrid Corn for Tennessee*, Knoxville, 1952.

Rochester, M. C., *Successful Farm Tenancy Practices*, Clemson, 1940.

Roy, Ewell P., and James M. Baker, *The Broiler Enterprise*, Baton Rouge, 1953.

Rush, J. F., and J. Sam Taylor, *Acreage, Production and Value of Commercial Vegetables in South Carolina, 1918–1949*, Clemson, 1950.

South Carolina Corn Statistics, Trends, 1870–1958, Clemson, 1959.

South Carolina Livestock, Dairy, and Poultry Statistics, Clemson, 1951.

South Carolina Yearbook of Agriculture, Columbia, 1954.

Streetman, Harold L., *Harvesting Hay in South Carolina*, Clemson, 1956.

Taylor, J. Sam, *South Carolina General Crop Statistics*, Clemson, 1952.

Tennessee, Agricultural Yearbook, Nashville, 1951.

Valleau, W. D., *Breeding Tobacco for Disease Resistance*, Lexington, Ky., 1952.

———, and others, *Tobacco Diseases*, Lexington, 1954.

Wasson, R. A., and A. G. Kilgore, *Louisiana Soybeans*, Baton Rouge, 1954.

————, and R. K. Walker, *Louisiana Rice*, Baton Rouge, 1955.

White, Morris, and others, *Cotton Production Practices in the Black Belt Area of Alabama*, Auburn, 1951.

————, *Cotton Production Practices in the Piedmont Area of Alabama*, Auburn, 1951.

————, *Cotton Production Practices in the Sand Mountain Area of Alabama*, Auburn, 1951.

Welch, Frank J., *The Problems of Low-Income Farm Families*, Lexington, 1955.

York, E. T. Jr., *The Contribution of Improved Technology to More Efficient Crop Production*, reprint, Plant Food Review, Washington, D.C., 1958.

INDUSTRIAL DEVELOPMENT

Atkins, Robert M., "A Program for Locating the New Plant," reprinted from *Harvard Business Review*, November–December 1952, Cambridge.

Mauer, Leonard, and Harry Wechsler, *Man-Made Fibers, A Modern Textiles Magazine Handbook*, New York, 1953.

"The Public Appraises the Electric Industry," *Executive Digest*, Princeton, N.J., 1955.

Pulpwood Production and Sawmill Logging, 1958.

Resources for Freedom, 5 vols., Washington, D.C., 1952.

Tomb, John O., "Should Industry Move South?" reprinted from *Harvard Business Review*, September–October 1953, vol. 31, no. 5, Cambridge.

Arkansas, *Business Trends*, Arkansas Chamber of Commerce, Little Rock, 1958.

Florida, *Industrial Florida*, Tallahassee, 1954.

Georgia, *Georgia Forestry*, 1946–1959, Atlanta.

Trees for Georgia, Biennial Report of Progress, Georgia Forestry Commission, Atlanta, 1954.

Action Program for Eastern Kentucky: Flood Rehabilitation Study, Frankfort, 1957.

Crawford, Thomas J., *Compilation of Coal and Petroleum Production Data for Kentucky*, Lexington, 1958.

Duer, William A., and R. O. Gustafson, *Management of Forests in an Eastern Kentucky Area*, Lexington, n.d.

Economic Security in Kentucky, 1955–1960, Frankfort.

Kentucky Agricultural Statistics, Frankfort, 1952.

Kentucky Economic Statistics Desk Book, Frankfort, 1954.

Kentucky, *Kentucky Resources*, revised edition, Lexington, 1958.

Louisiana, *Directory of Manufacturers,* Baton Rouge, 1954.
Louisiana Invests in Industry, Baton Rouge, 1954.
Louisiana Labor Market, vol. X, no. 4, Baton Rouge, 1955.
"The Louisiana Story," reprinted from the *Manufacturers Record,* Baltimore, 1954.
Louisiana's Industrial Expansion, 1946–1954, Baton Rouge, 1955.

Mississippi, Allen, Henry V., Jr., *Survey of Mississippi as a Location for a Chemical Industry,* ms., Jackson, n.d.
Balance Agriculture with Industry, House Bill 176 as amended by Senate Bill 180 and House Bill 495, Laws of Miss., Jackson, 1952.
Directory, Mississippi Manufacturers, 1950–1953, Jackson.
McLendon, James H., and others, *Manufacturing in Mississippi, An Historical Survey,* State College, 1952.
Mississippi's Business, vol. 13, no. 4, University, Miss., 1955.
Mississippi Magic, 1950–1959, Jackson.

Negro Employment: Bobcock, Stefan H., *The Negro in the Industrial Development of the South,* reprinted from *Phylon, The Atlanta University Review of Race and Culture,* third quarter, 1953.
Selected Studies of Negro Employment in the South, National Planning Association, reprints 1–5 from publication No. 6, Washington, D.C., 1955.

North Carolina, *Directory of Manufacturing Firms,* Durham, 1952–54.
Evidences of North Carolina's Industrial Progress with Relation to the Southeastern States, (ms.), Raleigh, n.d.
Industrial Dispersion Advantages in North Carolina, Raleigh, n.d.

South Carolina, *Annual Reports,* South Carolina State Development Board, Columbia, 1953–55.
Stepp, J. M., and J. S. Plaxico, *The Labor Supply of a Rural Industry. A Case Study of the McCormick (S.C.) Spinning Mill,* Clemson, 1948.

Tennessee, *Annual Report,* Tennessee Valley Authority, Knoxville, 1957.
Cassell, Robert, *Industrial Tennessee in 1953–1954,* Nashville, 1954.
Directory of Tennessee Industries, 1954–1955, Nashville, 1955.
Greenville Is Growing, 1950–1952, Greenville, Tenn., 1953.
Industrial Development of the Tennessee River, Knoxville, 1955.
Industrial News Letter, Tennessee, 1945–1957, Nashville.
Industrial Resources of Tennessee, revised ed., Nashville, 1948–54.
Tennessee Valley Authority, Shelton Barrett, *The Decatur Story,* Lake Success, New York, 1949.

Virginia, Black, Robert E., "Localities Organize for Industry," reprinted from the *Commonwealth,* December 1954, Richmond.

Directory of Virginia Manufacturing, 1955–1956, Richmond, 1956.
Labor Resources and Labor Income in Virginia, Department of Conservation and Development, Richmond, 1953.
Manufacturing in Virginia, Report of the Committee on Industry, Richmond, 1951.
"The Virginia Story," reprinted from the *Manufacturers' Record,* Baltimore, May 1955.

PUBLIC HEALTH

Alabama, *Annual Report of the Bureau of Vital Statistics,* summary Vital Statistics, 1927–46, Montgomery, 1947.
——, *Annual Report of the Bureau of Vital Statistics,* Montgomery, 1947–59, Montgomery, n.d.
Gill, D. G., *Health in Alabama, Then and Now,* Montgomery, 1956.
——, *Healthy People Are Wealthy People, Alabama Health Needs,* Montgomery, 1955.
Hosty, Thomas S., and others, *Hookworm in Alabama,* Montgomery, 1954.
——, *The Health of Your State,* Montgomery, n.d.
——, *Public Health Is Many Things,* Montgomery, n.d.

Arkansas, *Annual Report,* State Board of Health, Little Rock, 1946–59.

Florida, *Annual Report,* Florida State Board of Health, Jacksonville, 1923–32, 1945–59.
——, *Florida Morbidity Statistics,* Jacksonville, 1945–59.
——, *Life and Death in Florida,* Jacksonville, 1940–49.

Georgia, *History of Public Health in Georgia, 1733–1950,* Atlanta, 1950.
——, *Public Health and You,* Atlanta, n.d.
——, *Vital Statistics, 1945–1959,* Atlanta.

Kentucky, *Vital Statistics,* State Department of Health, 1945–1959, Frankfort.

Mississippi, Rice, M., and others, *Life Tables for Mississippi,* 1930, 1940, 1950, Starkville, 1954.

North Carolina, *Annual Report of Public Health, Communicable Disease, Morbidity Statistics, 1945–1959,* Raleigh.
——, *Health Progress in North Carolina from 1940–1950,* Raleigh, 1954.

South Carolina, *Annual Report of the State Board of Health, 1945–1959,* Columbia.

Tennessee, *Clean Water for Tennessee,* U. S. Department of Health, Education, and Welfare, Washington, D.C., 1953.

——, *Morbidity Statistics,* 1933–1959, Nashville.

Texas, *History of Public Health in Texas,* Austin, 1950.

Virginia, Bien, William, *The Virginia Department of Health, Survey of 83 Years of Progress,* Richmond, 1955.

——, *Clean Water for the South,* U.S. Department of Health, Education, and Welfare, Washington, D.C., 1953.

——, Garnett, Charles A., and Charles Burr, *Virginia Faces Its Population Future,* Blacksburg, 1939.

——, *Major Activities of the Virginia State Department of Health,* Richmond, 1953.

——, *The Organization and Services of a County Health Department,* Richmond, 1953.

——, *The Road to Health in Rural Virginia, 1900–1952,* Blacksburg, 1953.

——, *Statistical Annual Report of the Virginia Department of Health,* 1945–1959, Richmond.

COMMUNITIES

(PAMPHLETS AND BULLETINS)

Community Development for Better Living from Better Farming and Better Homes in Better Communities, Clemson, S.C., 1958.

Community Development in South Carolina, Clemson, 1956.

Garnett, William Edward, *Membership Relations in Community Organizations,* Blacksburg, Va., 1932.

——, *Negro Life in Rural Virginia 1865–1934,* Blacksburg, 1934.

——, *Virginia's Marginal Population,* Blacksburg, 1941.

——, *Virginia Rural Youth Adjustments,* Blacksburg, 1947.

Guideposts to Community Development for Extension Workers and Other Agencies, Clemson, S.C., 1957.

Guideposts for Community Development Club, Clemson, S.C., 1958.

Louisville Surveys Its Needs, Starkville, Miss., 1954.

Planning Guidesheets for Community Development Committees, Clemson, S.C., 1958.

Smith, T. Lynn, *The Situation and Prospects of the Population in the Black River Settlement,* Louisiana State University, 1940.

HIGHWAYS AND TOURISTS

Highway Statistics for 1955, U.S. Department of Commerce, Washington, D.C., 1957.

Travel U.S.A., Yearbook, National Association of Travel Organizations, Washington, D.C., 1958.

Your Community Can Profit from the Tourist Business, U.S. Dept. of Commerce, Washington, D.C., 1957.

Florida, *Know Florida, A Narrative and Graphic Guide to the Sixty-seven Counties of the State,* Tallahassee, 1955.

Twenty-first Report of State Road Department, Tallahassee, 1955–56.

Georgia, *Brunswick and the Golden Isles of Georgia,* Atlanta, n.d.

Chattahoochee Valley Attractions, Atlanta, n.d.

Happy Holidays for the Whole Family at the Ida Cason Gardens, Atlanta, n.d.

The Little White House, Warm Springs, Georgia, Atlanta, n.d.

More Thrills — More Fun — More Rest Await You in Georgia, Atlanta, n.d.

Okefenokee Swamp Park, Land of "Trembling Earth," Atlanta, n.d.

See Georgia's Boundless Relics of a Glorious Past, Atlanta, n.d.

See Scenic Southwest Georgia, Atlanta, n.d.

Georgia, *Twenty-sixth Report of the State Highway Department,* Atlanta, 1955–56.

You're Always Welcome in Savannah, Atlanta, n.d.

Kentucky, *Better Roads for All Kentucky,* Frankfort, 1959.

Boone's Tour, Frankfort, 1958.

In Kentucky, Frankfort (publicity magazine), 1940–60.

Report of the Tourist Commission of Kentucky, Frankfort, 1959.

Louisiana, *Arcadian House Museum,* Longfellow-Evangeline State Park, Baton Rouge, n.d.

Marksville Prehistoric Indian Park and Museum, Baton Rouge, n.d.

Louisiana, *Roads for the Future,* Baton Rouge, 1957.

State Parks and Recreation Commission, Baton Rouge, n.d.

Two Years of Progress, 1954–1955, Louisiana.

Walking Tour Through the Vieux-Carré, New Orleans, Baton Rouge, n.d.

Winter Vacations, Baton Rouge, n.d.

Woods Lodge on Black Lake Campti, Baton Rouge, n.d.

Mississippi, *Biennial Report of the State Highway Commission,* Jackson, 1953–55.

Nichols, Munro, ed., *Mississippi Today,* Gulfport, 1928.

Copeland, Lewis C., *Estimating North Carolina's Tourist Business,* Raleigh, 1959.

North Carolina, *Twenty-first Biennial Report of the State Highway and Public Works Commissioner,* Winston-Salem, 1955–56.

South Carolina, *Annual Report, Department of Highways,* Columbia, 1958.
Nothin' Could Be Finah than to See South Carolina, Columbia, 1958.

Copeland, Lewis C., *Estimating Tennessee's Tourist Business,* Nashville, 1954.
Tennessee, *Report of the State Highway Commissioner,* Nashville, 1956.

Texas, *The Tourist Industry, How the Tourist Dollar Is Spent,* Austin, 1958.

Virginia, *Forty-eighth Report, State Highway Commission,* Richmond, 1955.
History, Organization and Functions, Department of Highways, Richmond, 1942.

EDUCATION

(ANNUAL REPORTS AND PAMPHLETS)

Alabama Educational Association, *Only the Best Will Do for Us,* Montgomery, n.d.
Alabama Public School Laws, Bulletin 1954, Charlottesville, Va., 1954.
Alabama Schools by Name, Size, Address, Grades, Enrollment, Attendance, Montgomery, n.d.
Annual Report, Department of Education, Montgomery, 1925–56.
Public Education in Alabama, A Report of the Alabama Educational Commission, Washington, D.C., 1945.

Florida, *Annual Report of Superintendent of Public Instruction,* Tallahassee, 1954–56.

Hall, Robert H., ed., *Georgia School Laws,* Atlanta, 1958.
School Desegregation 1966: The Slow Undoing, Atlanta, Southern Regional Council, 1966.

Louisiana, *Educational Status of Louisiana's Farm Population,* Baton Rouge, 1947
Louisiana State Operated Trade Schools, Baton Rouge, 1953.

Mississippi, *Biennial Report and Recommendations of the State Superintendent of Public Education,* Jackson, 1953–54, 1954–55.
Higher Education in Mississippi, A Survey Report, Jackson, 1954, 1955.
Mississippi Education and Certification, Jackson, 1952.
Mississippi School Laws, General Acts, Regular Legislative Session, 1954.
Public Schools for Negro Children, Jackson, 1953–54.

North Carolina, *Biennial Report of the Superintendent of Public Instruction of North Carolina*, Raleigh, 1945–46.

Report of the Governor's Special Advisory Committee on Education, Raleigh, 1954.

South Carolina, *Annual Report State Superintendent of Education*, Columbia, 1945–56.

Mizell, M. Hayes, *School Desegregation in South Carolina, 1966: A Critique*, Columbia, 1966.

Moser, Ada, *Nutritional Condition of Children in Relation to School Lunches*, Clemson, S.C., 1945.

———, *School Lunches in Two Rural Communities*, Clemson, S.C., 1943.

———, *Some Dietary Attitudes and Habits among Rural Children in South Carolina*, Clemson, 1950.

Palmetto State Handbook, Columbia, 1945.

School Laws of South Carolina, 1952, Columbia, 1953.

Story of the Good School, Columbia, 1954.

Thompson, Henry T., *The Establishment of the Public School System of South Carolina*, Columbia, 1927.

Tennessee, *Annual Statistical Report of the Department of Education*, Nashville, 1954–56.

Educational Census Report, Nashville, 1952.

High Schools in the South: A Fact Book, Nashville, 1966.

Public Higher Education in Tennessee, Nashville, 1957.

Public School Laws of Tennessee, Nashville, 1957.

Rules, Regulations and Minimum Standards, Tennessee Board of Education, 1957–1959, Nashville, 1959.

Virginia, *Annual Report of the Superintendent of Public Education*, Richmond, 1940–59.

Garnett, Charles A., *Virginia Rural Youth Adjustment*, Blacksburg, 1947.

Bryant, Victor S., *Academic Freedom* (ms.), Durham, N.C., 1954.

Higher Education in the South, Chapel Hill, 1947.

The Negro and Higher Education in the South, Chicago, 1967.

Notes: 1967, Southern Regional Education Board, Atlanta, 1967.

Selected Bibliography

SEGREGATION-DESEGREGATION

(Special Articles, Handbills, Speeches, Bulletins)

Ackley, F. R., *The Bible Answers the Race Problem,* Denver, 1945.

Barnett, Albert E., "A Southerner Answers," reprint from *Christian,* New York, 1956.

Bloch, Charles J., *The Need for States Rights Councils and Citizens Councils,* Birmingham, 1956.

Brady, Judge Tom P., *Segregation and the South,* a speech delivered to the Commonwealth Club of California, San Francisco, 1957.

Cain, Mary D., *Congress of Freedom Meets,* "Where We Stand," n.d.

Callaway, T. F., *The Cause of the Confederacy,* States Rights Council of Georgia, Inc., Atlanta, 1956.

Carter, Hodding, "The South and I," *Look,* June 28, 1955.

———, "A Wave of Terror Threatens the South," *Look,* March 22, 1955.

Coleman, A. Lee, *Desegregation of Education in Kentucky — One Year After,* a mimeographed report, Lexington, 1956.

Copeland, Curt, *Messiah Is Found,* Star City, Arkansas, 1955.

Cox, Ernest Sevier, *The School Situation at Clinton, Tennessee,* 1957.

———, *Unending Hate,* 1955.

Dabney, Virginius, "School Crisis in Dixie," *United States News and World Report,* Jan. 18, 1960.

East, P. D., *Editorial Reprints from the Petal Papers,* Petal, Miss., 1957.

Eastland, James O., *The Supreme Court's "Modern Scientific Authorities" in the Segregation Cases,* Washington, D.C., 1955.

Faulkner, William, Benjamin E. Mays, and Cecil Sims, *Three Views of the Segregation Decision,* Atlanta, 1956.

Foster, L. H., *Race Relations Report,* Tuskegee Institute, Alabama, 1954.

Gillespie, G. T., *A Christian View on Segregation,* Jackson, Miss., 1954.

Horne, Lena, *A Letter,* NAACP, New York, 1954.

Kamp, Joseph P., *Trickery, Treachery, Tyranny, and Treason in Washington,* Westport, Conn., 1957.

Kaup, Verne P., *Satan Goes to School,* Madison, Wis., n.d.

King, Clennon, "I Speak as a Southern Negro," *American Mercury,* Jan. 1958.

McIntosh, H. T., *Memorial Day Reminders,* Atlanta, 1956.

Martin, John Bartlow, "The Deep South Says Never," *The Saturday Evening Post,* June 15, 22, 29, July 6, 13, 1957.

Mernagh, Patrick, and Deane Settoon, *The Pope on Segregation,* n.d.

Miller, A. C., *Progress in Race Relations — A Factor in World Peace,* Nashville, n.d.

Mobley, Marvin, *The Red Hens Are Coming Home To Roost,* Decatur, Ga., n.d.

———, *What Thomas Jefferson Wrote Against Race-Mixing,* Decatur, 1955.

Muse, Benjamin, "When and How the South Will Integrate," *Harper's Magazine,* April 1957.

Newman, Stewart A., *The Christian's Obligation to All Races*, Nashville, n.d.

Perez, J. H., *Racial Integration by Court Decree, An Address to Young Men's Business Club*, New Orleans, 1954.

Pittman, R. Carter, *The Supreme Court, the Broken Constitution, and the Shattered Bill of Rights*, Dalton, Ga., 1956.

Red, D. B., *A Corrupt Tree Bringeth Forth Evil Fruit*, Hattiesburg, Miss., n.d.

Sass, Herbert Ravenel, *Mixed Schools and Mixed Blood* (reprint from the *Congressional Record*), Greenwood, Miss., 1956.

Sims, Cecil, *A Lawyer's View* (ms.), Nashville, 1956.

Stainback, Charles A., *An Open Letter*, 1956.

Talmadge, Eugene, *You and Segregation*, Birmingham, 1956.

Vanderbilt, Paul, *The Most Ancient, Exalted, Royal, and Illustrious, and Military Order of Knights Hospitallers of St. John of Jerusalem*, Louisville, 1957.

Watson, Thomas E., *Equality, Can Man Improve on God?* Clarksdale, Miss., 1956.

Williams, John Bell, *Interposition, The Barrier Against Tyranny*, Washington, D.C., 1956.

——, *Where Is the Reign of Terror?* Washington, D.C., 1956.

The Citizens' Councils:

Citizens' Councils, Winona, 1956.

The Citizens' Councils . . . Their Platform, Homer, La., 1956.

Citizens' Councils of Kentucky, Inc., Louisville, 1959.

Conflicting Views on Segregation (reprints of a series of letters between Dr. D. M. Nelson, President of Mississippi College, Clinton, Miss. and an unnamed alumnus), Winona, 1956.

Congressional Committee Report on What Happened When Schools Were Integrated in Washington, D.C., Greenwood, 1956.

Cox, Eugene, *The Ugly Truth about the NAACP*, Winona, 1956.

Crime Report Reveals Menace of Integration, Greenwood, 1956.

Declaration of Constitutional Principles (signed by nineteen members of the Senate, and 77 members of the House of Representatives), Greenwood, 1956.

The Deep South Says Never, Greenwood, 1957.

The Educational Fund of the Citizens' Councils, Greenwood, 1956.

Gillespie, G. T., *A Christian View of Segregation*, Winona, 1954.

I Am the Bill of Rights, Greenwood, 1955.

Is Segregation Unchristian? From the Holy Bible, Greenwood, 1956.

Letter from the NAACP (reprint from Jackson, Miss., *Daily News*), Winona, 1955.

Letter from Robert Patterson to Paul Davis, Greenwood, 1957.

Letters and Bulletins, Association of Citizens' Councils, Winona, 1956.

McClary, Webster, *Prominent Kingstree Negro Makes Frank Statement* (reprint from *County Record*, Kingstree, S.C.), Winona, 1955.

Negro Senators from Mississippi, Greenwood, 1956.

Paddington Mercury, West London Star (reprint), Greenwood, 1956.

A Resolution, Association of Citizens' Councils of Mississippi, Greenwood, Miss., 1957.

A Review of Black Monday by Judge Tom P. Brady, Winona, Miss., 1956.

The St. Louis Story — Integrated Schools Hurting Both White, Colored Pupils, Greenwood, 1957.

To All Men and Women in Greenwood (reprint from *Jackson Daily News*) Greenwood, 1955.

Venereal Disease Infections by State and Race; Illegitimate Births by States, Greenwood, 1957.

The American Way to Jobs, Peace, Equal Rights, and Democracy, New York, 1954.

Arkansas Faith, Little Rock, 1955.

Closer Up, Year Eleven, Number Thirteen, Time for Truth Press, Miami, 1955.

The Coming Red Dictatorship, Common Sense, Union, N.J., 1957.

Congressman James C. Davis Speaks to the States' Rights Council, Atlanta, n.d.

Core-Lator, New York, 1955.

Deep South Wins First Round Against Court (*Washington Post*), Greenwood, 1956.

The Facts — This Is Just Not So, Mississippians for States' Rights, n.d.

Federation for Constitutional Government, New Orleans, 1955.

Friends of Cromelin, The Alabama Platform, Wetumpka, Ala., 1958.

Highlander Folk School (Communist Training School), Atlanta, 1956.

Impeachment Proceedings (against the United States Supreme Court) *Resolution No. 100* — House Repr. 174–554d, Georgia Gen. Ass., Atlanta, 1957.

Notice Circulated by a Negro Group in Atlantic City, Northside Union League Bulletin, 1955.

Now It's the South's Move (*Richmond News-Leader,* June 1, 1955).

Official News Letter White American News Service, vol. 1, no. 5, St. Louis, Jan. 1956.

Proposal for an Organization To Defend State Sovereignty and Individual Liberties, n.d.

Research Bulletin No. 4, Grass Roots League, Inc., Charleston, S.C., 1955.

Segregation of the White Race Must Be Preserved, A Declaration, New Orleans, 1956.

The South, the Poor South, reprint *Richmond News-Leader,* Aug. 16, 1956.

Subversive Affiliations of Rev. Adam Clayton Powell, Jr., Negro Congressman from New York City, Grass Roots League, Inc., Charleston, S.C., 1957.

Thou Shalt Not Bear False Witness . . . NAACP, New York, 1959.

Tract — Total Mongrelization, American Nationalist, Inglewood, Calif., 1956.

Truth About the Supreme Court's Segregation Ruling, Grass Roots League, Inc., Charleston, S.C., 1954.

Waxing, J. R., "The Southern Case Against Desegregation," *Harper's Magazine*, Jan., 1956.

We Are Opposed to; We Are for by Christian Association, Union, N.J., 1956.

What You Can Do as an Individual To Preserve White America, n.d.

Where the "Enlightened Sociological Department" Road Leads, New Orleans, 1955.

Within the Letter of the Law or the Power of a Jury, Birmingham, 1956.

THE SOUTHERN CHURCH

(PAMPHLETS, SPECIAL ARTICLES, AND STATISTICS)

"Atlanta Ministers' Statement," *The Christian Century*, November 20, 1957.

Baptist Program, Nashville, 1958.

Barnett, Henlee A., *Urban Culture Challenges of the Churches*, A Christian Life Report, The Christian Life Commission, Nashville, 1956.

The Bible Speaks on Christian Citizenship, Baptist Convention of Texas, Dallas, 1956.

The Bible Speaks on Moral Issues, Christian Life Commission of the Baptist General Convention of Texas, Dallas, 1956.

Brewer, Earl D. C., and others, *Methodism in the Changing South*, The Southeastern Jurisdictional Council, The Methodist Church, Atlanta, 1952.

Churches and Church Membership in the United States, An Enumeration and Analysis of Counties and Regions, National Council of the Churches of Christ in the U.S.A., Series A-D, New York, 1956–58.

The Egg and I, Nashville, 1956.

MacGorman, J. W., "A Vanishing Baptist Distinctive," *Western Recorder*, September 5, 1957.

"More than Two Million," *The Baptist Program*, Nashville, March 1958.

The Quarterly Review, A Survey of Southern Baptist Progress, Nashville, 1953–55.

Sapp, Phyllis Woodruff, *The Long Bridge*, Atlanta, 1957.

Southern Baptist Convention Annual, Nashville, 1940–59.

Southern Baptist Handbook, Nashville, 1946–52.

Southern Baptists and Race Relations, Social Service Commission of the Southern Baptist Convention, Louisville, 1950.

STATISTICAL SOURCES

County and City Data Book, Washington, D.C.

Statistical Abstract of the United States, 39 vols., Washington, D.C., 1920–59.

U.S. Census, 14th, 15th, 16th Decennial Reports, Washington, D.C., 1920–50.

Index